MUTINY OF RAGE

The 1917 Camp Logan Riots and Buffalo Soldiers in Houston

Jaime Salazar

Prometheus Books

Guilford, Connecticut

Prometheus Books

An imprint of The Rowman & Littlefield Publishing Group, Inc.
4501 Forbes Boulevard, Suite 200
Lanham, Maryland 20706
www.rowman.com

Distributed by NATIONAL BOOK NETWORK

British Library Cataloguing in Publication Information Available

Library of Congress Cataloging-in-Publication Data Available

ISBN 9781633886889 (cloth : alk. paper) | ISBN 9781633886896 (ebook)

∞™ The paper used in this publication meets the minimum requirements of American National Standard for Information Sciences Permanence of Paper for Printed Library Materials, ANSI/NISO Z39.48-1992.

In the spirit of Juanita Lourdes.
Written during the global pandemic
and racial unrest of 2020.
Dedicated to all who suffered.

CONTENTS

FOREWORD

Houston, Texas, my home since I retired from a twenty-two-year career in the U.S. Army, was recently recognized as the most diverse metropolis in the United States. America's fourth-largest city, home to a global seaport, sits at the crossroads of Latin America, the Caribbean, the Deep American South, and its rugged West. The area's vibrancy is apparent when walking the tidy footpaths of Memorial Park. Along the crushed pink granite trails, young families from every race, ethnicity, and faith stroll past native Texans whose roots go back centuries. An expansive arboretum abuts a manicured golf course. But beneath the surface of this picture-postcard public space for the Bayou City's leisure class lays a far more interesting yet sinister story that few Houstonians even know about. The truth behind that account, which took place on August 23, 1917, is painful, and its stain lingers to this day.

Hidden in the park's underbrush are the decaying ruins of what was once Camp Logan. Men with loaded rifles guarded this area, and many never returned from the Great War. The events described in *Mutiny of Rage* resulted in the largest single criminal trial in American history. The defendants were more than a hundred black soldiers of the 3rd Battalion, 24th Infantry, known from their frontier days as Buffalo Soldiers. But they may as well have been every black serviceman. Their only ambition was to serve their country in a time of war—yet their fate embodies one of the darkest chapters of America's post-reconstruction history.

Courage and honor are two character traits that define the profession of arms and have been at the very foundation of the U.S. Army since the Continental Congress created it on June 14, 1775. Since then, African Americans have demonstrated these traits and served with distinction in every war and theater of operation. The soldiers of the 3rd Battalion boasted an expansive campaign record, from policing the American western frontier to San Juan Hill in Cuba, to executing General "Black Jack" Pershing's punitive raid against Pancho Villa in Mexico. And in 1917, they were ready, willing, and able to carry the burden of confronting the nation's new enemies on the Western Front in France. That chance never came. Instead, they faced a far more formidable enemy: their own U.S. Army.

The explosion of racially motivated violence that tore through Houston on a sweltering summer night pitted these soldiers against a local community. It resulted in numerous casualties, dozens of court-martial convictions, and nearly twenty death sentences. It also generated widespread discussion about the treatment of African American service members and the military justice process that was far more about "military" than it was about "justice."

So why is so little known of this pivotal event in American history? I served in the army for twenty-two years, most of that time within the Judge Advocate General's Corps (JAG). There I prosecuted and defended soldiers tried by court-martial for every conceivable offense. This remains among the experiences of which I am most proud, as I continue to believe that the system of military justice I operated within served the interests of good order and discipline by ensuring a fundamentally fair criminal justice process—one that reflected the values of the nation I swore to defend.

But I also am painfully aware that the army did not always live up to its lofty mandate and often failed those who most needed the protection of a fair and credible process. This was the case for these servicemen, and the army they loved should have done better. The military justice system of today reflects a sea change that was a genuine result of the lessons learned from what happened to these soldiers.

This tragedy should not be an obscure blip in local history or the collective understanding of military justice. But only by confronting the injustices inherent in a segregated army, institutional prejudices in the highest echelons of government, the sad reality of the Jim Crow South, and the tragic consequences that result when men of honor reach a breaking point will meaning emerge from this misfortune.

Our nation failed to live up to the promise that "all men are created equal" during the Jim Crow era—the struggle for equality continues to this day. But it was especially dreadful for a nation to betray the men who pledged their lives to defend it and its constitution. This unvarnished story walks us through the chaos and fears these soldiers lived through when thrust into a hostile community and the wrenching moral and legal consequences of their actions. *Mutiny of Rage* does something few books have attempted before: it contributes to a present-day awareness of the tragic end that befell these soldiers. Written by one of my former law students, Jaime Salazar is a Mexican American and Indiana native, certainly not a person I expected to have a vested interest in this bit of African American military history. His only personal connection to this story was his devotion to the high American ideals of equal justice under the law. That is the most important testament to *Mutiny of Rage*. Salazar was compelled to bring this story out of the historical shadows.

Nonetheless, the real final chapter of this narrative has not yet been written. At the time of this book's publication, an initiative is ongoing to restore honor to these soldiers. I'm working with South Texas College of Law Houston faculty and students, several retired U.S. Army Judge Advocate officers, historians, and cadets at the U.S. Military Academy at West Point. We hope to someday restore the dignity of the innocents of the 3rd Battalion, 24th Infantry. At the very least, we must all understand these events and learn from this tragedy.

—Geoffrey Corn, Gary A. Kuiper Distinguished Professor of National Security Law, South Texas College of Law Houston, Lieutenant Colonel, U.S. Army (Retired)

I

GALLOWS AND UNMARKED GRAVES

When a man knows he is to be hanged in a fortnight, it concentrates his mind wonderfully.—Samuel Johnson

On December 10, 1917, the smell of freshly cut wood wafted about a grassy break surrounded by a mesquite bosk outside San Antonio, Texas. It was early in the morning and ominous dark clouds hovered above like omnipresent watchmen. A way off was the Alamo, where a century earlier, death arrived for a ragtag group of American frontiersmen before honor left. However, this day was different. Thirteen condemned Buffalo Soldiers—a number only one more than Christ's demi-platoon of apostles—were brought to the gallows to be hung until dead. Dew had settled upon the blades of grass, dampening the black servicemen's polished boots.[1] Decades earlier, Virginia slave Nat Turner, the most infamous and mythical slave revolter, was sentenced to be "hung by the neck until you are dead! Dead! Dead!" Turner, a self-taught polymath and religious visionary, led a gang of escaped slaves on a rampage that left upward of sixty-five whites dead.[2] "History doesn't repeat itself, but it often rhymes," quipped Mark Twain.

The men were awakened at five in the morning, ordered to dress, and escorted to awaiting army trucks. The wheels of justice turned slowly. One sergeant, four corporals, and eight privates had been anticipating their fate for weeks, not knowing if each passing day would be their last. There they waited for word of their destiny. The men prayed.[3] Several submitted themselves to Christ for the first time in their lives, "For by grace, you are saved through faith; and that not of yourselves."[4]

Nevertheless, those prayers seemed to do them little worldly good. In this instance, what awaited them was what they feared the most. The men had requested the option to die by firing squad strongly, in line with their service as riflemen and warriors.[5] Soldiers were meant to die in battle. However, the appearance of the wooden monstrosity that was the gallows made one thing clear—the army had instead opted for the most severe punishment possible under the military code of justice.[6] A bonfire burned in the background. Their hearts sank like those of condemned Celtic prisoners when they realized that they would be dispatched as live burnt offerings. Had they been condemned centuries earlier and on a different continent, their grisly penalty would have been that of Guy Fawkes, Britain's seventeenth-century Catholic insurgent. Dante designated the worst circles of punishment for traitors and mutineers.

By 06:20, the procession of deputies, military officers, and convicts arrived at the site of execution.[7] No friends or even family of the victims were allowed to witness. A more desolate spot could not have been selected. One hundred and twenty-five cavalry, one hundred infantrymen, and a black civilian minister accompanied them. The Army Corps of Engineers had already hastily built a large twelve-foot-high scaffold from the abundant but intractable mesquite wood. They worked the previous night feverishly by the light of bonfires.[8] Thirteen ropes, six on one side, seven on the other, hung on a beam above two large trapdoors. Military guards wearing khaki greatcoats turned up their collars against the morning chill. They resembled medieval executioners.[9]

No notice was given to the media or public. The sentences of hanging would not be formally announced until after the fact. Weeks prior, the high-ranking army officers who comprised the court-martial panel secretly deliberated the guilt or innocence of each soldier. The president of the panel promptly communicated those decisions to Major General John Ruckman, commanding officer of the Southern Department, for his final review. The decision to execute the men or to incarcerate them was entirely in his hands. Because the United States was at war against the German Empire, the swiftness of the executions was backed by the Articles of War, and an appeal was not allowed.[10]

The condemned Private Thomas Hawkins took solace in knowing that his mother would eventually read the letter written and mailed to her the night before his execution.[11] She would be blissfully asleep at the moment life escaped his body.

> When this letter reaches you, I will be beyond the veil of sorrow. I will be in heaven with the angels. I fear not death. Did not Jesus ask death "Where art thy sting?" Don't regret my seat in heaven by mourning over me. I now can imagine seeing my dear Grandmother and the dear girl Miss Bessie Henderson that I once loved in this world standing at the river of Jordan beckoning to me to come and O!
> I am sentenced to be hanged for the trouble that happened in Houston, Texas. Although I am not guilty of the crime, but Mother, it is God's will that I go now, and in this way, and Mother, I am going to look for you and meet you at the river. This is the happiest day I met with since Jesus spoke peace to my soul in Brookstone church.[12]

Some soldiers maintained that they were innocent.[13] For them, there were no deathbed confessions. It would have been difficult to understand the reasoning or benefit of taking hidden guilt to the grave. With death being the ultimate equalizer, even the vilest criminals admitted fault out of respect to the victims' families or as

a means of expiating their conscience. Thirteen God-fearing men
were about to meet their final judge, and indeed they wanted to
stand at attention with an untainted soul. For these prodigal sons,
animi cruciatus was the first step, through the Son of Man, toward
ultimate reconciliation. The necessary components were repentance, a desire for God over sin, and faith in redemption. In the
fourth century, ever-vigilant Saint Augustine was remorseful till his
dying day over stealing pears from a neighbor's tree as a youth.

The Sons of Ham were calm as they were escorted to the gallows. The conductors took their places, and the men for the last
time heard the command, "March!" As if on divine cue, they spontaneously broke into hymns. "Lord, I'm comin' home," sang Private Frank Johnson as ropes were fastened about the young men's
necks.[14] The others joined him, their voices crooning in a rich,
majestic tone. Tears welled up in the eyes of even the most battle-
hardened men hearing this last farewell.[15]

As the conductors took their places, the troops had chairs placed
before them, an increasingly ominous portent of their approaching
death. The symmetry and precision of the affair contrasted with the
random, violent act that was about to occur. Was the decorum a
mocking gesture by a corps that operated on order and procedure or
an attempt to give honor to the condemned? A black minister
climbed up the platform and offered up a consolation in a short
prayer.[16] All present removed their hats. One prisoner whispered to
the cleric that he hoped to meet him on the other side.[17] Reminiscent of Christian defiance toward the Romans, Private Johnson
declared that he was dying not for Uncle Sam, but God.[18] As soon
as the order was shouted, the condemned reflexively snapped to
attention and stood obediently atop the trapdoors. Military discipline was maintained. The troops were well-kept and shaven, even
for this last mission. After days of proximity, the men had befriended the white guards. The last exchange of words was the
soldiers saying, "Goodbye boys of Company C."[19] In 1944, French

schoolchildren tearfully bade "*Au revoir père*," as the Gestapo arrested headmaster Father Jacques de Jésus. "*Au revoir les enfants.* I will see you soon," he responded as he was led to his death.

Thirty years prior, Civil War veteran and writer Ambrose Bierce wrote movingly of Peyton Farquhar, a plantation owner who was about to be hung from an Alabama bridge by Union troops. Beyond them, armed sentinels stood at attention. The protagonist reflected on his family but was interrupted by loud clanging—the ticking of his watch. The soldiers dropped Farquhar from the bridge, but then, miraculously, the rope around his neck broke. He freed his hands and rose to the surface, a distance away. His senses were now much attuned, and he started the long walk home through an endless and surreal forest. Farquhar then began to experience hallucinations of distant galaxies and heard voices in indecipherable languages. The next morning, he found himself at his home's front door. He saw his family but then suddenly felt a heavy blow to the back of his neck, followed by a burst of white light. His life flashed before his eyes in an instant, and then all faded to quiet and darkness. He had imagined all the events during the split-second between falling through the overpass and the noose snapping his neck. His limp body swayed gently from the bridge.[20]

The rickety chairs were kicked out from beneath the Buffalo Soldiers, and the condemned dropped to their deaths.[21] There was a loud thud, and the massive beams trembled. The men were dispatched simultaneously, at 07:17, precisely one minute before sunrise, or the Office of Prime for the monastic monks nearby engaging in morning prayer. "Amazing grace, how sweet the sound."[22] Not a word was spoken, as it was over in less than a minute. Those soldiers met death in a courageous, dignified manner, silently but defiantly deriding the army's elaborate security measures.[23] Not a single man wept or begged for mercy.[24]

In an act reminiscent of Judas Iscariot, the army quickly removed traces of the deed by hastily disassembling every piece of scaffolding and burning it.[25] The intense purgatorial fire expiated the sins committed that day. Hidden from the view of the condemned, unpainted and unvarnished wooden coffins were placed alongside thirteen open graves. Mexican laborers performed the grizzlier tasks, such as removing the hangman's knots, some of which were so tight that they took minutes to disentangle.[26] The bodies were laid in coffins, each with a soda water bottle containing a typewritten slip of paper with name, rank, and date of death.[27] Stone mile markers numbered one to thirteen were placed at the head of each grave, the only reminders of that event.[28]

As soon as word got out, Americans of all races and colors were aghast—the army had secretly executed thirteen men before the public knew, before even the American president or secretary of war had reviewed the order. Major General Ruckman had little to say and showed far less contrition. He had chosen the time and place for the executions and righteously declared that he had acted in complete conformity with the 1916 Articles of War.[29]

Many white Americans, particularly those in the steamy Texas port city of Houston two hundred miles away, greeted the news with satisfaction. Theirs was the city in which the soldiers rioted during what was known as the Camp Logan Mutiny. They were pleased that justice was served and that the severity of punishment matched the brutal outrages committed by Negro soldiers.[30] The event shook race relations in Texas, birthed a regional surge of wartime racial activism, and inspired the black power movement decades later.[31]

In 430 BC, at the beginning of the Peloponnesian War with Sparta, Athens was hit by a plague that killed thousands of troops and a third of the city's inhabitants. Similarly, by 1918, Camp Logan cared for seven hundred Spanish influenza pandemic victims. Tragically, nearly 110 soldiers would die there. The contagion made its way into the barracks and trenches of World War I. It killed more people than the conflict itself. Nearly forty thousand

American doughboys died before ever reaching Europe, almost half perishing en route.[32] More American service members died of the Spanish flu and pneumonia than from bullets and bombs.[33]

A century later, hardly a trace of Camp Logan remained. Adventurists and historians identified several concrete structures, most of them taken over by the surrounding vegetation. The crumbling skeletons seemed more at home in northern France, connecting an abandoned wing of the Maginot line. The aptly named Memorial Park was built on the same grounds. The contiguous high-rent area was subsequently referred to as Rice Military. Ghosts of the camp's soldiers wandered aimlessly in the thick surrounding woods. Some carried red posies. Some were lost, searching helplessly for their units, while others were fleeing from gunshots. Many were pandemic victims. Still other spirits were children desperately seeking safety from a marauding mob of soldiers meant to protect them. In 1924, Houston bought the land and turned it into a park to honor the servicemen who died in World War I.[34]

A historical marker commemorated Camp Logan and the 1917 riot.[35] It was initially to be placed near Memorial Park's golf course clubhouse. Nevertheless, this was vehemently opposed by a prominent civic group. The city agreed that the marker would be better placed on the corner just outside the edge of the park.

> The black soldiers' August 23, 1917, armed revolt in response to Houston's Jim Crow laws and police harassment resulted in the camp's most heralded incident, the "Houston Mutiny and Riot of 1917."[36]

2

BUFFALO SOLDIERS

We sleep peaceably in our beds at night only because rough men stand ready to do violence on our behalf.—George Orwell

Henry Johnson, born June 11, 1850, was a member of the famed U.S. Army Buffalo Soldiers and a Medal of Honor recipient for his actions in the Indian Wars of the Wild West. He spent much of his life in its ranks. Johnson hailed from Boydton, Virginia, eighty miles from Southampton Country, where Nat Turner rampaged. His parents lived through that incident. Johnson was handsome, with pitch-black skin, and henceforth would become a motif for soldiers of fortune, romancers of war, and the likes of Che Guevara and Mad Mike Hoare a century later.

In 1866, Johnson enlisted in the army as an original member of the 10th Cavalry. He fought against the Cheyenne tribe on the Republican River. Johnson's unit patrolled southern Colorado just before the Meeker Massacre. On September 29, 1879, a group of Ute warriors ambushed a large group of soldiers and militiamen near Milk Creek. The troops along the creek created a perimeter around their wagons with their dead animals. After a week of fighting, only four wounded horses remained. The situation was fast becoming desperate. The enemy had the unit pinned, and its men had run out of water. Johnson was charged with securing the outposts. As he scrambled desperately, shots ricocheted off the rocks around him. He had to inspire his men and return with water. His death would have resulted in his men dying of thirst or at the hands of hostile tribes, notorious for their prolonged torture techniques.[1] The Utes were eventually defeated and ceded much of Colorado to white settlers. Johnson's Medal of Honor citation read: "Voluntarily left the fortified shelter and under heavy fire at close range made the rounds of the pits, fought his way to the creek and back to bring water to the wounded."[2] However, heroes are rarely saints. At the time of the award, he was merely a private. Johnson already had been promoted to sergeant three times but had been demoted most recently for brawling.

Johnson never rested on his laurels. His thirst for adventure motivated him to fight the Apaches for the next two years. Not one to give up so easily, Johnson reenlisted two months after he was discharged in 1883 to serve with the 10th Cavalry and was once again fighting the Apaches. His enemy had by now won a begrudging admiration for this "black demon." Again, after this five-year enlistment ended in 1888, he rejoined with the Ninth Cavalry. Johnson's final enlistment ended in 1898, when his ripened body simply could not continue, just before his unit was packed off to fight in the Spanish-American War. He died shortly after, living the life of a hundred men, embodying the term "hard to kill."[3]

Born in 1875, Buffalo Soldier David Fagen of Tampa, Florida, served in the 24th Infantry Regiment. He fought in the Philippine-American War.[4] His unit marched for weeks, often in waist-deep mud and through impenetrable undergrowth to the region of Luzon. Tropical diseases plagued the Americans. Ill and exhausted by the time they reached their objective, they subdued the enemy, captured a thousand combatants, and even flipped the area to the pro-American overlords.

Nevertheless, throughout the conflict, reports came of war crimes committed by American forces. Scathingly, the *Philadelphia Ledger*'s Manila correspondent wrote: "The present war is no bloodless engagement; our men have killed to exterminate men, women, children, prisoners, and captives . . . from lads of ten up." It continued, "the idea prevailing that the Filipino was little better than a dog."[5] The war resulted in the deaths of at least two hundred thousand Filipino civilians, mostly due to famine and disease. Some estimates approached a million casualties.[6]

Fagen witnessed and possibly participated in at least one such atrocity. It weighed heavily upon him. He detested the second-class treatment by U.S. forces toward black soldiers. Furthermore, he sympathized with the native Filipinos, whom the Americans regularly referred to as "niggers" and "gugus."[7]

He eventually defected to the Filipino army in 1899. There he acquired the rank of captain in the Philippine Revolutionary Army. He became a successful guerrilla leader, and his men called him General Fagen.[8] Besides clashing several times with American troops, his most famous action occurred during the fearless capture of a river steamer in Central Luzon. His crew seized the vessel's cargo of weapons and quickly melted into the jungle. By the time American forces arrived, not a trace of the marauders could be found. His exploits had begun to take on mythical proportions on both sides of the conflict. Fagen's cult triggered fear among army brass of mass black defections and called into question the fidelity of "Negro troops." White officers grew frustrated at their inability to capture Fagen, who became something of an Osama bin Laden–like figure of his time.

Fagen's elusiveness became an obsession with the U.S. military and the American public. A substantial reward was offered for his capture—"dead or alive." The course of his later life is uncertain. Some reports claim that a Filipino defector brought forth to the Americans his decomposed head. However, it was most commonly believed that Fagen took a young local wife and retired peacefully to live with her in the mountains.[9] His legend lives on in the jungle, his name whispered before smoldering campfires.

Bob Scanlon was a black American war hero who never served a day in the U.S. forces. Born in 1886, he was a natural athlete from Mobile, Alabama. Scanlon's options in life were limited at best. Being lynched simply for being a handsome black man was always a possibility. Yet, unlike most of his peers, he found a way out of poverty by becoming a prize-winning boxer, following the first black celebrity sportsman, heavyweight champion Jack Johnson. Making his way across the Atlantic in the years before the Great War, he fought in England and France. It was in Paris that Scanlon first experienced the freedom, acceptance, and opportunity denied him at home. When the call aux armes came, he paid his debt to France by joining the famed French Foreign Legion. He fought bravely in World War I, was wounded, and just managed to live to tell about it. After cheating death for years, either the Spanish flu or a jilted woman ended his colorful life.[10]

Buffalo Soldiers became an emblematic symbol of the American Wild West, depicted in comics and film as battling Native Americans and protecting settlers. They were originally members of the 10th Cavalry Regiment formed in 1866 at Fort Leavenworth, Kansas. The Buffalo Soldiers were established by Congress as the first peacetime Negro regiments, mostly out of gratitude for how well blacks fought in the Civil War.[11] Though they now had their own units, this allowance was seen as formalizing segregation in the army.[12] The Cheyenne tribe coined their nickname, the actual translation being "wild buffalo." The Apache refined the term, stating that the soldiers "had curly, kinky hair . . . like bison."[13]

This corps consisted of five regiments: the 9th and 10th Cavalry and the 24th, 25th, and the Second 38th Infantry Regiments.[14] From

1866 to the 1890s, Buffalo Soldiers served in the Southwest and Great Plains regions. They participated in most of the military campaigns in these areas and earned a reputation for excellence.[15] Nineteen enlisted men and officers from these regiments earned the Medal of Honor during the Indian Wars. In New Mexico, Buffalo Soldiers gave chase to Chiefs Victorio and Nana and their Apache warriors in Victorio's War. The 9th Cavalry spent the last months of 1890 guarding the Pine Ridge Reservation during the Wounded Knee Massacre. They removed Sooners from native lands before Oklahoma statehood. In 1918 Buffalo Soldiers fought in the last engagement of the Indian Wars, the small Battle of Bear Valley in Arizona against Yaqui natives. In total, Buffalo Soldiers disproportionately composed up to a fifth of all army infantry and cavalry personnel. To their detriment, they also served various undesirable morale-sapping roles, from building roads, guarding posts, to escorting U.S. mail.

During the peacetime formation years, the regiments were commanded by white commissioned officers and black noncommissioned officers. General of the Armies John Pershing was a divisive leader of the Buffalo Soldiers. He served with the 10th Cavalry Regiment from 1895 to 1897. Pershing had served as an instructor at West Point, where he was known as a disciplinarian with high standards. Cadets took to calling him "Black Jack" due to his respect for Negro servicemen that he led. In 1877 Henry Flipper became the first black graduate of West Point and the first black commissioned officer to lead Buffalo Soldiers. On September 6, 2005, the oldest surviving Buffalo Soldier, Mark Matthews, died at the age of 111. He was buried at Arlington National Cemetery.[16]

After the Indian Wars ended, the regiments fought in the 1898 Spanish-American War in Cuba. On February 15, nearly three hundred American sailors were killed when the USS *Maine* blew up and sank in Havana harbor. The fighting began when Major General William Shafter led an expeditionary battle force, including three thousand blacks, into Cuba.

Up to five thousand black civilians volunteered to join the fight. Some units had all-Negro officers. Negro regiments were nicknamed "Immune Regiments" since blacks were selected for the war under the ignorant belief that the "Negro race" was somehow resistant to tropical diseases. Never mind that successive generations of blacks had lived in North America. [17]

To prepare for the invasion of Cuba, Buffalo Soldiers were posted to the southeast United States for the first time in their history. They were initially billeted near Tampa, Florida, where overt racial discrimination was commonplace. Nevertheless, the worst racist act was committed not by locals but by northern whites in uniform. Troops from the Ohio National Guard entertained themselves by coaxing a two-year-old black child into the open to serve as a firing practice target. Shots were fired. The child's mother was in hysterics but powerless to intervene. The youngster was injured but not killed. In a response that would be repeated, incensed Buffalo Soldiers rampaged through the city, though nobody died. [18]

Called the most integrated corps of the nineteenth century, Buffalo Soldiers fought up the slope of San Juan Hill along with the famous Rough Riders led by then Lieutenant Colonel Theodore Roosevelt. Men from the 24th Infantry were the first to raise the American flag atop that hill. Roosevelt commented, "no one can tell whether it was the Rough Riders or the men of the 9th who came forward with the greater courage to offer their lives in the service of their country."[19] Twenty-six Buffalo Soldiers died that day. Lieutenant Pershing wrote, "They fought their way into the hearts of the American people."[20] The Buffalo Soldiers took solace in the notion, albeit disputed, that they were liberating an oppressed indigenous and black people from the European imperialists.

During one landing at Tayabacoa, Cuba, 10th Cavalry Privates William Thompkins and three others voluntarily went ashore in the face of enemy fire to rescue wounded American and Cuban comrades. Each was awarded the Medal of Honor. Thompkins was laid to rest at the Presidio's San Francisco National Cemetery, along with another 450 black volunteers. [21]

Despite their gallantry, Roosevelt turned his back on his men and wrote: "Negro troops were shirkers in their duties and would only go as far as they were led by white officers."[22] As the black bodies piled up in Cuba in his wake, there was little love toward the cavalier president from the blacks. Racial politics continued to downplay the black troops' contribution to the war. Although the Buffalo Soldiers comprised 12 percent of the army's infantry force and 20 percent of the cavalry, they received less than 4 percent of the Medals of Honor awarded. Government bureaucracy impeded the awards process, and the posting of blacks to desolate outposts reduced their visibility to the public eye. [23]

However, many blacks hoped that their young men's heroism in Cuba and later in the Philippines perhaps would lead to "a new era for the Negro race" in earning equal rights.[24] The media, in large part, honored the Buffalo Soldiers' service with books, pictures, and editorials. One newspaper editor stated, "We are proud of our colored troops, the heroes of the day."[25]

In 1899, Filipino nationalists led by Emilio Aguinaldo resisted the American presence and began attacking U.S. forces. At the time, the 24th Infantry was based in the mostly Mormon Salt Lake City, Utah, breaking with the tradition of being garrisoned in far-flung outposts. Mormon theology at that time held tenuous beliefs about blacks, believing that they were cursed and thus given dark skin. Modern interpretations suggested that Canaan was punished through Ham, his father, and that Ham had sex with the wife of his father, Noah.

The regiment's stay hinted at the troubles that followed in the years to come.[26] An editorial in the *Salt Lake Tribune* claimed that black soldiers were likely to attack local whites. An eloquent rebuttal letter penned by an uneducated 24th Infantry soldier stated that the men had "enlisted to uphold the honor and dignity of their country as [did] their fathers."[27] In a sad plea, he and his comrades "object to being classed as lawless barbarians. We were men before we were soldiers. . . . We ask the people of Salt Lake to treat us as such."[28] His somber words changed the locals' hearts more than any rifle. Soon, blacks were integrating into various facets of local society. Allen Allensworth, one of only two black chaplains in the army, became a popular figure in civic and religious institutions. At the Buffalo Soldiers' hero's send-off, with applause and flags, black and white crowds cheered for the unit's band and baseball teams. Their departure from Salt Lake City en route to the Philippines was somewhat better than that in Florida. The home newspaper even offered a contrite public apology for the city's previous attitude.

Nevertheless, within the black community in the United States, there was considerable opposition to intervention in the Philippines. Some troops openly questioned whether blacks should fight for a white government that treated them as second-class citizens. Many black leaders and black newspapers supported the idea of Filipino independence. Editors felt that it was wrong for the United States to subjugate colored peoples in a quest for empire building. In the jungle, Filipino insurgents exposed soldiers to propaganda, encouraging blacks to desert. Posters and leaflets addressed to the "Colored American Soldier" described lynchings and rampant discrimination in their home country, discouraging them from being an instrument of their white masters.[29] Black discontent with wars against brown-skinned peoples and the opposing side's courting of black defection continued throughout the century, most notably during the Vietnam conflict.

Filipino resistance finally collapsed with the capture of their independence leader and the gradual wearing down of the indigenous fighters by the better armed and skilled Americans. After the elation of victory, one black infantryman described the likely result of their service. Fed up with the endless guarding and road building, he said: "We're only regulars and black ones at that; they will [eventually] detail us to garrison the islands. Most of us will find our graves there."[30]

The American entry into World War I came in April 1917 after more than two and a half years of efforts by President Woodrow Wilson to keep America out. Apart from an Anglophile lobby urging early support for the British and an anti-Tsarist element sympathizing with Germany's war against Russia, public opinion reflected that of the president. This sentiment for neutrality was particularly strong among those of Irish and German descent and black church leaders. Even before the war started, American opinion was slightly more negative toward Germany. Emperor Wilhelm II increasingly seemed the aggressor after reports of atrocities in Belgium and the sinking of the passenger liner *Lusitania*. Wilson made minimal preparations for a land war, but he did authorize a major ship-building program for the U.S. Navy. The president was narrowly reelected in 1916 on an antiwar ticket.

In 1917, with Russia experiencing revolutionary upheaval, Germany made a secret offer to help Mexico regain territories lost in the Mexican-American War. An encoded message known as the Zimmermann Telegram was intercepted by British intelligence. Publication of that communiqué outraged Americans just as German U-boats began sinking American merchant ships in the North Atlantic. Texans were particularly incensed at the thought of ceding their independence back to their southern neighbor. Sam Houston, the city's namesake, was the hero of the battle of San Jacinto against Mexico. President Wilson then asked Congress for "a war to end all wars" that would "make the world safe for democracy."

Congress voted to declare war on the German Empire on April 6, 1917. American troops began significant combat operations on the Western Front under the beloved Buffalo Soldiers officer General "Black Jack" Pershing the following summer.[31]

At any particular time, there were nearly a dozen prominent Houstonians in Washington lobbying the government for a dollop of its largess. In response to the war, sixteen auxiliary army training camps needed to be hastily established. Houston got its wish two-fold, signing a $2 million contract for a sprawling 7,600-acre National Guard training center. Camp Logan would house and train more than thirty thousand soldiers, all living in neatly organized tents among the scattered oak trees. Local leaders wanted even more federal handouts and negotiated with the War Department for a separate aviation school, which would become Ellington Field Joint Reserve Base. Buffalo Soldiers assisted with its construction. It would later be shared with NASA.[32]

Black soldiers' dreams of being reposted to the Philippines to lounge with a local wife under the shade of a coconut tree were quickly shattered. The 24th Infantry was instead split up into separate battalions and ordered to perform guard duty at three new camps for the training of national guardsmen called into the war. The 1st Battalion was ordered to Camp MacArthur in Waco, Texas. The 2nd Battalion would remain in New Mexico. The 3rd Battalion, consisting of 654 enlisted men within I, K, L, and M Companies, were ordered to Houston for a short guard duty tour during the construction of Camp Logan.[33] The training camp was located approximately three miles from the center of town and one mile west of the city's limits. Many of the Buffalo Soldiers were combat veterans, and they were salty for action. They expected to be sent off to fight in France shortly, as they were ordered to pack up and bring their winter kit with them. As the camp was erected, they would police the premises and oversee a steady stream of Texas and Illinois National Guardsmen, including black units from the

latter, to man the barracks.[34] In the span of only a few months, a
camp half the size of Manhattan Island was built in a city whose
population only approached a hundred thousand.

In contrast to the more permanent Camp Logan, the 24th Infantry camp lay a mile west, near the city's edges, north of Washington Street and south of the Southern Pacific railroad tracks.[35] It was
essentially a bivouac nestled in the thick woods enclosed on three
sides by low-hanging barbed wire and a drainage ditch on the
fourth. A footbridge across the trough provided access to the camp.
To save time and effort, soldiers who approached from the west or
north regularly crawled through or over the fencing without much
afterthought by superiors. The bivouac was divided into five distinct sections. Each officer was assigned his own tent, all aligned
parallel to the drainage ditch. A short distance west was situated the
larger tents for the mass of rankers, arranged by the company. The
men would assemble before their tents on the street for roll call or
any other headcount. The supply tents were placed at the head of
each company, and the latrines were located to the rear. On the
camp's western edges were the guardhouses. In the settlement's far
northwest corner was a thickly wooded area that served alternately
as the drill square and also as recreational grounds where the men
could entertain lady guests.[36]

The seven guardhouses consisted of roughly two hundred men
who usually worked a twenty-four-hour shift. Soldiers guarded the
premises for two hours at a time and were off for the following
four. Similarly, men were assigned guard duty for one out of every
three days. The guards were instructed to protect all government
property and prevent unauthorized persons from entering the camp.
Each guard was issued merely five rounds of ammunition and ordered to load his weapon only in an emergency. He was also to
treat all authorized personnel with respect. The latter was stressed
more than the former.[37]

Initially, army officials decided against sending black recruits to the South for training and tours of duty, especially those from the North. They feared "embarrassing difficulties will arise in places of public entertainment from the demands of these troops who are associated with white contingents in Northern states."[38] Mississippi Senator James Vardaman said, "Whites are opposed to putting arrogant, strutting representatives of the black soldiery in every community."[39] This decision was revoked. However, commanders of southern camps were ordered to "exercise discretion and judgment to prevent any difficulty from arising."[40]

The battalion arrived on July 28, 1917. It was an assignment that neither the Buffalo Soldiers nor their white officers wanted due to the negative reputation Texans had toward black troops. Lieutenant Colonel William Newman, the 3rd Battalion's commanding officer, tried to get the order revoked. He cited an incident in Del Rio where one of his men was shot dead by a Texas Ranger for merely being black. The War Department ignored his plea. His underlings shared this sentiment. "Every time we have been in Texas, we have had trouble," commented one company captain.[41] A respected black sergeant confirmed that the troops also expected problems from white mobs from the start. Newman's superiors attempted to allay widespread fears. They announced that the Houston Chamber of Commerce had assured the War Department that black troops would be received by the citizens of Houston "in a spirit of patriotism."[42] The War Department cited troop shortages as the reason for posting black servicemen in southern cities, but the truth was more practical. As the army shunned sending blacks into overseas combat roles, it reserved less desirable stateside assignments for them, the consequences be damned. Newton Baker was the secretary of war who knew little of the military.[43] He likely saw the stationing of black troops in the South as purely a matter of administrative efficiency.

Similarly, during the Vietnam War, Robert McNamara, a General Motors "bean counter" with dubious military experience served as the secretary of defense. Whereas Baker could be criticized in hindsight, he made it clear that his decision was in line with military tradition, hinting that all fighting men are of the same race. His verdict might have been progressive for his time and the right course of action if the same situation presented itself decades after the civil rights movement.

The 3rd Battalion of the 24th Infantry arrived in Camp Logan, Houston, with a patchy officer corps with less than half of the sixteen leads originally assigned to it. Only one company had more than one officer. Although the commanding officers of two companies held the usual rank of captain, the other two units were commanded by first lieutenants.

The seven officers were generally considered to be of questionable competency. Most were careerists who were using their time with the black troops as a career steppingstone. Lieutenant Colonel Newman assumed command of the 3rd Battalion at the very last moment—more specifically, on the day it left for Houston. This slapdash appointment was an omen of things to come. He was a career soldier with twenty-five years of experience. Newman was born in Tennessee to a military family who had fought for the Confederacy. His style of leadership focused on detail and daily procedures—consistency and continuity. Unlike the other officers, Newman remained on base and kept abreast of every detail in his bivouac and Camp Logan. Daily he inspected each of the seven guardhouses and tramped both camps on horseback. He was also a devout husband and father. His son frequently dined in the officer's mess.[44]

The duties of battalion adjutant fell on the shoulders of Captain Haig Shekerjian, an officer with six years' service, who had been with the 3rd Battalion for only a few days by the time it arrived. The red-headed Shekerjian was a Christian born in Turkey and raised in Connecticut. He not only had the distinction of being the only Armenian holding a commission in the U.S. Army, but he also was the only one of the five officers in the battalion to have finished in the upper half of his West Point class. Next to Lieutenant Colonel Newman, he was the most professional of the officers and quickly gained the respect and affection of his men. Shekerjian oversaw the battalion's supplies and was also in charge of the military police (MPs). This heavy schedule of assignments kept him occupied with little time for the frivolous activities that so delighted many of his colleagues.[45]

Captain Kneeland Snow headed I Company. He had worked his way up from the ranks. With sixteen years of commissioned service, he was the veteran in the group. Snow also graduated near the bottom of his West Point class. What the company commanders had in common was aloofness when it came to noncritical daily tasks. They were rarely found in or near the camp but enjoyed the prestige of being seen in uniform in a city that revered the military. Snow, a married man, spent most of his time playing golf with a local businessman who subsequently was awarded many lucrative contracts by the base. When not golfing, Snow spent hours with several genteel lady friends.[46]

Captain Bartlett James headed L Company. An idealist from a respectable Virginia family, he was arguably the only promising leader in the bunch, despite being the most junior of all the officers. James also graduated from West Point at the bottom of his class and had never been considered a spectacular leader. He was a bachelor who lived with his younger sister, whom he adored. She spent much of her time tending to the wives of prominent businessmen. A thoughtful and dedicated officer, he abstained from the social climbing and womanizing of his peers. What James lacked in terms of rank, pedigree, and accolades, he made up for in natural leadership and work ethic. As such, James was a well-liked and respected leader among his men. He listened to his enlistees and was fair,

regardless of color. This hard-earned bonhomie would prove invaluable.[47]

In 1831, a continent away and under very different political circumstances, by royal decree, King Lois Philippe II of France came up
with a way to handle all the politically and ethnically undesirable
men roaming Paris streets. He corralled them into a military unit
known as the Foreign Legion. For centuries, it was commonplace
to pay foreigners to fight for France, to die in the most undesirable
corners of the French Empire, away from civilized society. The
Foreign Legion existed to protect and expand French interests. The
corps followed in the steps of the Roman Legion in that it con-
quered the enemy by building infrastructure. In addition to under-
taking the carving out of roads, units were tasked with constructing
an elaborate series of forts with a minimum of tools, often under
enemy fire. The prominent Algerian city of Sidi-bel-Abbes was
erected by legionnaires, as were swathes of the Trans-Sahara highway.[48]

Nevertheless, all the feats of civil engineering came at a high
cost. Being part of a throwaway army of undesirables meant that
the French-born officers were always in danger of being bayoneted
by their men. Months spent doing nothing but digging in the rocky
soil predestined that morale was always near suicide levels. To
prevent desert madness, commanders kept their men busy at all
times. The only break to the drudgery was war and violent death.
Legionnaires carried an extra round to use on themselves to avoid
capture and torture at the hands of North African tribes.

The Foreign Legion felt betrayed by President Charles de Gaulle
when he withdrew entirely from Algeria in 1962. Men from the
highly decorated 1st Foreign Parachute Regiment rebelled and took
part in a putsch against him. Legionnaires went so far as to prepare
for a paradrop over Paris to take command of the Fifth Republic.
Military and civil leaders again became aware that disenfranchised

soldiers packed off to far-flung corners of the empire, often with only a pickax, eventually burn down their master's house.

3

THE WHITE MAGNOLIA

There is no Negro problem. The problem is whether the American people have loyalty enough, honor enough, patriotism enough to live up to their own constitution.—Frederick Douglass

Even after the West was won, Houston was a steamy, muddy, rough-and-tumble town that regularly flooded. There were few more precise ways of settling disputes than via an Old West duel. Being "fast on the draw" did not mean a gunslinger drew a pistol quickly; it referred to aggression—someone who would pull his weapon at the slightest annoyance. In 1911, two grizzled men met on Main Street. The time of day was probably high noon, as was customary. Their hands trembled as they watched in anticipation of any sudden movements. For this American pastime, it was "two men enter, and one man walks away." The only anomaly to this mortal ritual was the fact that the two combatants were not outlaws or ruffians, but two Houston policemen who were settling a petty personal grudge. Residents wondered whether they would have to take cover from bullets fired by police or criminals. [1]

During the Civil War, Houston served as a headquarters for Confederate forces that used the city as a gathering point for the Battle of Galveston. By then, the city had emerged as a business and railroad locus for the export of lumber and cotton. Companies joined together to expand the railroad network. Spurs from the Texas hinterland converged in the new metropolis, where they joined other lines to ports along the swampy Gulf Coast. After the war, cotton barons pushed to widen the city's extensive matrix of bayous to allow more traffic between downtown and the nearby port of Galveston. By the turn of the century, due in part to its proximity to the Panama Canal, Houston was the logistics center of Texas, integral to the development of San Antonio, Dallas, and Fort Worth.[2]

Houston was designated as an official port of entry in 1870, its gilded age. Galveston was struck by a devastating hurricane in 1900, one of the deadliest in history, killing up to twelve thousand citizens. Houston was considered a more viable option for the region's deepwater port due to Galveston's vulnerability to the unforgiving Gulf Coast. The following year, the discovery of crude at the Spindletop field near Beaumont ushered in the Texas oil boom. By 1910, the city's population had reached seventy-nine thousand, more substantial than that of Galveston, almost doubling in a decade.

The port opened in 1914, seven years after ground was broken. By 1930, Houston was the most populous city in Texas, with Harris County the most populated county.[3] For decades to come, Houston remained approximately a third black and two-thirds white, categorizing Hispanics as white.[4] Land was cheap, and the zoning was lax. As such, nonwhites lived in lightly constructed homes situated on blocks close to the downtown district on large plots of land often next to commercial or industrial buildings.

In 1874, Houston completed its first permanent public transit system. At the time, every major American city was nearly buried in manure. Until 1891, transit vehicles were mule-driven streetcars, after which electric cars finally were implemented, in line with many of the great metropolises such as Paris and Berlin.

Houston was home to several hundred factories by 1890, hiring more than three thousand workers. Ten percent of that workforce was white-collar employees. More than a thousand citizens worked for railroad companies, many at Southern Pacific's large shops and other smaller "mom-and-pop" entities. Three years later, there were nearly a dozen railroads in operation.

By 1913, twelve oil companies headquartered in Houston, most notably Humble Oil, later known as ExxonMobil. Billionaire eccentric Howard Hughes was born in Humble, twenty miles from Houston, where his company was born. In 1912, the Rice Institute, afterward known as Rice University, opened several miles from downtown. Rice's original charter dictated that the university admit and educate, free from tuition, "the white inhabitants of Houston, and the state of Texas."

Mexicans fleeing the Mexican Revolution flocked to Houston after 1910 and remained a strong social and cultural influence in the city henceforth. Although anti-Hispanic prejudice was qualitatively different from the black sort, Latinos were arguably more economically and politically disadvantaged than blacks. Magnolia Park, seven miles downstream from the city center near the Houston Ship Channel, became one of the first Hispanic neighborhoods in the city. The construction of the channel and associated industries attracted mostly migrants from Mexico. Before the petrochemical sector was established en masse, Hispanic women commonly worked indoors, in home-kitchen eateries or shops, while the men toiled in construction, cotton processing, and cattle rearing.

Amid Reconstruction, Houston hired its first black police officers. The city had only a dozen uniformed men, and, surprisingly, it parsed half of the positions to blacks. Police procedure was drafted and formalized, and the salary was set at $60 per month. Soon after, the department employed its first two detectives and purchased a patrol wagon. The title "city marshal" was changed to "chief of police," yet it remained an elected position. In 1910, the city intro-

duced its first motorized police car and commissioned its first traffic squad to manage the increasingly bustling streets. Various administrations tinkered with doling out police jobs. A pay raise finally occurred in 1915, when it was increased to a paltry $75. Police
who were quick on the draw and also poorly paid made for a toxic
combination. At the time of the raise, the force was a hundred men
strong, with only a handful of blacks. One police chief admitted to
utilizing bloodhounds, much in the manner of antebellum plantation owners, "to exert a moral effect . . . especially upon the Negro
race."

Though the force was slowly evolving into a professional unit
on par with larger northern cities, there was little bonhomie or trust
from the populace. The aim of the force was primarily to curtail the
most egregious crimes and banditry. Being a police officer proved
one's virility. Frontier justice was still in effect, and citizens resorted to Old Testament variations of it. A famous black Houston
minister said, "Law-abiding citizens feared the police in getting
over the city at night more than they feared the highwayman."[5]

Puritanical police chiefs came and went, depending upon how
political winds blew during any given season. Not surprisingly,
reformers were unpopular among the rank and file since they imposed military-style discipline onto an ossified establishment.
Elected chiefs who were exceptionally ethical quickly made enemies and were eventually voted out. Houston Police Chief Clarence
Brock was one such reformer. He was previously the superintendent of parks and ill-suited to run a major police department with
an entrenched culture of machismo and nepotism.[6]

Different administrations with varied philosophies about law enforcement coupled with opposing economic policies created racial
discontent. The red-light district, also known as the reservation,
was a ten-block portion of the Fourth Ward, also known as Freed-
men's Town, abutting the San Felipe district. It was composed of
all races and ethnicities, with the sex workers mingling freely with

their black neighbors in the abutting districts. However, when the more priggish approach to law enforcement came into effect, it disrupted what was an orderly regulation of the reservation. Though all creeds lived among each other, their different economic backgrounds allowed white prostitutes to continue to ply their trade in more favorable parts of the city. Black sex workers were forced out of the brothels and onto the streets where they were easy pickings for overly zealous police.[7] Not surprisingly, the vast majority of johns and consumers of bootleg alcohol were whites.

Blacks were also overpoliced.[8] Their concentration in pockets of the city made them targets for the police's arrest quotas and provided the commissioners with favorable crime statistics. Many decades later, police forces across America would fall into those same sloppy practices, resorting to quick, easy fixes rather than long-term solutions. This culture fostered a rise in police brutality, foreshadowing the future woes of minorities and, at the very least, irreparably damaging any goodwill. Years later, this dynamic bore a child with the Rodney King beating and Los Angeles riots of 1991,[9] police militarization,[10] and nationwide racial unrest in 2020.[11]

Houstonians wondered if there was indeed an operational police force. During Prohibition, policemen capriciously enforced laws on alcohol. Often they actively participated in bootlegging. Lax enforcement of the legal drinking age was typical of the era and the South in general for many decades. Louisiana during Mardi Gras was a notable example. Bar and brothel owners donated funds to city officials who were sympathetic to their activities. Everyday frontier pastimes such as prostitution were technically illegal. Rather than ignore the vice, a harm-reduction approach tacitly permitted sex work in the reservation. Regardless of the sleaze, Houston police quickly turned a blind eye toward businesses that provided kickbacks or hush money.[12] Nevertheless, as in any gray-market or quasi-legal activity, the political complexity of allowing it grew geometrically as the vices' prevalence increased linearly.

The National Selective Service Act of 1917 was a provision that called for a five-mile buffer zone around military installations in which a saloon or house of ill repute would not be allowed.[13] This stipulation put many cities like Houston in an awkward position since they sought the economic activity of an army installation but had to balance that with lost revenue from their red-light districts. For decades before and after the Civil War, Houston had hosted out-of-state troops. The difference now was that the proposed troops were black. Those who opposed their presence coupled those sentiments with the idea that the 24th Infantry would cause an unprecedented rise in vice from gambling to dancing. Residents were befuddled. The angst of having to choose between two evils came to a head when a local committee ran an incendiary ad referring to a 1906 incident involving Buffalo Soldiers resulting in bloodshed. The *Houston Post* wrote: "3000 Negro Troops . . . Remember Brownsville."[14]

Amid this turmoil, there emerged the "uppity Negro" trope. "Uppity" described a person who took on a whiff of superiority or assumed liberties beyond one's social class. By the 1900s, the term was used to describe blacks who did not show the appropriate deference to even lower caste whites. Forgetting to address someone as "sir" or "ma'am" or looking a white woman in the eye proved that a black was surpassing his social status. Obtaining an education or speaking proper English was also discouraged. Blacks commonly stepped off the wooden sidewalks to let whites pass freely. It was believed that allowing black soldiers a foothold in Houston would give previously obedient local blacks a sense that they could also demand equal rights and a stake in society.

The first person of African heritage to arrive in Texas was Estevanico, who arrived in the sixteenth century. A black community already existed in the settlement by the time Houston was founded

in 1836. In 1860, half of the city's black population consisted of
slaves.[15] Those lucky enough to live within the city limits usually
held domestic or artisan jobs. Since the announcement of emancipation after the Civil War ended was delayed, blacks in Texas
remained in slavery for many months though legally free. In the
first half of the twentieth century, blacks left Texas by the tens of
thousands in what was termed the Great Migration. They sought
work and hitherto unknown civil liberties in northern cities, Chicago a notable destination. Those from the countryside that did not
migrate north relocated to Houston. Blacks who stayed in the area
hoped to build New Jerusalem. In the fifth century, Saint Augustine
presented human history as a conflict between the City of Man and
the City of God. This clash was predetermined to end in victory for
the latter. The City of God was inhabited by citizens who had
forgone earthly pleasures. To blacks, the City of Man consisted of
those who exploited their brothers and sisters.

Though Houston was already the largest municipality in Texas,
its cultural flavor was more closely aligned with the slave-owning
South. It was located in east Texas and known as Magnolia City,
after the delicate white and pink flower native to its marshy bayous.
It symbolized many antebellum traditions. The city was an island in
what was known as the "black belt." Houston suffered the
post–Civil War hangover, along with a lengthy occupation by black
and white Yankee troops.[16] Broad-based resentment was directed
toward northern carpetbaggers and the unfounded belief that former
slaves caused the new profound social and economic upheaval.[17]

Since Houston already had a large proportion of blacks, they and
the few previously freed slaves organized groups to help their new
compatriots obtain housing. The modern welfare state of the devel-
oped world was merely an economic theory at the time. Despite
charity, many of the new residents were relegated to abandoned
buildings and tent communities. Blacks were politically disenfranchised and poorly represented by the predominantly white state

legislature and city council.[18] Democrats regained power in the late
1870s, often after violence and intimidation suppressed black voting. Many former slaveholders and Confederate soldiers were
elected into office. Churches and schools were still segregated,
with blacks staunchly belonging to Baptist and Methodist denomi-
nations.[19] Although this separation may have kept the racial peace,
it also entrenched the notion that blacks and whites were irreparably different.

Early Houston was divided into four wards. The southeast ward,
known as the Third Ward, became a vital hub for black-owned
commerce and culture, with Dowling Street being the area's central
corridor. The largest black population was found in the San Felipe
district, located inside the Fourth Ward.[20] On any given night, the
heavenly smell of fried chicken, ham hocks, and sweet potatoes
emanated from any given doorway. Black Houston had four movie
houses, three weekly newspapers, and a professional baseball team,
the Black Buffalos. Blocks of ice were often lugged along the main
thoroughfares, and on Sunday mornings, immaculately dressed
families would queue for a scoop of ice cream and a cold glass of
sweet tea. Aside from the shoe shiners, laborers, and chamber-
maids, blacks were rarely found outside of their historic boroughs.
A mass exodus out of and back into the black districts before and
after the workday was a sight to behold. However, times were
good, and many enterprising blacks had done well for themselves
in their parallel city within a city, which housed its own law offices,
jewelry stores, and hotels. Tall buildings grew like weeds, and, to
an extent, the blacks rode the up-and-coming Magnolia City's pros-
perity boom. As long as racial tranquility was maintained, there
was no reason for the good times to end—even if government
violence was needed to enforce the peace. Houston and Atlanta
competed to become the Athens for black Americans.

As affluent whites moved to the suburbs, blacks who were previously forced to live beyond the outskirts of the city began to pur-

chase property in the heart of the San Felipe district. This swapping of real estate and racial shift was indicative of en masse "white flight," which other American cities would experience years later.

Nevertheless, the city did just enough to placate both struggling blacks and segregationist whites. It earmarked a considerable amount of social spending on blacks in the form of parks, libraries, and public services. Houston embodied a spirit of coexistence, which was more passive than the tenuous race relations of other major cities, reflecting the American West's rugged individualism. Politicians were well aware that blacks could be pushed only so far, as racial flare-ups in other Texas towns proved.

Unfortunately, slave emancipation was not synonymous with equality.[21] Many blacks returned to the same fields to toil under conditions indistinguishable from those during their bondage. When northern troops quit the South, they intended to leave behind a freer and just society. Instead, their departure ushered in the Jim Crow era.[22] Revenge was a dish best served cold. The South pushed back and got even with black and white Yankees alike via the judiciary. Jim Crow laws were state and local statutes that enforced segregation in southern states. They supplanted the South's previous "black codes." The origin of the phrase was attributed to "Jump Jim Crow," a black song-and-dance caricature performed by a white actor in blackface, which first surfaced in 1828.[23] He was used to satirize President Andrew Jackson's populist policies and later became a pejorative expression for "Negro."[24]

All laws were enacted in the late nineteenth and early twentieth centuries by white Democrat-dominated state legislatures. Twenty-seven passed in the Lone Star state, mandating segregation in all public facilities and resulting in a new state constitution.[25] Most notably, they disenfranchised blacks by making voting and registration unduly complicated and subject to white oversight. Blacks were often required to recite the Declaration of Independence. After federal troops withdrew from the South, southern states contended that the constitutional requirement of equality could be met in a way that separated the races. State and federal courts tended to reject pleas by blacks that their Fourteenth Amendment rights were violated, arguing that it applied only to federal, not state citizenship. As such, the federal government preferred to leave racial segregation up to the individual states.

"Equal but separate" doctrine was derived from a Louisiana law of 1890.[26] The legal principle extended to transportation, including interstate trains and buses. Amenities for blacks and Native Americans were consistently inferior and underfunded compared to those for whites. Often there were no facilities at all for people of color. Nuances and variations differed by state. Texas laws required separate water fountains, restrooms, and waiting rooms in railroad stations.[27] Young black female university students had to give up their seats on public transportation to sweaty white male laborers in overalls. In practice, nobody believed that separate could ever be equal.

In many ways, the second Morrill Act codified the basis of "equal but separate" laws. The federal government provided funding for each state's higher education budget but left the details to state legislatures. Yet seventeen states excluded blacks from access to their land-grant colleges without providing similar educational opportunities. Some states adopted laws prohibiting schools from offering access even if they wished to. As such, the act, which only touched on education policy, implicitly accepted an odious legal principle:

> That no money shall be paid out under this act . . . for the support and maintenance of a college where a distinction of race or color is made in the admission . . . but the establishment and maintenance of such colleges separately for white and colored students shall be held to be a compliance . . . if the funds received . . . be equitably divided.[28]

The only positive outcome was that, in response, seventeen states established separate land-grant colleges for blacks, which would be known as historically black colleges and universities (HBCUs).

The Plessy v. Ferguson decision of 1896 added the finishing touches to state-sponsored segregation. In 1892, Homer Plessy, who was of mixed ancestry but appeared to be Caucasian, boarded an all-white railroad car in Louisiana.[29] While the conductor collected passenger tickets at each seat, Plessy announced that he was seven-eighths white and one-eighth black.[30] He was then instructed to move to a colored-only car. Plessy refused and was promptly arrested.[31]

In court, Plessy claimed that his Thirteenth and Fourteenth Amendment rights were violated. The Thirteenth Amendment abolished slavery, and the Fourteenth granted equal protection to all under the law.[32] The case made its way to the Supreme Court. In its subsequent decision, the court ruled that the railroad had not infringed upon the Thirteenth and Fourteenth Amendments, thus formalizing separate but equal.

> The object of the [Fourteenth] Amendment was undoubtedly to enforce the absolute equality of the two races before the law, but . . . it could not have been intended to abolish distinctions based upon color, or to enforce social, as distinguished from political equality, or a commingling of the two races.[33]

The court decision meant that railway companies were required to provide equal but separate accommodations. Separate rail cars could be used, and the companies could deny service to passengers who refused to comply.[34]

In 1913, staunch Democrat Woodrow Wilson became the first southerner elected president since Zachary Taylor a half-century prior. Wilson's views on segregation were mainly in line with popular public opinion. He lamented the contamination of American bloodlines by the "sordid and hapless elements" coming from southern and eastern Europe.[35] Wilson considered the Negro question a "human problem," not a political one. Southern politicians celebrated his rise to the presidency of a country that was not yet a great power.

The federal government recently had pursued racially tinged policies toward Native and Latin Americans and had passed laws that specifically prevented Africans and Asians from immigrating to the United States.[36] Defenders of President Wilson claimed that his views on race were not as crude or vicious as those of other prominent segregationists. He rejected the Ku Klux Klan and lynching as un-American. Wilson's approach was to "promote racial progress by shocking the social system as little as possible."[37] Nevertheless, he appointed several open segregationists to his cabinet. His administration escalated the discriminatory hiring policies and segregation of government offices that began under President Roosevelt. In Wilson's first month in office, he allowed cabinet members to segregate their respective departments. By the end of 1913, many departments, including the navy, had separate workspaces, restrooms, and cafeterias. There was almost no opposition in Congress toward these policies, most of which remained in place for years afterward. Wilson defended his administration's arrangement, arguing that segregation removed "friction" between the races.[38]

President Wilson was critical of Reconstruction and held the prevailing view that the South was demoralized by northern carpetbaggers and overreach by the Republican Party.[39] As such, extreme measures to reassert white control of southern legislatures were justified. During Wilson's presidency, D. W. Griffith's infamous 1915 film *The Birth of a Nation* was the first motion picture screened in the White House. Although revolutionary in its cinematic technique, it glorified the Ku Klux Klan and portrayed blacks as savages.[40] One villain walked with a stoop and salivated as he fantasized about a young white woman, spittle a proxy for semen.

White femininity was held sacrosanct and protected from repulsive black masculinity. Wilson was quoted in the film three times. He compared the movie to "writing history with lightning."[41]

In 1935, when Nazi Germany set out to legally discriminate against Jewish citizens, it had precedent to fall back on. Germany closely studied America's Jim Crow laws and passed two profound pieces of racial legislation: the Reich Citizenship Law and the Law for the Protection of German Blood and German Honor. These Nuremberg Laws laid the legal groundwork for the persecution and extermination of the Jews. The Nazis studied how the United States had designated Native Americans, Filipinos, and other groups as noncitizens even though they lived within the United States or its territories. This framework influenced the citizenship portion of the Nuremberg Laws.[42] Nazis then reproduced the statutes that segregated blacks. However, there were challenges. Whereas blacks were poor, uneducated, and powerless, European Jews had considerably more economical and political power. As such, the German laws needed to be more stringent.

Contrary to the optimism of some Houston city officials, the black soldiers were not welcomed by the populace. Nevertheless, they were expected to behave in the same manner as the local blacks— accepting brutality, harassment, and racial slurs without recourse or retaliation. Texans always viewed servicemen favorably; however, many police and residents also felt that black skin negated an enlistee's status as a soldier. Even white construction workers at Camp Logan who toiled under a relentless sun for meager wages took delight in addressing the Buffalo Soldiers with racial slurs. No efforts were made by the army to discourage such transgressions.

The completed camp was an economic boon for Houston. The timber industry was especially eager to supply materials for the camp and merchant vessels used along the ship channel. Camp Logan also would drive increased federal funding to widen the waterway, opening the region to increased commerce.[43] Houston's port was the closest major U.S. port to the Panama Canal.[44] The engineering and construction contract was awarded to a local construction company at a running cost of roughly $1 million per week.[45] During the preliminary discussions, business leaders were aware of growing problems among white citizens, police, and black troops at Camp Logan. However, they refused to communicate them to the War Department for fear of losing the aviation school or reducing plans for Camp Logan.[46]

Officers from Fort Sam Houston and the quartermaster's department in Washington, D.C., eventually arrived in Houston. They leased two thousand acres of muddy, mosquito-infested woodland outside the city limits. The property was accessible from Washington Road, which became Washington Street closer to the city. Trains on the Southern Pacific railroad rumbled slowly just north of the site. Over several months the Army Corps of Engineers set to transform the area into a bustling camp composed of seven hundred buildings and a maze of ten miles of paved roads. Mess halls, infirmaries, latrines, showers, and stables were set up by soldiers and civilians alike, peaking at four thousand laborers.[47] Concrete and money poured into Houston in equal dollops.[48] Times were good and moneyed interests wanted it to remain that way. The Great Depression was nowhere in sight. A century later, Washington Road would be known as Washington Avenue, one of Houston's poshest thoroughfares, replete with upscale boutiques, martini lounges, and fine dining establishments. The land where olive tents were once erected would become among the most valued real estate in Texas. President George H. W. Bush and former first lady Barbara retired only a mile from where the camp once stood.

The Houston business community allowed the pursuit of profit from the war to override its civic responsibility. Treating black soldiers with respect should not have been a severe challenge to the white community. Elected leaders should have pressured local police into reining in their heavy handedness. Nevertheless, they refused to take even the most reasonable measures to prevent high-probability eventualities. In a surprisingly progressive tone, the *Houston Chronicle* sympathized with the Buffalo Soldiers and advocated welcoming them: "Can we conscientiously ask our [European] allies to quarter soldiers whom we ourselves profess to be afraid of?" the daily asked.[49]

A revered preacher and many older blacks felt that armed Negro troops would upset the hard-earned calm between the races; the agitation invited "a direct bid for racial troubles, in which blacks were likely to be all the worse off for it."[50] In a tone that Martin Luther King later reflected, the cleric emphasized the aim of a glorious afterlife to empower blacks. He implored them to "join hands to ameliorate our internal strife [so] that we may be better prepared to meet the external."[51] Decades later, King wrote: "Before I was a civil rights leader, I was a preacher of the Gospel. This was my first calling, and it remains my greatest commitment. . . . I have no other ambitions in life but to achieve excellence in the Christian ministry."[52] Nat Turner confessed, "devoting my time to fasting and prayer. By this time . . . hearing the scriptures commented on at meetings, I was struck with that particular passage which says: 'Seek ye the kingdom of Heaven and all things shall be added unto you.' I reflected much on this passage—as I was praying one day at my plow, the spirit spoke to me."[53]

Although civic leaders only feared that there might be trouble, officers of Camp Logan knew from firsthand experience that trouble was imminent. Lieutenant Colonel Newman went out of his way to placate the local populace by stressing that the only men allowed to carry arms would be the sentries on duty. Troops would be allowed into the city on a case-by-case basis; only those who had shown impeccable behavior would receive a pass from the base. Recruits would not be allowed off base for some weeks until they proved their trustworthiness. It was doubtful whether even military regulations allowed for such arbitrary and capricious rules for off-duty soldiers. White service members did not serve under such an onerous regime. Treating highly trained troops like children simply reflected the patronizing way white society viewed blacks in general—affable but helplessly childlike and, on rare occasions, beastly.

A clerk of the 33rd Division said, "The Negro likes to go to church because God gives him equality. . . . And in the Army he wears good clothes, eats three meals daily, sleeps in a bed at night, and at the end of the month, has a little money in his pocket." This treatment caused resentment within the ranks, even though Manila, Philippines, awarded the 24th Infantry with a ceremonial two-handled cup in gratitude for their impeccable off-duty conduct in that country.[54] The San Francisco police chief extended an open invitation to several guards to join his force after their enlistment. Even Nat Turner's lawyer underestimated his natural intelligence. As Turner sat in his cell, his counsel asked if he could document their conversation. Turner began with his childhood. His master mistreated him and considered him incapable of advanced reasoning. The condescension fueled his rage. He explained stoically:

> The manner in which I learned to read and write. . . . I acquired it with the most perfect ease. . . . I have no recollection whatever of learning the alphabet—but to the astonishment of the family, one day, when a book was shown me to keep me from crying, I began spelling the names of different objects—this was a source of wonder to all in the neighborhood . . . and this learning was constantly improved at all opportunities . . . whenever an opportunity occurred of looking at a book, when the school children were getting their lessons, I would find many things that the fertility of my own imagination had depicted to me before; all my time, not devoted to my master's service, was spent either in prayer, or in making experiments in casting different things in moulds made of earth, in attempting to make paper, gunpow-

der . . . that although I could not perfect, yet convinced me of its practicability if I had the means. [55]

After the interview, when questioned about the science of manufacturing those various items, he was well informed on those topics.

4

EAST TEXAS STORM CLOUDS

The greatest pleasures are only narrowly separated from disgust.—Marcus Tullius Cicero

Jesse Washington, a black man, was stripped of his clothing and
dragged on the street. Concrete, tarmac, and rocks scraped away his
flesh, leaving a trail of blood. He struggled to minimize the agony
by shifting his weight onto harder portions of his body, such as his
heels or elbows. However, bits of soft tissue still grated away the
top layers of skin and subcutaneous fat. Soon it would be bone. All
the while, he was beaten with sticks by an angry white mob. The
thrashing was perhaps an act of mercy, as he might have lost consciousness. Soon, men with sharp instruments appeared. Others
grabbed both his legs and forced them apart. As he writhed in
terror, the mob castrated him.[1]

Contrary to stories about farm livestock, this was not a matter of
a few quick snips. Washington's genitals were grabbed, pulled, and
slashed for several excruciating minutes. His ravaged flesh was
torn away as he struggled and shrieked. Nevertheless, the pinnacle
of Washington's torment lay ahead.[2]

Tradition held that Lucifer was cast out of heaven and allowed
to rule the worldly realm. In rare instances, humanity glimpsed
actual hell on earth. In the spring of 1916, horror visited the town of

Waco, Texas. Lucy Fryer, the white wife of a small business owner, was raped and murdered. Washington was accused of the
crime.[3]

On May 15, Waco's courthouse quickly filled in anticipation of
the trial. More than two thousand observers also filled the streets
and wooden sidewalks outside. The judge asked Washington for a
plea and explained the potential sentences. Washington muttered a
response that the court interpreted as guilty. It heard testimony
from the arresting officers and the physician who examined Fryer's
body. The doctor discussed how the woman died, but he did not
mention rape. Washington's limited intellectual capacity was apparent to all present. The prosecution rested, and Washington's
attorney asked him whether he had committed the offense. Washington replied approximately, "That is what I done" and then quietly apologized.[4] The trial lasted merely an hour. The mob roared in
approval upon hearing the lead prosecutor declare that the trial was
conducted fairly.

The jury's foreman announced a guilty verdict and the sentence
of death.[5] Court bailiffs attempted to escort Washington away but
were pushed aside by the mob, which seized Washington and
pulled him outside. A heavy chain was placed around his neck, and
he was forcibly dragged toward city hall by the growing throng. By
the time the morbid procession arrived, a group had already prepared wood for a bonfire beside a tree.[6] Washington, semicon-
scious and covered in blood, was partially hung from the tree by the
chain. To increase his suffering, he was doused with oil, and the
kindling was lit. Washington was repeatedly raised and lowered
into the flames by somebody who ensured that he was always con-
scious and who presumably was familiar with how flesh reacted to
heat. That chain handler likely would savor grilled meats with his
family the following weekend without a shred of guilt. After Washington repeatedly climbed the piping hot chain, the crowd cut off
his fingers and broke his arms. Shouts of delight were heard as

Washington burned. Children from nearby schools watched, some climbing trees for a better view. Many parents considered participation in a lynching as a rite of passage for young men.

Photos were taken of the dangling charred stump of what was once a living, breathing human. Even his mangled form showed his natural muscularity, masculinity that white men subconsciously feared. Many in the crowd were smiling as the photo was taken. The torture not only broke Washington's body but rendered him unrecognizable. Amid a Sunday picnic atmosphere, the spectacle drew a large crowd of up to fifteen thousand at its peak, including the mayor and the police chief. Nobody intervened. Some blacks were purportedly present, though it was not to revel in mob sadism. Doubtless one of the blacks watching this ritual torture was Washington's mother. The sight of her weeping for him may have been the last thing he saw. Similarly, in revering Saint Bartholomew's suffering, St. Theresa Church, founded in 1946 on the grounds of Camp Logan, displayed a stained-glass window depicting the knives used to skin alive one of the twelve apostles.

The fire was extinguished after several hours. Bystanders swarmed to collect souvenirs, including Washington's bones and chain links. One scavenger claimed a part of Washington's genitals. Children pried Washington's teeth from his skull and sold them. His corpse was removed from the tree and dragged behind a horse throughout the town.[7] Americans would be reminded of this horror in 1998 after James Byrd Jr. was lynched in Jasper, several hours from Houston, by being dragged from a pickup truck. In 2004, the charred and mutilated bodies of American military contractors were hung from a bridge in Fallujah, Iraq. In Conrad's *Heart of Darkness*, Kurtz's last dying words were: "The horror! The horror!"[8]

More than a century earlier, England had banned the practice of drawing and quartering convicts, deeming it a cruel act that a civilized nation ought not conduct. For centuries, "death by a thousand cuts," or slow slicing, was practiced in China for serious crimes, often high treason or regicide.[9] The drawn-out ordeal could last up to three days. Ribbons of flesh were rumored to be thrown to onlookers for use in traditional Chinese medicine. In 1905, French troops stationed in Beijing witnessed and photographed such executions. Circulation of those published images shocked the world and fueled xenophobia. Many organizations sensationalized the practice as typifying Eastern barbarism. Others even fetishized the act as the highest form of Oriental sexual sadism. The West prided itself in its modern penal code, although slow slicing was abolished a decade before Washington met his agonizing death. In her 2003 book *Regarding the Pain of Others*, social activist Susan Sontag bizarrely described a photo depicting slow slicing. In it, a criminal, while being laboriously executed, rolls his eyes heavenward in "transcendent bliss." Sontag was known to frequently stare at the image for minutes on end and meditate upon it.

British Special Forces member Andy McNab was captured and tortured by Iraqi forces during Operation Desert Storm. He understood firsthand the unspeakable cruelty of which civilized humans were capable. He wrote of his tormentors: "they had a job to do as well. It's just that some of them enjoyed it a bit too much."[10] Many compared Washington's lynching to a blood sacrifice. Prior to the Waco siege of 1993, historians considered that cursed event as "the most infamous day in the history of central Texas." Upon reviewing the facts independently decades later, most legal experts concluded that Washington did, in fact, murder Fryer.

As Camp Logan was rising from the marshy soil, in southern Illinois, up to 250 blacks were killed in what would be known as the East St. Louis Massacres.[11] A toxic cocktail involving race and jobs ignited one of the deadliest race riots in American history. East St. Louis, with its stockyards and meatpacking plants, was a microcosm of its big brother Chicago, conjuring images of Upton Sinclair's *The Jungle*. It was a rough industrial city where saloons outnumbered schools and churches and where blacks also began overwhelming the myriad of European ethnicities. Most of the whites were Catholics of Slavic extraction. The new immigrants and their ancestors never owned slaves. Local Ku Klux Klan chapters saw little distinction between papists and Negroes. Sociologists described what was termed a racial tipping point, when the percentage of nonwhite faces finally empowers those outsiders to group with their own—not integrate—and embrace their identity.[12] It is often also the point at which the native population no longer feels at home. The phenomenon has been applied to bars, social clubs, and schools. In 1910, approximately 10 percent of East St. Louis's population of fifty-eight thousand was black. By 1917, that proportion had nearly doubled.

Overseas, the Russian Revolution was in full swing. In North America, this period was one of frequent labor violence, most notably in industrial cities. Employers used force to suppress organized labor and strikes. Since established white Americans were more likely to work in the service sector, many industrial workers were recent immigrants from the less prosperous parts of Europe. Though American unions had ties to international labor movements, they were not color-blind and favored their white constituents. During strikes, they strengthened their appeal by excluding black workers. Mostly bystanders in the labor disputes, blacks were hired as "scabs," or strikebreakers, fueling racist sentiment. Competition for finite resources and tribalism was rife among ethnicities, but more so between races. White workers feared they would be undercut by blacks who were willing to accept lower wages without union representation.

The generally accepted concept of a minimum wage, which would later be seen as empowering minorities and the economically disadvantaged, resulted from nefarious motives. In 1925, a minimum-wage law passed in the Canadian province of British Columbia, with the intent and effect of pricing Japanese immigrants out of jobs in the timber industry. Australia passed a similar law to "protect the white Australian's standard of living from the invidious competition of the colored races, particularly of the Chinese," who were willing to work for less. [13]

In the summer of 1916, twenty-five hundred white meatpacking workers went on strike. In response, numerous companies imported black workers to replace them. [14] Ultimately the striking workers won a wage increase, but the companies still retained nearly eight hundred blacks. This result only exacerbated growing racial tensions. In early 1917, the aluminum smelting laborers went on strike. The company hastily recruited hundreds of Negro workers to replace them. Again, after the incident, hundreds of blacks were retained, but many whites were also fired. Tensions reached critical mass after rumors spread of black laborers fraternizing with white women. [15]

In retaliation, several thousand white men marched into downtown East St. Louis and began attacking blacks on the streets, buses, or streetcars. From there, they rushed into the black sections of town, south and west of the city, and began rampaging. The mob indiscriminately beat and shot blacks, including women and children. A policeman was inadvertently killed when he was mistaken for a white shooter. This death further incensed the white mobs. During the killings, the black quarter was set alight. After sabotaging the fire department's water hoses, white insurgents burned adjacent sections of the city and shot black residents as they escaped the flames. Rioters claimed that "Southern Negroes deserved a genuine lynching." Several blacks were hanged. In that town, on those nights, black skin was a death warrant. Fifteen teenage girls wielding clubs chased a Negro woman in the small hours of the morning, pleading with the rampaging men to kill her. Like refugees fleeing war, columns of blacks crossed the Eads Bridge over the Mississippi River to escape into St. Louis. It seemed odd for former slaves to flee a northern state into a southern one for safety.[16]

The local police were either indifferent or encouraged the rioting. To suppress the violence, the governor finally called in the Illinois National Guard, yet a significant portion of it was ineffective or idle. Numerous witnesses claimed that guardsmen joined in the attacks. No organized effort was made to protect the Negroes or repel the onslaught, even though the aggressors were leaderless and disorganized. A mere dozen dedicated police could have prevented the worst of the bloodshed.[17]

In the aftermath, the ferocity of the attacks and the government's failure to protect lives contributed to the radicalization of many blacks in the region and, eventually, the nation. What would be a pernicious mistrust by blacks of the police was conceived in historical fact. In 2014, the embers of this insurgency lit the nearby Missouri town of Ferguson on fire after black teenager Michael Brown was shot dead by a white policeman.[18] Echoing the spirit of previous struggles, the Black Lives Matter movement was born.

The mostly Hispanic south Texas town of Brownsville seemed an unlikely place for racial strife. Since arriving at Fort Brown in 1906, the Buffalo Soldiers of the 25th Infantry, sister regiment of the 24th, were required to obey existing Jim Crow laws and customs. The mores included showing not just respect for whites but submission. In the mostly Hispanic town, many local women befriended the soldiers, which incensed many of the menfolk who still practiced an antiquated form of Latin machismo.[19]

A reported attack on a white woman on a hot summer night so incensed the townspeople that army commanders implemented an early curfew the next day to avoid trouble. To make matters worse, on the following night, a well-known bartender was killed. Gunshots also wounded a policeman. Murder in a sleepy, dusty town shocked the region. The Buffalo Soldiers would experience the less-known form of brown-on-black prejudice. Though nobody was sure who the culprits were, Brownsville residents immediately blamed the outsiders. Nevertheless, the Fort Brown commanders confirmed that all troops were in their barracks at the time of the shootings. Citizens, including the mayor, disagreed vehemently.

Alleged witnesses combed the premises and provided evidence of the 25th's part in the shooting by producing spent bullet cartridges from army rifles. Despite contradictory evidence showing that the shells were planted to frame the Buffalo Soldiers, government investigators accepted the statements of the local whites and mayor. An officer with the Texas Rangers was called in to investigate and interview twelve soldiers. However, the local county court did not return any indictments based on that official report. Civilians continued the fight and managed to get the attention of army brass.[20]

At the recommendation of the army's inspector general, President Roosevelt ordered 167 of the black troops to be dishonorably discharged because of their "conspiracy of silence." The legal basis for such a discharge was dubious, even within the unique military penal code.[21] Despite a lack of evidence or reliable testimony, city and federal officials including Roosevelt merely presumed the entire unit's guilt. The Old Testament's notion of the sins of the father lived on. A dishonorable discharge was not merely a red stamp on a document but akin to a scarlet letter for cowardice. This judgment would prevent those enlistees from ever working in a military or civil service capacity. Many soldiers had been in the army for decades. Others who were close to retirement forfeited their entire pension.

Upon learning of this mass injustice, prominent black educator and activist Booker T. Washington, "the wizard of Tuskegee," asked President Roosevelt to reconsider his decision. The president caused a stir by personally meeting with Washington in the White House. Nevertheless, Washington left disappointed.[22] Blacks had historically been staunch Republicans, favoring the party of Lin-coln. However, Roosevelt's decision may have been the event that disillusioned blacks, pushing them to the Democratic Party. Al-though the incident became a political football for decades, no real relief was offered until 1972, when the army found the soldiers innocent. A Senate Military Affairs Committee Report suggested the incident was staged by townspeople or instigators to have the black servicemen removed. At its recommendation, President Rich-ard Nixon pardoned the men and awarded them honorable dis-charges—but without back pay. Regardless, it was too little, too late, as there were only two surviving soldiers from the affair. A year later, Congress approved a tax-free pension for the last survi-vor, Dorsie Willis, who received $25,000. Before he died, he was subsequently honored in the nation's capital. In 2007, Louisiana State University graduate student Ricardo Malbrew convincingly argued in his thesis that the shots that started the rioting came from a white captain who should have been found guilty.

Despite the unpopularity of the war in Europe, a week after Presi-dent Wilson's declaration, the War Department had to stop accept-ing black volunteers because its quotas had filled so quickly. Law-makers must have felt it necessary to limit the number of men willing to die for their country. The lack of black representation in the war effort caused a backlash from patriotic blacks, which prompted the War Department to eventually establish the black 92nd and 93rd Divisions, both combat units.

Nevertheless, the involuntary draft was a different matter, as those efforts were disconnected from the black quotas. Draft panels were composed almost entirely of white men. Blacks were told to tear off a corner of their registration cards in order to easily identify and process them separately. Instead of turning blacks away, the draft boards did all they could to rope them into the war. One Georgia county exemption board medically discharged 24 percent of white registrants but only 3 percent of Negros. Black men who owned their farms or had families were regularly drafted before single white farmhands. Other times, southern postal workers deliberately withheld the registration cards of eligible blacks so they would be arrested for dodging the draft.

While still discriminatory, the army was far more progressive than the other military branches. Even then, most blacks were limited to labor battalions. Black servicemen sometimes went for months at a time without proper clothing. Some were issued little more than old Civil War uniforms. Others were forced to eat outside in the winter and to sleep in pitched tents rather than barracks. Even basic training was segregated.

So eager were some blacks to fight for their country that many joined foreign militaries, such as France's Foreign Legion. Eugene Bullard, the famous ace pilot, transferred to the French air force via the Foreign Legion and became a legend. Proud and battle-ready Buffalo Soldiers were barred from overseas combat roles. They were instead sprinkled throughout American-held territory to slog under the sun like foreign legionnaires, building roads and guarding encampments. Secretary of War Baker opposed this policy, arguing that "black soldiers have performed brave and often conspicuously gallant service for the nation since the American Revolution."[23] In reality, he knew the United States was about to enter the European war and needed every man who could shoot a rifle. Those who made it to France were tasked with digging the infamous trenches, building latrines, and handling unexploded shells. Like ancient caste systems throughout the world that Christians frowned upon, blacks were relegated to handling and disposing of the dead. Often, logistics units that loaded and unloaded war matériel worked backbreaking twenty-four-hour shifts. Morale in most Negro units was undoubtedly low. Blacks could not serve in the marines and could serve only in limited and menial positions in the navy and the coast guard. However, in 2020, a U.S. aircraft carrier was named after one of those humble black rankers for his heroism during World War II, Messman Third Class Doris Miller, born in Waco, Texas.

America entered World War I with approximately eighteen thousand regular army and National Guard officers available. Approximately twelve hundred were black. The army allowed Negro officers to lead only black troops, whereas white officers commanded both whites and blacks. In major cities, blacks protested their lack of representation in the officer corps, which had the authority to lead their young men to death. The War Department finally agreed to act upon those demands, but only because they believed that more Negro officers would reduce the risk of mutiny. The army chose to create a segregated but equal officer training camp. In the spring of 1917, Fort Des Moines in Iowa opened its doors to black officer candidates. It was headed by the former second in command of the 24th Infantry. Mixed-race units, with a diversity of backgrounds and combat experience, benefited from the cross-pollination effect. Knowing that these units were more battle ready than white ones, the War Department, fearing racial uprisings, sacrificed effectiveness for a predetermined racial homeostasis. Social engineering within the U.S. military would continue even a century after the Great War.

Several other factors began to change the attitudes of military brass. West Point cadets now mingled with the handful of black cadets and were impressed with their commitment. Aside from their reputation for bravery, black servicemen had a high reenlistment rate, which meant that officers were spared the drudgery of training novices. Some junior officers sought the prestige of commanding black troops that were stereotyped as savage and undisciplined. Many Buffalo Soldiers were previously black vaqueros of the West. Aspiring cavalry officers volunteered to lead Buffalo Soldiers to learn horsemanship from the very best original cowboys. Some officers with genuine Christian or social justice senti-

ments volunteered to lead the Negro regiments due to principle
alone.

Although blacks could now serve as officers, the privilege did
not result in equal treatment. The army did not hold to the universal
principle of respecting men who led other men into battle. Blacks
were often barred from officer's clubs and quarters. The War Department rarely interceded, and discrimination was usually overlooked, sometimes condoned. Mandating that white enlisted men
recognize Negro officers' positions of authority was problematic.
Black officers were often advised by their superiors to avoid de-
manding salutes from whites when passing them on the street or in
camp. Even white soldiers who recognized a black officer's rank
found ways to show contempt. Many saluted but added, "Damn
you!" under their breath.

Because many southerners protested out-of-state blacks being
placed in local training camps, the War Department understood that
it was sitting on a powder keg. Nevertheless, they still tossed proud
black soldiers into the gauntlet of antebellum racism. One half-
baked measure stipulated that no more than one-fourth of trainees
in any army camp on American soil could be black. Overseas installations, by nature of their isolation, allowed a higher proportion
and better self-policing against a black mutiny.

In Houston, young children played in the streets with wooden rifles
in eager anticipation of the guest soldiers. Although locals were
happy to host a military camp, they had subtly and not forcefully
lobbied the army to send white troops instead. The Houston Chamber of Commerce suggested the Texas National Guard. The military was unsympathetic. Backing down and reluctant to show in-
gratitude, the chamber responded by stating clumsily for the record,
"The people of Houston are not Negrophobes."[24]

Once the political wrangling ceased, two battalions of the 24th
Infantry rolled out of Columbus, New Mexico, en route to the green

marshy woodlands of East Texas.[25] So opposed were many Texans to the sight of black men in uniform that trains carrying black troops were often fired upon. Commanding officers regularly requested military escorts so that the men could "pass through an area which they were supposed to protect without danger from hidden assassins."[26] However, the original orders were for the men to remain in Houston for merely seven weeks, which may have been a compromise and optimistic projection.[27]

Though the units seemed up to scratch, they were a rather motley bunch. Their most senior and experienced noncommissioned officers (NCOs) were missing. They were transferred to Iowa for officer training, where success required "absolute obedience . . . and exemplary conduct." The old hands were replaced by inexperienced men unprepared for promotion. Moreover, the unit size was inflated by fifty additional rookies. Discipline, the glue holding the units together, was severely compromised. Of particular concern was the loss of their beloved first sergeant. This position was both essential and highly sensitive, as he was not only the senior enlisted man but also a liaison between the white officers and black soldiers. He needed to be exceptionally diplomatic and guard the hard-earned trust and loyalty of his men. Like half-mad legionnaires stuck in a desolate Saharan fort, the fighters were salty and eager for war. The prospect of guarding an installation was unappealing and morale sapping.

Nearly eight hundred enlistees and eight white officers arrived in Houston to considerable fanfare. Once word got out about the exotic troops from afar, a crowd of several thousand black and white spectators gathered to watch. The Sons of Ham were nevertheless a jolly bunch. With boyhood fascination, one remarked that after seeing "nothing but sand, rocks, and sage brush" in Arizona, Houston's "tall green grass, real trees, fresh water close to the camp, watermelons and roasting ears in season, and plenty of our folks to mingle with . . . everything looked mighty good, sir."[28] The

Houston Post went on to paint the soldiers as lovable buffoons who "grinned happily" before city officials.

Houston's Mayor David Moody patronized the troops by using colorful language and exotic comparisons, likening their fighting spirit to a bearcat. In allaying the fears of the populace, he added that discipline in the ranks was near perfect. As if beholding prized racehorses, Moody added that the soldiers consisted of "the best and most intelligent Negroes in the country." He lavished extra praise on the white officers, who must have been exceptionally talented to be able to lead such sex-starved, incorrigible fighters.[29] Indeed, in the French army, the finest officers were the top academy graduates who volunteered to lead the "foreign regiments" consisting of criminals and refugees.

Moody had stepped in as acting mayor after the sudden death of his predecessor, who was known for playing fast and loose with the rule of law. A political novice, he had large shoes to fill and a leviathan government to run. Moody took a hands-off approach toward the police department, sought consensus, and quickly delegated tasks to others. Moody also knew that the police chief was underqualified and incapable of managing the actions of a handful of rogue policemen.

In due course, businesses that cared more about the color of money than that of a man's skin sprung up around camp. Frustrated that the black throngs scared away all his white clients, one Baptist business owner converted his refreshment stand to an establishment referred to as the "dance hall" for those same black soldiers. Lieutenant Colonel Newman was delighted and fully supported the gesture, as it meant that his enlistees would remain close to the base and not wander too far into town. The owner marveled at how the Buffalo Soldiers danced and always had a jolly good time. The troops behaved impeccably, although the owner complained of the numerous unescorted females with dubious reputations. Every business owner catering to the troops swore on the holy Bible that he was not selling them alcohol. Apparently, the sale of soda water kept those businesses in good financial health. A few enterprising soldiers' wives rented a vacant studio across the street from the dance hall, situated a used piano in it, and made a decent profit by allowing dancing in the evenings.

Color and vibrancy emerged in this corner of Houston. Jazz bands filled the air with melodies of that distinctive age. Few realized that those slapdash clubs were giving birth to a unique genre of American music. Texas blues became prevalent in the early 1900s among blacks who worked in ranches, oilfields, and military bases. Its regional style was characterized by swing and jazz influences. Later variations were compared to southern rock and blues-rock. In the 1920s, Blind Lemon Jefferson contributed to the style with improvisation and a single-string guitar. During the Great Depression, many bluesmen moved to the major cities of Galveston, Houston, and Dallas. From these urban centers, a new wave of popular performers appeared, such as Lil' Son Jackson, Lightnin' Hopkins, and eventually Stephen "Stevie" Ray Vaughan.

Fifty miles away on the Gulf Coast, boxing legend Jack Johnson continued to break barriers both in- and outside the ring. Nicknamed the "Galveston Giant" during the height of the Jim Crow era, he became the first black world heavyweight champion. He held on to that title from 1908 to 1915. Johnson became a legend after defeating white boxer James Jeffries in what was known as the "fight of the century." Whites rioted after the match. Transcending boxing, he became a lightning rod for sports and race.

Johnson was fond of dressing in a derby and three-piece suits, reminiscent of an English dandy. He pioneered the image of the flamboyant and trash-talking boxer in the days when fighters still observed Marquess of Queensberry rules. A century later, British boxer Naseem Hamed and Irish mixed martial artist Conor McGregor were known as much for their fashion sensibility as for their championship titles. Johnson lived a lavish lifestyle with all the material trappings, including fast cars and amorous pursuits. Johnson flouted conventions regarding the social and economic "place" of blacks in American society. He broke a strong taboo by consorting with white women. Newspapers reported the succession of females coming in and out of the champ's hotel room. When asked about the secret to his vigor, Johnson replied, "Eat jellied eels and think distant thoughts." He enraged white America with his audacity and verbally taunted white and black detractors alike. Nevertheless, his flamboyance did not escape the high-minded idealism of some black leaders. Booker T. Washington said it "is unfortunate that a man with money should use it in a way to injure his own people, in the eyes of those who are seeking to uplift his race."[30]

In 1912, Johnson opened a fashionable restaurant and nightclub with his white wife. He eventually was arrested on what many felt were trumped-up charges of violating the Mann Act, which forbade transporting women across state lines for "immoral purposes." In a manner reminiscent of the Dreyfus affair, the media sided with Johnson and claimed that he was selectively persecuted merely for being a wealthy black athlete married to a white woman. Sentenced to a year in prison, he fled the country and continued boxing abroad until 1920. He eventually returned home and served his prison sentence at the federal penitentiary in Leavenworth, Kansas. Doubtless, many starry-eyed youths wanted to be Johnson and admired him for his in-your-face rejection of societal prejudice.

Lieutenant Colonel Newman took a progressive approach toward recreation. He allowed lady guests into the camp and established liberal visiting hours. This allowance was not due to laxity but to keep his men off Houston's streets and out of trouble. Doubtless some visitors were prostitutes, but others were simply male preachers or bible study participants. Many of the youthful females were locals attempting to improve their lot in life by marrying a young man in uniform—ideally one that could read and write. Although Newman's gestures may have seemed benevolent, his motivation stemmed from a desire to expose the men to the upper classes of black society living in Houston. As such, he hoped to civilize his unruly brood.

With the war raging in Europe, the 24th Infantry was eager to get to France. The Moulin Rouge was in its golden age, and stories of love, liberty, and freedom abounded. Men believed that the French accepted all people as long as they spoke French. *Fraternité* was an idea, not a skin color. Blacks were treated so well that American officials complained to the French that those servicemen were being spoiled and would not be given such deference upon return. Jazz culture dominated Paris nightlife. Montmartre was home to clubs such as Le Grand Duc and Chez Florence. Black boxers, artists, and Harlem Renaissance writers, later including James Baldwin, were warmly welcomed. The Nazi invasion of Paris in 1940 halted the "corrupt" influence of jazz in the capital.

Yet trouble hovered over Houston like East Texas storm clouds ready to unload a torrent. Washington's lynching was still fresh in the public's mind. Many of the educated men in the 24th Infantry were avid readers of W. E. B. DuBois's *Crisis*, the publication of the National Association for the Advancement of Colored People (NAACP), and the *Chicago Defender*, a militant black anti-southern newspaper. The soldiers indeed debated whether respect was earned through Christian meekness or violent resistance. The 3rd Battalion was accustomed to being treated fairly in western parts of America, such as Cheyenne and San Francisco. Lieutenant Colonel Newman knew his soldiers would suffer in Houston.

Since "the Texan's idea of how a colored man should be treated was just the opposite of what these [soldiers] had been used to," the men took too many liberties and veered dangerously close to the domain of the so-called uppity Negro.[31] Several tussles occurred on public transportation, against police or store clerks. City officials and employees wanted to make it abundantly clear to the new visitors that their status as servicemen did not elevate them to the same class as whites.

In 1955 Rosa Parks heroically defied the law regarding segregated buses and changed American civil rights. She was credited with speaking truth to power. Nevertheless, decades earlier in Houston, the Buffalo Soldiers also took a visible and undocile stand against Jim Crow laws. A group boarded a streetcar, but the rear black area was already filled. Rather than sit on the aisle's floor, the uniformed men defiantly took their places in the whites' section. In other instances, men took down the "colored" signs inside streetcars and tossed them out the window. Others kept the signs as war booty, a powerful gesture for a small victory in a seemingly unwinnable battle. A Buffalo Soldier swaggering about town wearing a "colored" sign around his neck must have seemed the ultimate "fuck you" to the white establishment. One placard was ungraciously ripped from a restaurant. The dismayed owner was threatened upon pain of death never to exhibit it again. It was time to turn the tables. Righteous anger was on full display, and the upright God of Daniel looked approvingly upon those men. On justice and rage, medieval saint and church doctor Thomas Aquinas said, "but he that is angry with cause shall not be in danger: for without anger, teaching will be useless, judgments unstable, crimes unchecked."

Similarly, a young Mahatma Gandhi traveled to South Africa in 1893 to practice law. In Natal, he was subjected to racism and anti-Indian laws. His tipping point into activism came after he was roughly removed from a first-class white railway compartment. Losing a subcontinental empire taught British leaders that proud brown men must not be kicked off trains.

In another incident, as the soldiers' curfew approached, they crammed into a streetcar, leaving downtown. Again, there was no room for all of them in the black section. A police officer was within earshot. After they took places in the white section, the conductor brusquely ordered the troops off the trolley. The Buffalo

Soldiers begrudgingly complied but expressed their disdain out loud and threatened to overturn the entire streetcar in protest. This scorn unnerved the other passengers and later put all other conductors on notice about the black soldiers' violent nature. Upon boarding the second streetcar, the Buffalo Soldiers threatened the conductor with violence by announcing upfront that they "would just love to see the first son of a bitch that would try to put them off."[32] There was no indication that this conductor was hostile to them. Furthermore, in a surprisingly gracious gesture, he even moved the white passengers forward so that the Buffalo Soldiers would have enough room.[33]

Bystanders were often the first victims of war. Bombs did not discriminate between the guilty and innocent. Lieutenant Colonel Newman repeatedly reminded his men that streetcar conductors were not the authors of segregationist policies and were merely bound by the ordinances of their jurisdiction.[34] Many conductors were doubtless sympathetic to the Buffalo Soldiers but were nonetheless menaced by packs of them on the weekends. We always hurt the ones we love, according to a familiar aphorism.

Shocked or infuriated whites riding on the streetcars either muttered under their breath or threatened the conductors with disciplinary action if they did not set the Buffalo Soldiers straight. Houstonians were caught off guard by the level of black disobedience. The lack of white retaliation was not indicative of weakness. They were simply biding their time.

Temporary bandage solutions to mitigate racial animosity were proposed by the city, such as dispatching additional streetcars during peak hours. However, such gestures largely failed to address blacks' real grievance—their second-class treatment. No amount of kind words or separate accommodations could assuage that sentiment. And only in the 1960s would that boiling energy lead to meaningful racial equality—an entire century after slave emancipation.

Nevertheless, there was a shot over the bow that those in power underestimated, misunderstood, or ignored. Similar racial scuffles involving the 24th Infantry occurred in Waco when it was assigned guard duty for Camp MacArthur. As Waco was a far more racially homogenous town than Houston, the discrimination experienced there was more pronounced. Worried commanders forbade their men from carrying loaded weapons in the city. This seemed a dishonorable slight for soldiers whose raison d'être emanated from the barrel of their Springfield rifles.

On one uneventful Waco evening at midnight, word leaked to a commanding officer that a dozen soldiers had slipped out of camp and into town with loaded weapons. Additional troops were sent out to intercept those men who were angry, trained, and more than ready to assault the local police. When the two squads made visual contact within the city, a firefight broke out. The renegades mistook the troops for the police. Miraculously, there were no injuries, and all the men eventually were corralled into camp. The army made a desperate public relations effort to downplay the severity of that incident. A captain insisted that only half a dozen men had fired their rifles and that they were rookies with only a few months of service who had not yet been acclimated to army customs. A lesson that was not learned from Waco was that the local police should cede control of an insurgency entirely to the military. Another forgotten basic training lesson was to always correctly identify the enemy before firing.[35]

Despite the military establishment's best efforts, the Waco incident fueled white Americans' lingering fears that blacks could not be trusted with firearms. An unceasing debate about guns and race would continue for decades. An offspring from this dispute was the 1967 formation of the Oakland-based Black Panther Party, which made the public display of guns central to its charter. The group proclaimed: "The gun is the only thing that will free us."[36] A few years earlier, Malcolm X appeared in an iconic photo in *Ebony* posing with a rifle, visually embodying his "by any means neces-sary" philosophy for justice. Led by charismatic figures like Huey Newton, the Black Panthers movement was younger, more revolu-tionary, and more militant than the one led by Martin Luther King. The apostles Paul and James preached that a byproduct of anguish at the hand of this world was perseverance. A transformed man and former Christian, Malcolm X retorted, "There is nothing in our book the Koran that teaches us to suffer peacefully."[37]

Several prominent black pro-gun groups, such as Black Guns Matter, formed decades later in the wake of the civil rights move-ment. Firearms historically had been entwined with privilege. In colonial America, only landowners could carry guns. They be-stowed that right to low-caste whites only as a means to quell slave or Indian uprisings. Nat Turner's revolt depended upon comman-deering weapons from dead white victims. Later, a principal aim of the Ku Klux Klan was to disarm blacks. White politicians hotly debated the issue of gun control after blacks began arming them-selves.

As news of the Waco incident reached Camp Logan, Lieutenant Colonel Newman made what many considered to be a deal with the devil. Houston's Acting Police Chief Brock met personally with the colonel at camp. They decided to "split the baby." Newman assured the chief that additional resources would be dedicated to police the Buffalo Soldiers under his charge. As a result, a military police (MP) detachment was established consisting of eight NCOs and eight privates. They were explicitly assigned to monitor areas known to be hotspots for trouble, most notably downtown and the San Felipe district. In return, the police chief agreed to cooperate with the army's efforts and allow them the breadth to handle their men.[38]

However, Lieutenant Colonel Newman overestimated the police chief's authority within an entrenched and often splintered police force. Vested interests in city hall were actively working against

Brock. Newman did little to verify that the police were indeed cooperating with the army. In a good-faith gesture, he stripped his MPs of their regulation Colt M1911 pistols, and as such, they ventured onto Houston's mean streets unarmed. Newman's concessions may have never even been relayed to the policemen on the street. In reality, the Houston force treated Newman's MPs with the same contempt as they did "any nigger civilian." The physical assaults and verbal abuse they endured were not from random drunks or ruffians but the uncooperative police officers.[39] Newman's failed attempt to compromise with the city only sapped the paternal confidence his men had in him to maintain discipline.

Most disappointed about the turn of events was the local black populace, who idealistically saw the Buffalo Soldiers as guardian angels who would lead them out of bondage in Egypt to the New Jerusalem. They also hoped that the MPs would temper the brutality they faced from local police and allow the citizens a semblance of civil rights. At the very least, they wished to be policed by their kind. Nevertheless, this idealism faded quickly as the weeks passed.

However, racism even existed in one place where the soldiers should have been respected—their military camp. An Illinois National Guard captain had nothing but praise for their courtesy and conscientiousness, saying they were "well-disciplined and thoroughly instructed in regard to the method of guard duty."[40] Though the soldiers could maintain their professionalism when accosted on the streets, it was quite something else for a stranger to enter one's home, take a seat at the dining table, and address the owner with a slur. White workers who labored throughout the camp in a variety of roles humiliated the Buffalo Soldiers daily. The troubles began when whites complained about showing proper identification to the black sentries upon entering the base.[41] Again, camp commanders went out of their way to placate both parties, designating the Buffalo Soldiers as backup security while a white clerk verified the visitors.

Nevertheless, trouble continued, as any shared resource, such as drinking water, became a lightning rod. In defiance, the guards purposefully drank from the "whites" barrels to the workers' horror.[42] Tit-for-tat name-calling ensued, with laborers insulting black guards point-blank. After reaching their tipping point, the guards snapped back, grasping their Springfield rifles tightly, and said, "I ain't no nigger"—a challenge for anybody to proclaim otherwise. After an egregious racist comment comparing the value of a black man's life to that of a dog, a Buffalo Soldier drew his pistol. The workers complained to Lieutenant Colonel Newman after that dust-up, but he refused to take disciplinary measures.[43] Although a moral victory for the guards, it did not resonate well with white Houston. Workers quickly spread word in the town of the black troops' insolence.

The goings-on in the camp gave the city the overwhelming feeling that the black soldiers were too "uppity" for their britches. Moreover, whites feared that allowing the soldiers such latitude in the camp only empowered black locals to demand better treatment. Not only were the black troops unwelcome, but they were now seen as revolutionary figures hell-bent on sowing discord and disunity among the locals. Indeed, many of the men who befriended residents in the black community expressed sympathy and vowed to use their positions as members of the armed forces to help. On several occasions, soldiers intervened when they saw a fellow black being mistreated, responding to violence with violence.

As the camp's completion neared, the number of workers tapered off. Illinois National Guardsmen took their places. The nearly two thousand Texas National Guardsmen were quartered in several buildings downtown, en route to France via Camp Bowie near Fort Worth.[44] Many in the Texas contingent were from neighboring rural "cotton belt" counties around Houston. Local members lived

at home. Although the Buffalo Soldiers and the Texas National
Guardsmen occupied different universes, they often crossed paths
in the city. The encounters were not always amicable. The same
issues of race, class, and rank dogged both parties. The embodi-
ment of the southern warrior spirit was the 1876 establishment of
the Texas A&M University Corps of Cadets in College Station.
Texans proudly revered military service. Imbued with European
notions of valor, honor, and heroic death, they could not understand
why the federal government would allow peasant servants to wear a
fighting man's uniform to battle other civilized men. Added to this
toxic animosity was the fact that not only were the Buffalo Soldiers
in uniform, in contrast to the guardsmen, but they were full-time
professional federal troops.

Young recruits on both sides were unfamiliar with the rules of
conduct involving other military branches, even when no racial
animus existed. Both groups narrowly avoided bloodshed in similar
but separate incidents when confronted by an outside officer or
NCO who demanded that he be saluted.[45] The Texas National
Guard was led by General John Hulen, a railroad executive and
longtime Houstonian. His contempt for blacks was evident when he
posited that the black soldiers "seemed to think they had greater
privileges than other Negroes in the community."[46]

However, disrespect and racial slurs were commonplace as the
weeks went on. In a perverse twist of fate, Illinois National Guardsmen who quelled the East St. Louis riots were transferred to Camp
Logan. Many in the 24th Infantry donated money to a fund to help
the black victims. Some guardsmen openly boasted of siding with
the whites during the bloodshed. In return, many blacks made it a
point to "fix those whites from the [German, Irish] Chicago slums
before their time in Houston ended."[47]

Camp officers were now inundated with complaints by Houstonians about Negro soldiers running amuck, to the point at which the
reports could no longer be taken seriously. Added pressure came

from avid prohibitionists who pushed the police to crack down on lascivious consumption in the black quarter. That would not be the last time they voiced their opinion. Houston police were now openly forbidding any black soldier from talking to black civilians. Houstonians were afflicted with mass paranoia by the thought that there were unpatriotic and treasonous blacks in their midst. In return, local blacks paid a heavy price for sympathizing with the Buffalo Soldiers. The reservation was suddenly heavily policed, and even non-sexually oriented petty crimes were harshly yet capriciously punished. Youths were arrested for playing cards in alleyways. Prostitutes were locked up and brothels raided. Black men were arbitrarily arrested and intimidated, often by being handcuffed and fired at with empty pistols.[48] Morale plummeted both inside the camp and beyond the barbed wire. An eerie quiet descended upon Houston, and the remaining camp laborers openly quit in droves, citing a real fear that troubles lay just beyond those storm clouds.

The somewhat sinister term "fifth column" originated in Spain in the 1930s during the early phase of its civil war. Hemingway wrote at length of this nebulous entity. It reflected a statement made by dictator Francisco Franco. In a conversation, he referred to a total of five nationalist columns, four of which were approaching Madrid. When asked about the fifth, he chillingly replied that it would be composed of local citizens and "arise from inside the city."

5

GOMORRAH

To hell with going to France. Get to work right here.—Anonymous, 24th Infantry soldier

Gavrilo Princip was born in the remote settlement of Obljaj, Serbia, in 1894, the second of his parents' nine children, most of whom died in infancy. He was named Gavrilo at the insistence of the family's Eastern Catholic priest, who felt that naming the underweight infant after Archangel Gabriel would help him survive.[1] Princip's parents were Christian serfs living under Muslim rule. A born revolutionary, Princip was expelled from school in 1912 for participating in a demonstration against the Austro-Hungarian government.[2] He eventually joined the infamous Black Hand, the first revolutionary insurrection group in the Balkans and inspiration for similarly named movements—and rock bands—across the West. Its immediate aim was to create a unified Greater Serbia. In Sarajevo on June 28, 1914, nineteen-year-old Princip executed the most remarkable feat of any young revolutionary—political assassination.[3] On that day, he made last-minute adjustments to his positioning, as his target deviated from the planned course without notice. The driver applied the brakes upon learning that he was going the wrong way. While doing so, Princip, with FN Model 1910 pistol in hand, stepped to the car's footboard and shot an imperial couple point-blank.[4] The husband's last words were, "Sophie, Sophie! Do not die! Live for our children!" Archduke Franz Ferdinand of Austria and his wife were dead by noon.[5]

The assassination led to a month of diplomatic maneuvering between Austria-Hungary, Germany, Russia, France, and Britain. Anti-Serb rioting broke out in Sarajevo and various other cities within hours following Ferdinand's death.[6] Germany demanded that France remain neutral. Europe was racked by chronic instability and militancy compounded by incompetent leadership. These rulers, who prided themselves on modernity and reason, sleepwalked through crisis after crisis and convinced themselves that war was the only answer. Within weeks of the tragedy, Europe was at war with itself. The conflict would fell more than fifteen million souls, destroy three empires, and permanently alter world history. Princip died of tuberculosis in prison shortly after his arrest, while the war that the teenager triggered with one act of violence raged on.

"I am getting tired of the way they're treating us here," a random construction worker innocently overheard one soldier bemoan to his peers.[7] "You keep your damned mouth shut. These sons of bitches will get what's coming to them when the time comes," was the chilling response from another.[8] The accidental eavesdropper thought nothing of the conversation—for a time.

In immaculately pressed uniform, Lieutenant Colonel Newman stood before his boys and bade them farewell. To the army, changing one commander for another amid an eventless assignment was a mere formality. Nevertheless, Newman knew that he was walking away from a powder keg. He was confident that he performed his duties as expected and with honor but was nevertheless eager to put space between him and that troublesome little outpost in the woods. The camp was intact and orderly on the day he left. What happened afterward was anybody's guess. Newman was subsequently posted to the western-sounding Camp Dodge in Iowa. Camp Logan, however, was not happy to see the back of Newman's head. Although he was not beloved, he was competent. He rarely personally met with his troops but made great efforts to respond to fluctuating camp morale. The press praised him for the discipline and order displayed by his men, blissfully unaware of the problems simmering beneath the surface.

The army appeared to neglect proper due diligence in selecting Major Snow as Lieutenant Colonel Newman's replacement. Snow recently had been promoted to major and was considered inexperienced to command a unit of that size. He may as well have been Ichabod Crane from *The Legend of Sleepy Hollow*. The novel's protagonist worked as a teacher but spent his days daydreaming, writing love letters to local ladies, and eating meals they prepared for him. As such, Snow was much less of a disciplinarian than Newman. This detail may have stemmed from a difference in leadership philosophy or simply apathy, as Snow was seldom seen with his men.[9]

Meanwhile, roaming Houston's mean streets were two equally pitiless and unruly policemen. These hulking mounted officers were as intimidating to the locals as the first conquistadors to the diminutive Aztecs. Even off his horse, Rufus Daniels was a mountain of a man. Known for his brutality, he was feared among the black population. His no-bullshit attitude earned him the nickname Daniel Boone, the rugged frontiersman of yesteryear. Lee Sparks was an average-sized man at roughly five foot ten. However, what God takes from a man in terms of size or intelligence, he gives in other ways.[10] Sparks compensated for what he lacked in size with his blistering temper. He never allowed any black the upper hand or benefit of the doubt.

Officer Sparks represented a type of antebellum policeman who saw himself as a self-proclaimed guardian of a vanishing "southern way of life," which perhaps never even existed. White peasants who labored next to slaves somehow felt that the grand plantations represented their heritage. Raised in neighboring and racially charged Fort Bend County, a center for plantation slavery, Sparks had a history of brawling with blacks. As an officer, he made it a point always to let black suspects know that whites were squarely in charge. As an aging municipal policeman, he was likely unhappy with his lot in life, enraged that younger, fitter, more virile black men in uniforms with medals were issued Springfield rifles and sent to fight on his behalf. He was suspended previously for ten days by Police Chief Brock for verbally assaulting a woman as he arrested her son.

Nevertheless, the police department did little else to curb Officer Sparks's notorious abuses. What made his attitude so destructive was not that he did not understand the plight of blacks, but that he understood it all too well and wanted to cement their inferior status in society.[11] His colleagues recognized him as a bully and sadist. Mounted police often volunteered their horses for service, as did he. However, Sparks overly relished his Übermensch status atop his black beast of burden. Petty street hustlers and prostitutes were the favored objects of torment for this duo. As Marquis de Sade once quipped intelligently, "Why is your pain more important than my pleasure?"

It took the proliferation of consumer technology to effect police oversight and accountability. In 1991, motorist Rodney King was stopped by police and brutally beaten by several officers, though he was unarmed. An event that historically would have gone unnoticed and difficult to prove in a court of law was finally captured by a bystander with a home video camera.

As the black districts in Houston continued to be selectively policed, Officers Daniels and Sparks triggered a perfect storm of events. On the morning of Thursday, August 23, the humidity was already near 100 percent, and the day was set to be the summer's hottest. Locals often quipped that nothing good happened after ten o'clock or on days over a hundred degrees. The officers were called to investigate alleged gambling by black teens in the Fourth Ward. In an alley along San Felipe Street, two youngsters were seen throwing dice. It was unknown if any money was involved. The teens heard the police horses galloping toward them and fled on foot. Sparks pursued one of them, the chase leading into the home of black resident Sara Travers, a mother of five. She was ironing clothes when Sparks barged in. Alone and not expecting guests, she was woefully underdressed. [12]

"Did you see a nigger jumping over that yard?" Officer Sparks barked at Travers. She had seen nothing of the sort. Not satisfied with her response, he proceeded to turn the house inside out, searching for the culprit. Officer Daniels waited outside on his horse. Still with no sign of the suspects, Sparks vented his fury on Travers, calling her a liar among other slurs. "Since these . . . sons of bitches of nigger soldiers came here, you are trying to take the town," he exclaimed. "We do not allow niggers to talk back to us. We generally whip them down here." Having a basic understanding of her civil, property, and constitutional rights, Travers protested his intrusion into her home. Neglecting proper police procedure and the concept of probable cause, Sparks responded with violence. He slapped Travers. She let out a scream, and Daniels rushed in, not to assist her, but to help Sparks by grabbing one of her arms and dragging her away from the house. She protested that she was underdressed, but Sparks muttered that Travers would be taken away even if she were naked. Sparks later claimed that she was arrested for, of all things, abusive language. For being a "biggety nigger woman," they intended to give her ninety days on the "pea farm," referencing the practice of leasing slaves to other landowners. Sparks's official account of the incident differed, as he denied slapping Travers and insisted that she was adequately dressed when he entered. [13]

Travers was arrested, roughly removed from her home, and led to a call box. Since the officers were horse mounted, they phoned for a patrol wagon to take her away. Hearing the commotion from the start and seeing Travers in cuffs, neighbors stood by helplessly in fear. Among the crowd of two dozen happened to be Private Alonso Edwards, who was in the area on a twenty-four-hour pass from camp. He empathized deeply with the woman. Edwards may have smelled of alcohol or still been tipsy from the night before. However, in comradely fashion, he pleaded with the officers to allow him to pay any fine on Travers's behalf.

Officer Sparks was in no mood to justify an arrest to a Buffalo Soldier who should have minded his own business. He told Travers to stay put, and then he approached Private Edwards with his revolver. The trooper stood his ground but was pistol-whipped across the head five times, causing severe injuries. Echoing the arrest of George Floyd in 2020, Sparks later stated, "I was not going to wrestle with a big nigger like that." When the patrol wagon finally arrived, both Edwards and Travers were hauled off to the city jail. Travers was soon released without charge; however, Private Edwards was charged with interfering with an official arrest and thrown into a cell where he would remain for several days.

Corporal Charles Baltimore was known throughout camp as a model soldier and mentor to many new privates. He was also a senior military police (MP) with authority over the soldiers. Baltimore happened to be in the Fourth Ward that afternoon. As he exited a streetcar, he was met by an excited soldier who witnessed the arrests and beatings. Baltimore approached Officers Sparks and Daniels to get a complete picture of the situation. Sparks did not like the tone in which he was questioned. Baltimore explained to the officer that he customarily had arresting authority over his men in those matters. "I don't report to no niggers," Sparks retorted. He was in no mood to consider additional information and struck Baltimore over the head with the barrel of his gun. He later claimed that

Baltimore had approached him roughly, used profanity, and made a sudden movement into his pockets. Nevertheless, later under oath, even Daniels refuted Sparks's story.

Corporal Baltimore was off duty at the time but completely unarmed. With the first blow to the head, he fled for his safety into an unoccupied home nearby. Officer Sparks revealed his genuine contempt for blacks when he later compared Baltimore to a fleeing greyhound and hollering dog. Although Baltimore had not committed a crime, Sparks fired three times at Baltimore's back and into a street full of women and children, according to a witness. Sparks managed to chase him down and pulled him out from under a bed. Baltimore again tried to explain himself but was instead greeted with another two blows to the head with Sparks's pistol. Baltimore was subsequently arrested, shoved into a patrol wagon, and thrown into a cell with his comrade Private Edwards. [14]

Then Corporal Baltimore died—or so everybody thought. However, rumors and exaggerated accounts of his murder quickly made their way back to camp. Alleged eyewitnesses were on the phone with Major Snow, describing how they saw Baltimore's dead body lying in the street unattended. Others offered slightly different first-hand accounts. [15]

In a droll but unfortunate turn of events, just as Major Snow received news of the incident, he was approached by two police detectives who were investigating unrelated reports of shoplifting committed by his men. The detectives were not yet aware of the altercation with Corporal Baltimore. Snow naively allowed them to rummage through the soldiers' personal belongings, searching for stolen merchandise. Nevertheless, the soldiers interpreted the detectives' presence as validation of Corporal Baltimore's death and pretext for further harassment or framing of crimes. Snow should have simply rescheduled what was a petty inquiry in light of that morning's events.

Before the detectives left, Major Snow received official confirmation that Corporal Baltimore was severely beaten but very much alive. In what could be described only as a failure of leadership, Snow did not immediately convey the news to his men. His paternalistic and aloof leadership style proved toxic. By rubbing elbows with businessmen and society ladies, he had squandered the opportunity to connect with his troops from the very beginning of his command. Merely making the rounds about camp and chatting with his men would have revealed the consternation and rage slowly simmering beneath the surface. In camp, groups of men began talking in muffled voices. Soldiers who were usually loud and gregarious whispered to each other. Men retold stories of abuse by the police and acts of racism by the locals. Ad hoc meetings were organized in tents. Despite the icy mood across the camp, Major Snow was oblivious.[16]

Before any historical calamity or man-made disaster, there are always obvious red flags that are ignored. In camp, a young private recalled overhearing others in his unit talk about "getting" the policeman who murdered Corporal Baltimore. Female visitors warned camp commanders that the boys were "going into town to raise the devil with the white people." Still others complained about the leaders in their camp. The first embers of the insurgency were kindled when soldiers muttered, "no white son of a bitch is going to keep us from going. . . . I will kill every one of them if they don't let us all go to town."[17]

In the form of shuttle diplomacy feverishly conducted before any war, Major Snow sent Captain Shekerjian to the police station to meet with Police Chief Brock. Both men were hoping to expeditiously prevent any uprising.[18] Brock was surprisingly conciliatory in handling the triggering incident, as he broadly agreed that Officer Sparks's actions were unlawful.[19] He preemptively assured Captain Shekerjian that no charges would be brought against his men. He also vowed to suspend Officer Sparks long enough to allow Major Snow the opportunity to press charges against the errant cops. He even offered to personally visit the camp the following day to discuss their ultimate objectives. [20]

Captain Shekerjian was posed with three possible courses of action. The police chief could temporarily suspend Sparks pending final approval by the internal civil service commission; the army could file charges of assault; or they could wait for the district attorney to indict Sparks and present his case before a grand jury. The last option seemed the least attractive since both Shekerjian and Brock knew that a local all-white jury would not find a policeman criminally guilty of beating a Negro. In either case, Sparks's immediate fate was left up to the army. In a small symbolic victory for the Sons of Ham, Brock agreed to bar his men from hurling racial slurs at the soldiers. [21] In an age where epithets were commonplace, a small stride toward human dignity was achieved, though at a cost. Words can hurt deeply.

Corporal Baltimore could be forgiven for mistaking Captain Shekerjian's face, when it appeared behind the bars of his jail cell, for Archangel Saint Michael, leader of God's army against the devil. Nevertheless, in a cruel twist, Baltimore was left to molder in his cell for an additional night in order to heal, precisely because he was beaten so severely. In his wisdom or folly, Shekerjian feared Baltimore's bloody and lacerated condition would outrage the camp. Shekerjian also needed time to obtain fresh clothing for the soldier. [22] However, keeping the rest of the camp uncertain about Baltimore's fate for an additional night only fanned the flames of rage already fulminating. It is unknown whether Baltimore knew of the troubles that his beating had stirred up. Shekerjian stressed that upon Baltimore's return to camp, he must play down the entire incident as if nothing serious had occurred. "I understand," the excellent soldier responded. [23]

No sooner did the men from the 24th Infantry leave the police station than Officer Sparks erupted in a furious rage against his

boss. In what was an unheard-of act of insubordination, an indication of his depraved character, or both, he verbally accosted Police
Chief Brock. Showing extreme patience toward his subordinate,
Brock insisted Sparks go home and stay there until the incident was
settled. Sparks was even offered paid leave. Nevertheless, he continued to berate Brock, going so far as to accuse him of taking the
side of the soldiers over his men. "[You're] no better than a nigger."[24] Brock did not take this lightly and demanded that Sparks
surrender his pistol. He refused.

Ever the progressive reformer, Police Chief Brock sought to
manage the police department along the lines of a well-run business, emphasizing transparency, accountability, and customer service. He embraced the radical idea that police existed to serve the
public and ought to do so with courtesy and professionalism. However, in an American region known for banditry and outback justice, this was a tall order. The old guard still existed, and its loyalty
was to the previous chief who ran the force as a good old boys'
club. Officers manifestly disregarded Brock's orders and conferred
with the previous chief. Some executives attempted to indict Brock
on spurious charges. The chief walked a fine line to maintain his
leadership while preventing outright revolt. There is a well-known
maxim in leadership circles that, when dealing with superiors or an
entrenched bureaucracy, one can be right, and one can be dead
right.

Police forces are colored by the chiefs who led them, for better
or worse. New York City detective Frank Serpico risked his career,
reputation, and life by exposing police corruption in the 1970s. He
was one of the few police reformers who succeeded. After Rodney
King's beating, Los Angeles police chief Daryl Gates became the
poster child for ineffective leadership and police militarization. The
widespread backlash eventually resulted in his ouster and a shift
toward community policing.

Police Chief Brock may not have been a man of letters, but a cursory understanding of Dostoyevsky's *The Idiot* would have revealed to him that the world destroys the righteous man. The title was an ironic reference to the central character, Prince Myshkin, a young idealist whose goodness, open-hearted plainness, and generosity convinced those around him that he was an affable imbecile. He is, in fact, a pastiche of the Christian messiah, a "positively good and beautiful man" who is abused and discarded by the world.[25]

The whispers and ad hoc preparations by the troops were not completely secret. The rumor circulating the Fourth Ward was that "they were going to do to Houston as the 9th and 10th done to Brownsville."[26] Nevertheless, the government missed one alert after another about the impending catastrophe. One notable white neighbor, a single elderly woman who lived on the outskirts of the camp, had established friendly relations with the Buffalo Soldiers, perhaps out of fear or for some mutual benefit. She was one of the few in the area with a telephone in her home, and she allowed the soldiers to use it at nearly any hour of the day.

However, on August 23, she noticed a marked difference in both the tone and content of their phone conversations. Soldiers who were always joyous or raucous were now stone-faced and sober, imploring their girlfriends to stay inside their homes that evening because there was trouble brewing. Others requested that their lovers not come to the camp because "Houston was about to be set alight at eight o'clock."[27] Since her phone was in use by the soldiers, she relied on a neighbor to inform the camp of what she overheard. Unfortunately, that neighbor was not considered reliable by camp commanders, as he had habitually pestered them with gossip and other false alarms.[28] In this instance, ignoring him proved a fatal mistake.

Several whites unlucky enough to be in the camp that evening were fortunate to escape with their lives. A local boxing promoter and his assistant who were working with one of the soldiers suddenly found themselves surrounded by a mob of blacks and were ordered to "get the hell out of here."[29] Another soldier interjected dismissively, "we're going to cut the rest of their throats a little later, anyway."[30] Then the group began removing the bayonets from their rifles, prompting the visitors to flee to their vehicles.

Behind them were two dozen soldiers in hot pursuit. The civilians nervously attempted to crank the engine but failed on the first try. "You better start the car, you son of a bitch" yelled one trooper.[31] Luckily for the whites, the second time was a charm, and they vanished in a cloud of dust.

Major Snow eventually took precautionary measures at the behest of Police Chief Brock. Committing a major blunder, the chief himself refused to take similar steps, insisting that he lacked jurisdiction over the military.[32] Snow doubled the number of guard posts. By the evening, he also had sent a corporal and three MP privates to police the streetcar loop to ensure that nobody slipped out of camp. The dance hall was closed to avoid luring men from the camp. Any available soldiers monitored several wards. Despite Snow's best intentions, the soldiers were still forbidden from carrying sidearms.[33] Despite the beatings of Corporal Baltimore and Private Edwards and the city's incendiary mood, MPs had nothing but their bare hands to protect themselves against citizens and vengeful municipal police.[34] Many troops privately disobeyed orders, considering the request tantamount to a suicide mission.[35]

Finally, Corporal Baltimore returned to base, like Lazarus, to what must have been a hero's welcome. Captain Shekerjian's plan seemed to have worked. Baltimore assured the captain that he would not stoke the flames and would calm any hotheaded ringleaders. Sheepishly obedient to the officers, Baltimore did not dare ask what sort of justice would be sought on his behalf. Confident that Police Chief Brock would keep his word and assured of Baltimore's docility, Shekerjian neglected to inform the men that action would be taken against Officer Sparks.[36] Baltimore's passive mood immediately changed once he was alone with his fellow enlistees. The Buffalo Soldiers had already given up hope that their officers could ever understand their plight. Like a married couple just before divorce papers were served, the soldiers made no complaints and went on as if nothing was about to occur. The chain reaction already was set irreversibly in motion.

Major Snow's aloofness blinded him, and he failed even to alert the police department of the latest flare-ups. He flippantly requested feedback from the black noncommissioned officers (NCOs) about the troops' morale. His orders trickled down the chain of command. Not surprisingly, the reports cited nothing of significance. What would later become obvious was the fact that the NCOs who reported back to Snow were either sympathetic to the plotters or actively preparing to mutiny. Major Snow rebuffed one exceptionally loyal NCO who did report disquietude among the ranks, chastening the sergeant for expressing the men's petty grievances rather than merely sticking to the facts regarding any actual misconduct or treason. The sergeant returned, somber faced, to his troops. Convinced that there was nothing of note to attend to, the camp commanders blissfully assumed that all was well. They kept their dining engagements in the city and left base for a splendid evening of leisure.

The only officer at camp that night was Captain James, the duty officer that day. Major Snow decided that the previous policy of having one officer at Camp Logan and another at his camp was not worth the drain on manpower. However, just before Snow got into his vehicle, acting First Sergeant Vida Henry rushed up to him. He was distraught and somewhat incoherent. "Major, I think we're going to have some trouble tonight."[37] Snow questioned him, but Henry was evasive and nonspecific, saying he was not sure and just felt a premonition of bad things to come.[38]

First Sergeant Henry was in his thirties and had served in the
army for thirteen years.[39] He was a native of Kentucky, a state with
frosty winters and clean waters, which made the best whisky west
of Scotland.[40] He may have been of mixed race, considering his
light complexion. Doubtless, his colleagues teased him, calling him
"mulatto," a slang term for light-skinned blacks. Henry was a stately and finely built man with a robust, athletic frame consisting of
two hundred pounds of muscle—a pious protagonist from a Dostoyevsky novel. He had a scar above his right eye, likely from a
boyhood scuffle. His physical prowess was matched by his faithful-
ness as a soldier. Every superior described him as an exceptional
serviceman. Subordinates seemed to delight in obeying his orders
without question, not out of fear, but out of respect. In a troop
replete with teenagers, he held a grandfatherly reverence. What he
lacked in formal schooling or measured aptitude, he made up in raw
leadership ability—to a fault, since he was often overly harsh.[41] As
such, he was promoted to first sergeant in his company. He peppered his commanders with his men's petty peccadilloes, whereas
most NCOs left such matters at the platoon level. He was a man of
contradictions, with unwavering allegiance to his white officers and
the backbone of the black enlistees. It is unsure if he knew where
his allegiances lay or whether he ever resolved the conflicts that
dogged him till his final day. Was the disquietude self-hatred or
internalized racism? Even among the downtrodden, mulattos were
commonly disparaged by their ebony brothers. The blood of both
the enslaver and the enslaved coursed through their veins like mag-
ma. Slavery was long over, yet the progeny of the bondage masters
and female slaves carried on.

As Major Snow and First Sergeant Henry made their rounds
through the camp, a suspiciously high number of soldiers milled
about outside the tents. Conversations ceased abruptly as the major
approached. Snow suspected his command was not entirely bullet-
proof. He now walked a fine line between leadership and appease-

ment. Though his authority needed to be apparent, Snow knew that if he pushed too far, the results could be catastrophic. Trying to display power while holding a weak hand was nerve wracking. After the pair passed one company's supplies tent, they spotted several shadowy silhouettes scurrying into the darkness, laden with stolen ammunition. Dropped rounds were scattered about the grounds. This event was the wake-up call Snow needed, as there was no reason for his men to smuggle out armaments other than mutiny.[42]

Major Snow ordered a bugler to make an officer's call. The four officers in camp were commanded to take account of all their men. All companies were thus assembled without their weapons, an odd occurrence in the evening, outside of working hours. Every man was to be accounted for, including those on duty, on leave, at the infirmary, or in jail. In addition to the strict head count, every tent was searched for ammunition or unauthorized weaponry. However, the rounds scattered about the grounds from raiding soldiers were nearly impossible to collect in the pitch black. As such, Snow ordered that all weapons be collected and locked inside one supply tent under heavy guard. Although a reasonable decision at the time, this proved to be catastrophic.[43]

As Major Snow personally began supervising the disarming of I Company, he received a phone call from the Houston Chamber of Commerce chairman and the former police chief, who relayed rumors that the Buffalo Soldiers were about to "go shoot up the town."[44] Only then did Major Snow realize the seriousness of the actions being planned beneath his nose.

Captain James oversaw the securing of ammunition and arms, which continued frantically into the night.[45] A head count was again taken by lantern, with the light shone on every man's face to confirm that no others were substituting for him. In one of his only personal gestures toward his boys, Major Snow instructed them to form a semicircle around him. By his side were Captain Shekerjian

and their trusted First Sergeant Henry. Snow's manner was far less
authoritarian and formal as he posited in a fatherly tone that men
were stealing ammunition in an attempt to take the law into their
own hands. He assured the rankers that the detested Officer Sparks
had been suspended from the police force and awaited formal punishment and that Police Chief Brock would give the wronged men
of Camp Logan a "square deal."[46] In a question that would resound
throughout the black community for decades to come, one soldier
spoke up and asked, "What are we going to do when a policeman
beats us up like this?"[47] Another broke his silence and lamented,
"We're treated like dogs here."[48] If the police could assault a model
soldier like Corporal Baltimore, they reasoned, not a single soldier
was safe from abuse. Some realized that this was not the time to
turn the tables. In sad tones of defeat, other men simply asked if the
entire regiment could pack up their things and leave Houston altogether.

The rifle collection on a company-wide basis was in full swing
when a first sergeant ordered his corporals to collect the remaining
weapons. The command was met with silence until a private barked
from the darkness, "Don't a man budge."[49] The troops held fast and
gripped their rifles tightly. Many were willing to follow the first
sergeant's orders but feared the others who refused. Some soldiers
later compared the situation to suicide. Troop loyalty now switched
from their officers to their peers, a dangerous tipping point in any
insurgency. A mutual lack of understanding contributed to the dispute. Many soldiers were convinced that a rumored white mob was
about to overrun the camp and that they were intentionally being
disarmed in preparation for the invaders.

A plucky lieutenant stepped up to try and rectify the situation
using a classic divide-and-conquer technique. "I'll give you two
minutes to get those rifles up here," he shouted as he glanced at his
watch.[50] Again, the response was silence. A first sergeant then began reciting the men's names alphabetically, explicitly calling the

NCOs first, who had a longer tenure with the army and thus more
to lose by insubordination. Several sergeants manned up and turned
in their rifles. The first sergeant hoped this would prompt the rankers to follow suit. It seemed to be working, as most of the men
stepped up. Just then, soldiers from distant companies took notice
of what was happening. A platoon-sized group approached menacingly from the darkness, some of the men trotting in double-time.
Their shouting made their disapproval clear. "Cowards!" they
shouted.[51] Some of the mutineers were motivated more by grief
than rage; "tired of seeing soldiers come in there with their heads
all beat up," one wailed openly.[52]

Meanwhile, Major Snow and First Sergeant Henry continued
making their rounds and overseeing the attempts to gather the ammunition, when they ran into a group of thirty men. Before the
major or first sergeant could apprehend the unidentified soldiers,
the duo was ordered in explicit terms to extinguish their lantern.
For the first time in his career, subordinates barked hostile orders at
the major. Something had gone wrong. A voice growled, "If you
take another. . . damned step, we will bore you."[53] The distinct
sound of brass casings clanking on steel followed as mutineers
loaded their rifles. "Let's kill the son of a bitch" yelled one soldier.[54] "No," another responded as an argument ensued.[55] Snow
remained calm and spoke the sad truth when he pleaded with his
enlistees: their actions would be "putting their heads in nooses."
However, the rifles, locked and loaded, now aimed directly at him.

The proud major somehow fled the immediate vicinity on foot
with his life intact. Accurate information is scarce. Major Snow
tried to phone the former police commissioner to warn him of the
impending conflagration, but the line suddenly went dead. Bullets
from the soldier's rifles severed the phone lines. Snow, believing
that the other officers had been killed, sneaked out of the camp and
searched for the nearest telephone to alert the police. He made it to
Brunner Fire Station 11, where he got through and talked briefly

with someone from police headquarters. A Good Samaritan drove
him to Dwyer's drugstore. The pharmacist recalled seeing Snow
"unarmed, very pale, panting heavily and very distressed." He continued, "I was alarmed at his appearance and gave him aromatic
spirits of ammonia to quiet his heart action."[56] Others recalled that
Snow "was not in physical or mental shape to take command."
Hours later, a stern written message to Snow instructed him to
report immediately to General Hulen at his temporary headquarters
in downtown Houston.[57]

Back at the camp, the soldiers were momentarily distracted by a
distant howl and call aux armes: "Get your guns, boys! Here comes
the mob!"[58] In quick succession, a single shot was fired into the
ebony sky, a shot heard across the entire city of Houston. Every
man within earshot began hollering that a white mob was about to
overtake the camp. Pandemonium ensued, and the troops rushed
the supply tents in which all the weapons had been temporarily
stored. A brave lieutenant stood between the mob and the rifles and
was immediately overwhelmed and nearly impaled on a tent peg.
The stores were quickly looted.

With cold, oiled steel now in their hands, the men fired their
weapons indiscriminately. Many shot straight into the sky, presumably as a celebratory gesture. Others did so at forty-five-degree
angles, as a nonlethal show of force. Nevertheless, some deliberately aimed at occupied buildings or houses near the camp or toward
downtown Houston. The night was near pitch black, and the soldiers, arguably, had no idea in which direction or at what they were
firing. The sky lit up with an array of muzzle blasts and cheers. For
a few moments, the men's feelings of oppression were discharged
with every red-hot round. No longer were they under the thumb of
white America or the army. Most of all, they were free to defend
themselves as they saw fit. Unlike their grandfathers, they were
now more than simply freed slaves—they were men with rifles.
Those who instigated the panic knew that it would later be impos-

sible to trace fired or discarded weapons to their rightful assignees since they were grabbed randomly. By goading the men into firing their guns within the camp, it also thwarted government investigators from using evidence of the rifles being fired as proof that they were used in the insurgency. The leaders knew their history and gambled on the likelihood that even if caught and punished, they would, at worst, be dishonorably discharged, as were those involved in the Brownsville affair. As one young private later stated, "If one or two men go, they will get punished, but if a crowd go they can't do nothing but kick them out."[59] The surrounding residential homes received a downpour, not of the typical fat, sweet East Texas raindrops, but of hot lead.

Then the momentary elation transformed. Amid the bacchanalia, a young Private Wiley Strong fell to the ground, almost unnoticed. A bullet had penetrated his abdomen.[60] One of the very first mutiny casualties was one of their own. In the Book of Judges, Jephthah led the Israelites in a battle against Ammon and, in exchange for defeating his enemy, vowed to sacrifice whatever creature would come out of the door of his house first. When his loving daughter stepped out to greet him, he immediately regretted the vow but nonetheless carried it out, ever remorseful for the death that his flippancy wrought.

Participants scattered and took cover wherever they could to avoid the bullets spraying in every direction.[61] Some resorted to hiding in the latrines. The bonhomie had worn thin, and the men realized that their orgy of firing was likely to get many of them killed.[62] Infighting is typical in any revolutionary movement. While the embers of the hard-won Russian revolution were still smoldering, the country suffered another bloody civil war, this time between the Bolsheviks and the White Russians. Without knowing it, the 24th Infantry rabble was firing at itself in the darkness. I and M Companies, embroiled in a firefight against each other, caught K and L Companies in the crossfire. There was no racist mob to be found. The death and mayhem had come from within—the fifth column had emerged. Nevertheless, despite the lack of invaders, later investigations revealed that the camp was indeed fired upon from the outside.

Captain James successfully ordered his company to lock their rifles. Captain Shekerjian then saw the opportunity to calm the rest of the horde. He rushed out to shake up the men into realizing that there was no mob and that they were devouring their own children. Ten minutes passed before the shooting quieted somewhat. The captain, running and shouting while covering himself from the gun-fire, affected little until the company bugler sounded a call to cease firing. The chaos ceased momentarily and then erupted again be-fore finally quieting long enough to restore a semblance of order.

Almost immediately, men began shouting out what action the mob should take. "Let's go clean up the . . . damned city," one shouted.[63] Less enthusiastic men in the swarm began to feel uneasy. Calls for racial solidarity were made, as well as appeals to righting prejudice. "Stick to your own race," was shouted.[64] However, the rallying cries soon turned into outright coercion. One soldier who remained hidden under a tent overheard one of the ringleaders talk about returning to camp afterward to shoot any stragglers or those who refused to participate. Ruffians rounded up any nearby men in tents and press-ganged them into joining the movement. By creat-ing panic and confusion, the instigators intended to recruit all men by sheer social momentum before they had a chance to change their minds or flee into the woods.

Nat Turner often went to nearby farms on Sundays to preach to his fellow blacks. A stocky man with a large bulbous head that many people took as a sign of his intelligence, he was considered a relig-ious zealot by some, a dirt-floor prophet by others. In 1831, on Lincoln's twenty-second birthday, an annular solar eclipse was vis-ible in Virginia. Turner envisioned this as a black man's hand reaching over the sun. He already believed that certain atmospheric conditions were an omen to begin preparations for a rebellion against slaveowners. It was a sign from God. The rivers would soon run blood red. The time was now.

Turner planned to kill white families, pick up guns, and recruit slaves on his way to Jerusalem, thirteen miles away. Before midnight, Turner deviated somewhat from the planned trek and led the band to the farm where he had toiled as a slave. It was the stately home of Turner's master, his wife, and their young children. They were sound asleep just before awakening to the face of their killer.

Somewhere in Houston, a cock crowed and First Sergeant Henry snapped. Clouds shrouded the moon much like a black hand. It had been a long, dry summer. The torrid Gulf Coast air was blowing and humid enough to slice with a machete. The black overcast sky was finally ripe for a downpour. During a pivotal moment in the mutiny, the model "squaddie," mentor, and loyalist became the self-appointed rebellion leader. What Henry wrestled with and the triggers that led him down that path would never be revealed. What was unwavering was his resolve and determination, which he had previously exercised in service to the U.S. Army and the commander in chief. "Fall in," he barked in a roaring voice that every man heard. Two sergeants who were also his personal friends approached Henry and tried to talk sense into him. Stoically, the First Sergeant simply snarled back, "Go. Get in there."[65] They acquiesced. Even those trying to escape the madness snapped to attention and followed the orders of their respected NCO. Some obeyed out of fear. "Get plenty of ammunition and save one for yourself," spoke Henry eerily, foretelling what lay ahead. "Fill your canteens . . . we are in it now."[66]

The column, numbering more than a hundred men, formed. "Right face," First Sergeant Henry shouted proudly.[67] The Houston police headquarters lay ahead, and the soldiers would have to fight to reach their objective. The men moved, hooting and hollering, much like the Vandals in the year 455. Pope Leo the Great received their leader and implored him to abstain from murder and arson and be satisfied with pillage. Those wise words saved Rome. The road to hell was unpaved.

The exodus out of Egypt had begun, with Moses leading his belligerent tribe. But the unknown wilderness lay ahead. The rebels had scarcely marched fifty meters before First Sergeant Henry ordered a halt. He called on Corporal Larmon Brown to gather the remaining men from the other companies. Henry then proceeded to address his men, emphasizing the gravity of his actions. "This is serious business," he stated morosely, adding vaguely that he might follow in the footsteps of his father, a soldier who had "gone down."[68] If anyone underestimated his earnestness, he made his intentions abundantly clear by ordering a handful of his most trusted corporals to guard the column rear. Now somewhat recouped from his injuries, Corporal Baltimore—exhibit A of all the past and future troubles—was one of those corporals: "Kill the first man that falls out of ranks."[69] The historical lesson that Henry failed to appreciate was that, since the Jewish rebellion against the Romans, revolts were fiendishly difficult to maintain. Toussaint Louverture's feat in Haiti a century earlier was the exception that proved the rule. Moreover, even after liberation, the nation faced centuries of crippling debt and misery.

Cracks in First Sergeant Henry's command began to appear. As Corporal Brown rounded up the remaining men, Captain James stepped up and ordered his boys to stand by him. "Stick with your race," the rebels extolled the wavering men.[70] The commander replied courageously in a booming voice, "L Company stands by its captain."[71] His men took heart and chanted, "We stay by our captain!"[72] One corporal still seemed unsure and, with tears rolling from his eyes, bemoaned to Captain Shekerjian, "Captain . . . we ain't gonna' be mistreated."[73] The voice of a rebel then shouted,

"Put a bullet into him and shut his . . . damn talk. We have got work to do."[74] As the column departed, the rebels reminded the nonparticipants of their intention to kill them all when they returned from victory.

Some still believed that a white mob was closing in, but the real threat was of the mutineers doubling back to shoot up the battalion. Captain James's men formed a defensive battle line on the west side of the camp. The men of M Company also joined in, facing west, with those of L Company facing north. It was distressing for the soldiers to consider that they might have to shoot and kill their black brothers in arms. Captain Shekerjian ordered a check of the men at approximately 21:10.[75] L Company was so angry and on edge that James hesitatingly decided to delay the count for more than an hour until the smoke had cleared. Consequently, the checks in all four companies were not completed until nearly 23:30, when it was discovered that 151 men were unaccounted for at that time.[76]

News eventually spread to all seven guardhouses around Camp Logan. Eighteen men were on guard duty at the distant Lower A Division, located on the northwestern corner of the base near the commissary warehouses. From there, they lazily watched trains pass along the lonely tracks. They soon heard word of the mutiny and abandoned their posts to join the rebels, albeit as a separate group for the time being. They still believed that Corporal Baltimore was dead and were determined to recover the body of their fallen brother. Several privates thought that the camp was under attack and suggested they rush over to defend it. Corporal John Washington, the senior NCO, objected. "What's the use to go to camp? You will get killed trying to get in."[77] One guard who also had been beaten by Officer Sparks was in no mood to turn the other cheek this time. God forgives, but they were not God. "I will shoot every white son of a bitch on Washington Street."[78] Three Lower A Division guards remained at their posts. It had begun. The time was now.

The Spanish Legion, also known as los Tercios, was founded as an elite unit of the Spanish army. It was historically was open to foreign volunteers and modeled on France's own Foreign Legion. It was raised in the 1920s during the last days of Spain's dwindling empire to serve as its Army of Africa. Domestic conscript units were ineffective in policing the colonies and fighting unpopular wars. The legion was symbolic of Franco's right-wing forces during the Spanish Civil War as well as a response to the internationalist troops such as the Abraham Lincoln Brigade, which fought for the leftist Republicans. In the newly formed ragtag legion, there were, among others, one Russian, one Chinese, three Japanese, and one black American. The corps was referred to as a legion, evoking Spain's military supremacy and Catholic Christendom. Organized into *tercios*, the legion gained a reputation for invincibility in Spanish Morocco. Legionnaires considered themselves *novios de la muerte* (bridegrooms of death). When in trouble, a legionnaire shouted *¡A mí la Legión!* Those within earshot jumped into action to help. Legionnaires never abandoned a comrade on the battlefield. A goat mascot wearing a legion cap accompanies the unit on parades. On Holy Thursday morning, during the Holy Week processions in the cobblestoned center of Málaga, legionnaires carry on their shoulders, with great reverence and devotion, the heavy life-size Christ of Good Death crucifix. Contrary to usual military practice, legionnaires are allowed to sport beards and wear their uniforms, both traditional and service, wide open over the chest. Firmly committed to die a glorious death for Spain and the church, the legion's motto is *¡Viva la muerte!*

6

VIVA LA MUERTE

As victors, we will parade prominently
For we don't just have weapons
But the devil marches with us.
—French Foreign Legion, 2^e REP Regimental Song

On that fateful evening, the tone-deaf Houston Chamber of Commerce had planned a festive "watermelon party" at the ironically named Emancipation Park to welcome the black servicemen respectfully. The Lower A Division guards' demi-platoon had different plans. It started its march along Washington Street, the unsightly and sparsely inhabited road that was initially the route to Brenham in Washington County. Fifteen armed black troops seemed out of place to a group of onlookers before Miller's eatery, near the dance hall, two of which happened to be Illinois National Guardsmen. The Buffalo Soldiers raised their rifles and aimed. "Halt," shouted a trooper at the whites.[1] "It's a damned good thing you've got on a uniform."[2] The respect among soldiers, regardless of color, spared the guardsmen's lives.

While the gawkers escaped unharmed, blood already had been shed, albeit unintentionally. During the shooting orgy in camp, at roughly the time that Private Wiley Strong was hit, an automobile carrying four residents returning from a day of shopping passed along Washington Street. The car was struck by several bullets, one of which penetrated the front passenger door and somehow lodged itself into the upper right thigh of Eck Thompson.[3] The party traveled a mile past Camp Logan before Thompson realized that the nagging numbness in his leg was from a bullet. By that point, he was covered in blood. The driver tried desperately to find a doctor, but the roads were closed off by the Illinois National Guard. Every attempt to get to a hospital was in vain, and it was hours before Thompson finally staggered into the St. Joseph's Infirmary downtown.[4] By this time, it was too late.

At roughly the same time that Thompson was hit, Manuel Gerardo, a Mexican laborer who had finished a backbreaking shift, took a well-deserved break. Working away from his family, he lived in a boarding house on Washington Street and went into the backyard, perhaps because all the bunks were filled, to lie on a bench. A bullet pierced his chest near his heart, and he never again opened his eyes.

Shortly after the encounter at Miller's eatery, the lights of an oncoming vehicle shone upon the soldiers. The men signaled and shouted, ordering the car to halt. It slowed without stopping completely. Both the occupants and soldiers made eye contact. During what might have been the most tense and excruciating seconds of their lives, the soldiers let loose a volley of shots directly at the vehicle and its occupants. It is unknown whether they fired out of fear, nervousness, or pure malice. Whatever the case, they wrought hellfire upon all six of the occupants. The driver, E. M. Jones, father of six children, was killed instantly.[5] A backseat passenger was severely wounded and would need to have his arm amputated. After drawing first blood, the group scattered in three directions, some back to the 24th Infantry camp, several further into town, still others back to their guard post about Camp Logan. None joined the leading group of rebels, which had begun in earnest the march into Houston.[6]

The soldiers who did not join the two groups marching into Houston terrorized the locals in close vicinity. Citizens emerged from their homes upon hearing strange, popping noises. They suspected that nearby electrical cables were shorting out. Others supposed that a nearby building might have caught fire, since neighbors customarily summoned help in those situations by firing guns into the air. Other civilians simply thought that the incessant clamor was from live-fire exercises inside the camp. Charles Wright ran out of his home, ready to help extinguish a house fire. He headed onto Washington Street to investigate. A group of black soldiers with rifles immediately surrounded him. He instinctively froze in place and raised his arms in unequivocal surrender. He posed no threat. However, his submission was not enough to appease the mob. Shot through both arms, Wright fell to the ground. The Buffalo Soldiers casually walked past him and shot at his head to finish him off. Luckily for him, the bullet only passed through his hair, sparing his life by a fraction of an inch.[7]

Two residents who lived just west of the city exited a streetcar and were walking along Washington Street. They had a way to go before getting home. The pair froze in their tracks upon hearing shots fired in the immediate vicinity. They wisely sought cover behind the nearest home they could find. Neither could determine where the shooting was coming from. However, they waited until the blast frequency lessened so that they felt safe enough to retreat hastily. This move proved to be a mistake. They had no idea that the firing was coming from trained soldiers, potentially snipers. Venturing out scarcely thirty feet from where they sought cover, Adam Carstens immediately doubled up in agony and fell into a ditch where he died. E. H. Neumeyer threw himself into the same trench and lay motionless for two hours. During that time, G. W. Butcher, mounted on a horse, passed by. Neumeyer had no idea if the rider was a friend or foe. The following morning, the horse was found nearby, shot and killed. Butcher was also hit but survived. It was an excruciating evening of cat and mouse, hiding from the sniper, a feat that only one of the three men survived unscathed to tell about.[8]

One unfortunate white laborer, done with his shift, was trying to catch a streetcar but made a wrong turn and came face to face with a group of rebels. They advised him to run in the opposite direction. He did so, whereupon the gang fired over his head and near his feet, having a jolly time terrorizing him. His flight to safety was not yet over. He encountered another group of soldiers. Like the Aztecs of centuries past, he was forced to run the gauntlet in order to save his life. They stood him against a wooden fence and practiced tracing his body's silhouette with bullets. After plenty of hooting and hollering, the soldiers allowed him to scamper to safety as long as he did so holding his hands up. Though humiliated, he survived. He leaped onto the next streetcar—a vehicle that caused such anguish among the soldiers—and put Camp Logan behind him as quickly as possible.[9]

Though First Sergeant Henry had marched off with a large number of men, a still more substantial number chose to remain in camp along with the handful of officers. Their motives were not necessarily pure or owing to fidelity. Many may have been sympathetic to the rebels and sought to do their part precisely by staying behind. A good number of them still believed that a white mob was approaching the camp. Other blacks were simply loyal to their officers and understood well the folly of insurgency. Nevertheless, by the end of the night, more than a hundred of the soldiers who chose to stay at camp eventually vanished. Perhaps they joined the column, believing it preferable to die for a cause, skewed though it may have been, rather than to survive as complacent stooges of the establishment.[10]

Two millennia prior, Xenophon accompanied the Ten Thousand, a large army of Greek mercenaries, to conquer Persia, ill fated as it was. The Gurkhas, a brigade of Nepalese nationals within the

British army, carried a curved knife into combat. By a strongly held tradition, they were not allowed to sheath their weapon until it made contact with human blood. In the same vein, First Sergeant Henry's column attached bayonets to the ends of their rifles, a weapon utilized for close-quarter combat.

The March to the Sea during the American Civil War was led by Major General William Tecumseh Sherman of the Union Army. It began with his troops leaving the captured city of Atlanta and ended with the capture of the port of Savannah a month later. The soldiers followed a "scorched-earth" policy, destroying military targets and infrastructure, industry, and civilian property, disrupting the Confederacy's economy. The operation broke the rebels' will and led to eventual surrender. Sherman's decision to operate deep within a hostile territory without supply lines is considered one of the first modern examples of total war.

First Sergeant Henry was equally determined to march on Houston, blazing a trail of destruction on the way to his objective— vengeance upon the Houston police department, come hell or high water.[11] There were two particular men at the top of the mob's kill list, Officers Sparks and Daniels.[12] Any of the San Felipe district's mounted police or patrolmen also were high-priority targets. However, along with truth, one of the first casualties of war is discipline. Not long after leaving the camp's gates, the rebels resembled a rabble of uniformed men. Many of them were not wholly aware of their purpose. Most were undoubtedly enraged by the injustices that the 24th Infantry had suffered, but not all were willing to kill others in return.

Though the leaders wished to restrict the violence to the guilty, a sizable number of men were eager to slay anybody resembling a police officer and those who got in their way. Some wanted to hunt the reviled streetcar conductors or particular business owners. Sadly, there were still others who desired to kill any whites they came across, regardless of circumstance.[13] The noncommissioned officers (NCOs) succeeded, to varying effect, in quelling the tempers of the most bloodthirsty of the lot.

Nevertheless, in terms of mayhem and destruction of property, these rebels were more restrained than the highly organized and disciplined white mobs that marched en masse into black East St. Louis neighborhoods earlier that year. In Houston, most of the property damage was committed by whites trying to defend themselves or fleeing from the Buffalo Soldiers.

Gaining in confidence and intent, the mob now resembled a symmetrical column. It picked up the pace and approached Shepherd's Dam Bridge, several blocks from Washington Street. Here, First Sergeant Henry's main column drew its own first blood—that of innocents.[14]

The file was ordered to extinguish all illumination and blend into the night. Citizens in the immediate area had received word of the ongoing mayhem and steered clear of any uniformed men on the streets. Residents turned off the lights in their homes to avoid attention. Families huddled in silence, waiting for the trouble to pass. The troops now moved stealthily through Houston neighborhoods, like ships passing in the night.

As the soldiers approached the Winkler home, three teenagers inside took an interest in the odd sight, ventured out onto the porch, and turned on the entrance lamp. The light shone on some of the soldiers, who took cover immediately. One yelled, "There they are!"[15] An NCO instantly ordered the men to "shoot that light out."[16] With textbook precision, two soldiers dropped to one knee, located the target in their sights, and fired without hesitation. A second later, Freddie Winkler, one of the youths, slumped over, and his body fell to the floor. The light was quickly extinguished, as was the victim. The other teen survived, although his arm nearly was blown off.[17]

When the group of soldiers reached the corner of Brunner Avenue, they spotted four policemen two blocks away on the now infamous Washington Street. The policemen were not military trained in camouflage and were gathered under a bright arc lamp. They were sitting ducks for the Buffalo Soldiers. Police Chief Brock made the mistake of sending out small groups of officers to subdue a hundred armed soldiers. Detectives T. A. Binford, L. G. Bryson, Tom Goodson, and a citizen bystander were attempting to maneuver the seriously injured Butcher into a civilian car, since no ambulances were readily available, when shots rang out.[18] No assailants could be seen as they stealthily maneuvered into position to finish off the police. Scant thought was given to sparing the lives of those assisting the wounded. This disregard was a principle of total war—a battle without rules.

Upon hearing shots, the car's driver peeled away, causing the men to drop Butcher, on a makeshift stretcher, in the middle of the street. Incapacitated, he remained there, an easy target, as the officers scrambled for cover. Butcher was hit yet again, this time by a military-grade round to the groin.[19] Another diabolical shot glided through the muggy air and hit Binford square in the kneecap, shattering it—and any hopes of ever walking on that leg. The assisting civilian was hit in the arm.

The uninjured police retreated and, as soon as possible, alerted headquarters that they were no match for the professional troops and needed massive reinforcements. Not wanting to draw attention or fire upon their position, the soldiers swiftly moved on. As the group continued marching down Brunner Avenue, they split up into three files, one down the middle of the street and another on each side of it. The violence meted upon bystanders followed no rhyme or reason. A car occupied by an entire family accidentally ran right into the moving column. Soldiers pointed weapons at the vehicle and ordered it to halt. The father behind the wheel knew about the conflagration and did not believe that the shots heard were from live fire exercises nearby. In an attempt to spirit his family away from danger, he drove straight into the prophets of rage. The soldiers held their fire but searched the vehicle and interrogated the occupants. After a brief exchange of words, the family was allowed to drive away to safety. [20]

Just then, another nearby car occupied by two teenagers trying to get home was stopped. Rain began falling as a dozen soldiers surrounded the vehicle. They were in no mood to argue. The occupants were told to "crawl out of there."[21] The car's jammed door latch nearly cost those young men their lives. They tried to exit the vehicle but struggled to open the door. The soldiers discussed killing both of them on the spot and raised their rifles. The driver finally managed to exit the car and immediately threw himself into a ditch. His broad hat fell off his head and saved his life when the soldiers shot several rounds into it. He feigned death. Rounds were then fired into the vehicle. The passenger was struck but survived. Soon after, a third car approached. Before the Buffalo Soldiers could menace it, they saw that it was carrying blacks. Without much ado, the vehicle was redirected with instructions to avoid Camp Logan. A soldier eventually shouted, "On to victory, boys, on to victory!"[22]

The column kept moving. After crossing Shepherd's Dam Bridge, the soldiers continued down their symbolic road to Damascus—San Felipe Street—into the San Felipe district, where the events that sparked this sad calamity began and would come to an equally sad end. Officers Sparks and Daniels were within smelling distance, but the police would not give up their bad apples without a fight. Like the Jews led out of slavery by Moses, First Sergeant Henry's men began to complain. All were tired and thirsty. Rather than trudge on like legionnaires in the Sahara, Henry allowed a brief halt. By this time, he was aware that he was hemorrhaging men from desertion and was down to roughly seventy-five. In an eerily symbolic omen, the group rested in one of the few cemeteries designated for blacks, College Park. There the NCOs discussed the finer details of the planned attack while the souls of passed blacks looked on from behind the tall grass.

The longer the organizers talked, the more restless their men became. They complained not only of fatigue but of being forced to participate in acts that they disagreed with. Some felt that the killings that they already committed were quite enough. Others were genuinely remorseful about aiding and abetting the deaths of innocents. A trickle of men quietly vanished into the night, blending into the tombstones and trees, communing with the dead after giving up the fight. Little did the raiders know, but this cemetery would be where some of them would be laid to rest in paupers' graves.

When First Sergeant Henry was made aware of the latest desertions, he flew into a rage. "Any of you who want to go back to camp? Step out and let me know."[23] It was a risky venture, as an ultimatum could reinforce the morale of his men or invite a mutiny against his mutiny. To Henry's relief, not a man spoke up. Emboldened, he ordered Corporal Baltimore to again guard the rear ranks. Anybody who dared fall out was to be shot on the spot. He made sure all the men knew this. "Yes, let's kill the first one," the men roared.[24] It was a moral victory for Henry.

By this time of night, more Houstonians had received word of the unfolding rampage. The calm that the column encountered on their march thus far would not last. Civilians near Washington Street now sought safety in the downtown district, for there was a gun behind every blade of Texas grass. Illinois National Guardsmen stationed in Camp Logan were hastily mobilized into an anti-riot force. Although the white mob's attack on Camp Logan was fictitious, a very real white mob was materializing. Members of the Harris County Patriotic League were told to assemble at Houston police headquarters.

Awoken from a peaceful slumber, Police Chief Brock made his way to police headquarters. Along the way, his car was shot at. He arrived by 22:00. [25] There Brock summoned Houston residents into a posse comitatus to help the existing officers with policing. [26] However, not all of the white volunteers brought weapons. In a legally dubious gesture, Brock handed out guns to the citizens, many of whom had no firearms training. Several businesses were looted for their weapons, and other gun shops loaned out arms on an honor basis to any able-bodied white man. [27] The number of volunteers grew markedly once word got out that weapons would be provided free of charge. Not surprisingly, few of the guns were ever returned. Harris County Sheriff Frank Hammond was as unprepared as Brock. He was an hour away, relaxing in the resort community of Seabrook, when the riot broke out. He did not make it to Houston until 02:00. In the interim, his assistant in Houston organized a posse for him composed of 250 angry civilians.

A crowd of more than a thousand whites assembled in front of the police station exchanging lurid stories of the rioting or volunteering to fight on behalf of the honest, law-abiding citizenry. "The colored soldiers are killing the whites" could be heard. [28] Indeed, after centuries of calm, the apocalypse was finally upon God's children. Hot gusts of wind from the Gulf Coast felt like the devil's breath. The crowd pondered why blacks were so incensed. Nearly every white family employed a black nanny, chauffeur, or grounds-keeper, and they seemed like splendid people.

Many in the crowd were already armed with short-range pistols or shotguns. Others were carrying little more than wooden clubs and rocks. Some simply found the situation to be the perfect opportunity to get drunk. Police wisely refused to provide those residents with arms. Centuries after the Middle Ages, the crowd resembled the non-church-sanctioned Peasants' Crusade to Turkey.

Upon hearing word of the uprising, many whites who were at home grabbed their personal weapons and took off by streetcar or automobile toward the hot spots. However, the armed citizens were a danger only to themselves. Many of the city-dwelling whites had never even thrown a punch, much less fired a weapon. Whites believed that Negroes were cowardly and incapable of fighting. Bravery and honor were attributes intrinsic to the white race. They seriously misjudged the dangers posed by a hundred black, combat-hardened soldiers with Springfield rifles. On several occasions, utter pandemonium and hilarity ensued when a volunteer tripped and accidentally discharged his own weapon. Creatively interpreting the facts on the ground in what would be called "fake news" a century later, the *Houston Chronicle* went so far as to claim that by standing down, the militia "saved the Negroes from annihilation."[29]

Compared to the Illinois National Guard's professionalism, city and county government, including the sheriff, were caught unprepared. They were almost as disorganized as the civilian mobs. That afternoon, Police Chief Brock timidly ordered officers to take strong precautionary measures against the possibility of violence. He struggled to coordinate manpower and come up with a plan to contain the riot. Unfamiliar with weapons or tactics, he directed policemen equipped with only close-quarter shotguns and six-shooters into the throng of soldiers armed with long-range rifles. Later that night, a colonel with the Texas National Guard was sent to Brock to help coordinate efforts with General Hulen. He found the chief in a state of utter confusion. Brock could not even tell the military officer the number of policemen on duty. The colonel listened as long as he could while Brock rambled incoherently about how his car had been riddled with military-grade rounds. The colonel eventually pleaded directly with Mayor Moody to remove Brock from his command on the spot because "he was not fit to command men,"[30] but Moody ignored him.

Houston was in danger of falling into the hands of either marauding black soldiers or a disorganized gang of white hooligans. At that critical moment, someone needed to fill the vacuum of leadership left by an indecisive acting mayor, a weak police chief, and an absent county sheriff. Somebody needed to step in and

assume command. The uncertainty motivated General Hulen to
take measures into his own hands. He phoned the governor, who
gave him free rein to restore order by whatever means necessary.
Hulen then placed Houston under martial law. He followed up with
a call to the commanding officer of the Southern Department at
Fort Sam Houston in San Antonio, who promised to send four
companies of the 19th Infantry and authorized Hulen to take command of all U.S. troops in the city. Furthermore, he instructed
Hulen to, in diplomatic terms, disarm the 3rd Battalion. After that
call, Fort Crockett in Galveston also immediately dispatched two
companies of the Coast Artillery Corps to Houston.

The white vigilantes moved out in front of Brunner Fire Station
11, only six blocks from Camp Logan. In the mix were Illinois
National Guardsmen, including many of the loathed men from the
East St. Louis riots, who happened to be downtown at the time and
were not under official orders. In no time, the crowd became irate,
animated, and prepared for war. Ugly calls to "lynch them" rang
out.[31]

Simultaneously, a separate mob of whites gathered on Washington Street near the station. A captain with the Illinois National
Guard arrived on the scene, leading an entourage of thirty military
trucks crewed by nearly nine hundred soldiers. He had been tipped
off by a lone private who had witnessed the rebels amassing and
then marching into the city. Foreseeing the possibility of an escalat-
ing race riot, the captain stood on the hood of a vehicle and pleaded
with the angry white crowd, telling them not to take the law into
their own hands. He stressed that they were up against trained
soldiers with military-grade kit.[32]

Although there was confusion as to where the rebels currently
were, word came to Captain Joseph Mattes, also from the Illinois
National Guard, that the Buffalo Soldiers were on San Felipe Street
"shooting everything in sight."[33] Several servicemen who were
thoroughly familiar with Houston claimed to know of a shortcut to

the Fourth Ward. They offered Mattes a lift there in a civilian automobile driven by Texas National Guardsman Corporal Zemmie Foreman. In this motley mix were his colleagues Corporal Melvin "Happy" Everton, Private Alpens Jones of the Coast Artillery Corps, and Houston Police Officer E. G. Meineke. Mattes accepted the ride and was accompanied by another captain and a motorcade of fifteen army trucks. He was determined to intercept the insurgents and inform the others of their location. Tragically, due to road closures and the cordoning off of entire swathes of the city, Mattes's car was separated from the motorcade, which made it to the San Felipe district as planned—but not before three other cars unexpectedly ran into the black mutineers.

The Fourth Ward was rather calm at that moment, as the rebels were taking a break for refreshments and cigarettes at what was likely a black-owned eatery. By coincidence, a streetcar ominously approached the mutineers from the darkness. It was an otherwise slow evening, and the only occupants were a black man and a white man. The motorman and conductor rode near the front. A soldier boarded the streetcar and ordered the black man to exit. There was no ill will toward him. The trooper then menacingly approached the motorman and pilot. A tussle for the controls ensued. Other soldiers tried to derail the streetcar. As soon as the soldier jumped off, the shooting started. A bullet grazed the conductor's hair. He throttled the car forward at breakneck speed and just barely managed to drive it past the bend to safety without running off the tracks.

While the soldiers finished their repast, they spotted a vehicle approaching slowly. Something was notably different about this particular car at that particular moment. The hair on the back of the men's necks stood on end. A local businessman drove the vehicle, which was likely commandeered by the government, for inside were four police officers: W. C. Wilson, Horace Moody, C. E. Carter, and in a droll twist of fate, the dreaded Officer Daniels. This was the prize the troops were waiting for. Upon hearing shots fired,

the civilian stopped the car. The policemen immediately jumped
out. First Sergeant Henry sprang into action, executing textbook
military ambush technique. He commanded his men on the north
side of the street to position themselves in the drainage ditch and
those on the south to take cover in the city cemetery, using the
tombstones of the dead for protection. As the police walked into the
open, a rebel shouted, "Let's get them!"[34]

Officer Daniels was armed with nothing more than a borrowed
pearl-handled pistol. Police Chief Brock essentially sent Daniels
and the rest of the small group to their deaths. Showing extreme
heroism or folly, Daniels charged the entrenched soldiers. He stood
no chance and was mowed down instantly by a volley, its explo-
siveness powered not only by the shells' powder, but also by the
mutiny's rage. The three other officers ran for cover into a garage.
They might have survived uninjured had they not fired back, giving
away their position. Instantly the soldiers returned the favor and hit
Moody. "My leg is shot off!" he cried.[35] Carter applied a tourni-
quet, but the policeman died from his injuries. The officers offered
no more resistance.

First Sergeant Henry ordered "Cease fire!" and the troops surveyed the area.[36] They did not know that Officer Daniels was
among the dead until they approached his bullet-riddled body and
quickly identified him. "There is the white trash we got," a rebel let
out.[37] Another private wrestled the pearl-handled pistol from Daniels's clenched hands, war booty of sorts. In a macabre celebration,
the Sons of Ham then proceeded to bash Daniels's face in with their
Springfield rifle butts—comeuppance for the pistol whippings he
and Officer Sparks inflicted upon scores of others. Other soldiers
bayoneted his body, clad in an olive uniform. Desecration of the
dead always had been the reserve of victors animated by extreme
rage and prejudice. In many societies, cannibalism was the ultimate
form of retribution, a way of consuming the enemy's power. In this
total war, there was no respect for the vanquished enemy.

No sooner had the smoke cleared than First Sergeant Henry ordered the group to continue marching. However, many men had not emerged from the cemetery or eatery. Desertion was a real option for those who had lost heart for a lopsided battle. And then the rebels suddenly suffered their first battle death—but not at the hands of the police. A soldier spotted a group of uniformed officers and, in his zeal to pick them off, shot one of his own in the back, young Private Bryant Watson.[38] Not all the mutineers realized it was an accident. Nevertheless, Watson's death provided an opportunity for Henry to reinforce the directive that anyone who surrendered or was captured would be shot by their men.[39] This command may have been an idiosyncratic act of mercy, sparing the captives from torture or dishonor. In 1942, Joseph Stalin issued to his troops the infamous Order No. 227, coining the phrase "not a step back," which obliged the Red Army to shoot any soldier who refused to fight, retreated, or surrendered. It generally had a detrimental effect on troop morale.

The column began moving again, and residents waved and offered words of encouragement, like Parisians cheering the Allies after ousting the Nazis. Food and drink were offered as the troops passed. Some able-bodied citizens volunteered to help in any way they could. "Pray for us," responded one soldier. "If we die, we will die like men."[40] The troops were retaliating not only on their own behalf but also on behalf of the black locals who did not have the means of resisting and suffered in silence. A few black Houston policemen and a smattering of Illinois National Guardsmen joined in the bonhomie and expressions of gratitude. However, unlike Nat Turner's gang, First Sergeant Henry's bunch failed to amass significant local blacks for the cause. Doubtless many enlistees realized their actions would be punished severely but, out of principle, carried on. A smaller number knew that those actions would cost them their lives.

Private George Bivens was among the first men to desert. He and several others made their way back to camp but were intercepted by two armed whites. The Buffalo Soldiers fled, but Bivens was shot twice in the leg. A Texas National Guard lieutenant and several corpsmen reached the injured Bivens before the whites, who would have executed him on the spot. Nevertheless, Bivens's medical treatment in Houston was haphazard. By the time he made it to Fort Sam Houston in San Antonio and had his leg amputated, gangrene had taken its toll. However, just before Bivens died, he made a deathbed confession that an unknown soldier had forced him at gunpoint to participate in the rioting. The good centurion was killed by those whom he wished no harm upon.[41]

As the column neared Heiner Street, three blocks from the last shooting, scouts caught sight of another slowly approaching civilian car with dimmed headlights. First Sergeant Henry immediately ordered his men to take positions on both sides of San Felipe Street. The vehicle, traveling at approximately 25 miles per hour, was driven by its teenage owner, James Lyon. In tow were several others, including another teen, Asa Bland, local civilian Eli Smith, and two police officers. The policemen had commandeered the car, and the young hangers-on decided that engaging in a firefight with soldiers would be a fun adventure on an otherwise dull evening.[42] It proved to be a fatal mistake. The police provided the youngsters with weapons, including a sawed-off shotgun.[43] They had traveled only several blocks on San Felipe Street before forty armed soldiers suddenly surrounded them.

All occupants were ordered out. As the police were exiting, they took a gamble by flexing their authority. "We are officers," one said.[44] "We know it, you white sons of bitches," came the curt response.[45] John Richardson was one of the especially loathed mounted officers. He was slow to raise his hands when ordered to. "You don't want to throw your hands up for a colored soldier?" a trooper asked with abhorrence.[46] Without hesitation, he broke his rifle's wooden butt over Richardson's head. At that point, Officer Ira Raney, a proud father of eight, Bland, and Smith took off in a desperate sprint for their lives.

Nevertheless, no matter how fast they ran, they could not outrun a bullet. Raney darted away from the vehicle but in plain sight of the headlights, which made him easy pickings. He was shot dead. Smith and Bland were both knocked down before they reached the wooden sidewalk. The same soldier who killed Raney stuck his rifle in Smith's chest and pulled the trigger. Luckily, the round only hit Smith in the arm. Lyon ran wildly in zigzags, trying to avoid getting shot. He was tagged by buckshot from the shotgun found in his car but managed to survive the ordeal.

Before the soldiers had a chance to make sure that Richardson and Bland were dead, another vehicle approached. First Sergeant Henry again ordered his troops to take position. About forty men reloaded their rifles and aimed. However, this vehicle was not crewed by the expected police officers. Captain Mattes stood at the helm along with three other enlisted men. He came in peace to reason with the rebels, not to fight. The headlights' glare made recognizing him nearly impossible. The captain approached with both his hands up. His uniform was olive drab, the same color as those of the Houston police. He shouted, "wait."[47] The soldiers commanded the vehicle to halt. Nevertheless, it did not, and the rebels let forth a deadly hail of bullets. Mattes's head was blown off. Police Officer Meineke, sitting in front of the captain and to his right, was also killed instantly. The second volley eventually ended Corporal "Happy" Everton.[48]

However, Private Jones survived because Captain Mattes's body shielded him from subsequent shots. Corporal Foreman, the driver, ducked, and the vehicle veered off the road and onto the wooden sidewalk, crashing into a building. Senator Satton, a young barber, heard the commotion. He and another citizen ran out, firing their pistols at the miscreants. Satton, no match, was shot dead before he could wound any soldiers. His partner fled. Ironically, hours before Satton's demise, his associate had exchanged pistols with Officer Daniels, offering his pearl-handled piece for protection. The juju had not worked for Satton or Daniels.[49] Jones and Foreman feigned death until it was safe to leave the area, though they were fearful of being discovered by the local blacks who peered at them through the shutters. Jones was the only one able to slither from the vehicle and hobble his way to safety, promising the others that he would return with help.

Thirty minutes after the mutineers had left the area, a party of 150 men was sent to the San Felipe district to find Captain Mattes, come what may. In the meantime, a hysterical Private Jones reappeared at the Brunner Fire Station 11 and reported the ambush that took the lives of Mattes and the others. After reaching the Fourth Ward, the search party came upon the bullet-ridden, blood-soaked vehicle containing the corpses of the captain and Meineke. Next to them, clinging to life was both Corporal Foreman, behind the wheel, and Corporal "Happy" Everton on the rear passenger floor.[50] Smith lay dead close by. Foreman, the pie-faced "good old boy" from Livingston, had several dozen wounds but would survive. "Happy" Everton died on the operating table.[51]

Only after the smoke cleared and the rebels evacuated the area did the seriousness of their actions dawn upon them. The soldiers marched on the double, yet their swift feet could not spirit them away from the massacre, which trailed them like a malevolent spirit. A grim silence fell upon the entire unit. Few talked, though all understood that they had escalated the rebellion to a new level by killing a high-ranking military officer, one who had come in peace. Like Oedipus Rex, who gouged out his eyes in anguish after mistakenly having sex with his mother, many soldiers repented participating even indirectly in the killings. Men held their breath and blinked, hoping the nightmare would end. Soldiers wished they had never left the safety of Camp Logan's gates. Although military life was hard, the fences and barracks were also motherly arms that kept those men safe. *Legio patria nostra*—the Legion is my homeland—was a popular military maxim.

When Captain Mattes's body was recovered, it was found not only headless from the initial gunfire but mutilated beyond recognition—by whose hands and for what reason remained unclear. Tepid participants realized that the movement was now devouring its offspring. The original intent was to avenge many injustices, but the radicals had hijacked the movement. In 2020, the widespread nationwide protests against racism were eventually taken over by a narrow cadre of white, university-educated Marxists.

Soldiers mumbled. The column gathered near the West End Ballpark, where weeks earlier, a 24th Infantry company led by its natural athlete Private Roy Tyler had played a friendly match against the local Black Buffaloes—how the wheels had turned. Fretting before a lit baseball field where children usually chased balls, the column also had injured men to tend to. At this point during the rampage, any straggler or man otherwise incapable of marching would be fresh meat for the roaming packs of white vigilantes. Their best hope would be to surrender to the Illinois National Guard. March or die.

Even the movement's leader, First Sergeant Henry, had a silver-dollar-sized wound to his shoulder. The city jail, the initial objective of the rebels, lay too far ahead. An alternate plan would be to raid the county jail. Instead, Henry chose to push his men no further. The mass of diehard stalwarts was matched by scores of those who simply wanted to get back to camp.

Shouting ensued, but this time the NCOs were the ones in disagreement. First Sergeant Henry managed to quash the bickering and ordered a strategic retreat to regroup. He led his men southward and then halted. Taft Street had come to a dead end, a symbolic omen. During the night's first silent moment, they proceeded off-road into Baker's Pasture, a large open tract of woodlands. They

cut the barbed wire and slipped through, like the ghosts of Gettys-
burg who continue to march in file through Pennsylvania thickets.
The column did not stop until it reached the lonely tracks of the
Southern Pacific railroad. There the men gathered under a china-
berry tree.

With a renewed sense of urgency, First Sergeant Henry insisted
on completing the original mission, but Henry was now only one of
three distinct factions with their own differing objectives. Henry's
closest friends heeded the other two voices. One faction rejected
the idea of returning to camp, viewing it as a guaranteed death
sentence. Cognizant of the blood of innocents on their hands, this
faction believed that National Guard units were sent out with shoot-
to-kill orders. By hiding out in the forest or in the homes of black
partisans, they presumed they'd have a better chance of surviving
the night. They then would desert the army and live the rest of their
lives on the run. The third faction feared being cornered by the
locals and lynched if they chose not to return to camp. There were
no good options. Despite the opposing opinions, the principal faction was hell-bent on returning to camp, with or without Henry and
the others.

First Sergeant Henry was smarting from a hot lead slug and
hardly in fighting shape. His authority was bleeding out, much like
his body. Infuriated by the timidity of the doubters, he berated his
boys for "coming out and leaving him in this manner."[52] As if he
were the Apostle Thomas inspecting Jesus's side to prove that he
was real, Henry pointed to Corporal Baltimore, still a trusted disciple. "Look here how this boy is beat up," he implored the others,
using the corporal as a visual aid in a persuasive speech.[53] Try he
did, but the movement had simply given up the ghost. The raiders
would continue no further. At a pivotal moment of the night, Henry
finally conceded that they would not attack the police. As the shepherd of his men, he chose the better part of valor. Some of the
Buffalo Soldiers were still eager to complete the mission. Others

simply wanted to see their mothers again. This dilemma bore on Henry's subsequent decision. Judas Iscariot, too, was the most trusted and loyal disciple. In the Gospel of Nicodemus, he chose to commit suicide because he feared that Jesus would rise from the dead and punish him. Many faithful prayed that Judas repented immediately after he jumped and just before the noose snapped his neck.

First Sergeant Henry remained on the ground with the look of a beaten man. In the depths of their souls, his men somehow knew what would become of him. He was a resolute man who did not often speak but meant every word when he did. Henry had proclaimed to all that he would not return to camp. The others got to their feet. The NCOs lovingly pleaded with him to call it a night, get up, and join them. "You all can go in . . . ain't going to camp no more," he responded.[54] This was not just a good-bye.

First Sergeant Henry called his most trusted men and asked them to do what no leader should ever demand of his subordinates. He requested that one of them shoot him dead. Yet even his most faithful boys could not obey. Such an oxymoronic command was akin to the theological paradox of whether God could create a boulder so heavy that the Creator could not lift it. It was a non-command. The cajoling continued, but the remaining men knew what would transpire. They imagined the sacrificial body of their light-skinned leader indignantly sprawled by the railroad, black and white blood needlessly spilled, soaking into the nutrient-poor clay soil.

· As a last request, something akin to a death row inmate's last meal, First Sergeant Henry asked to shake the hand of every one of his men. They all solemnly gave his non-injured hand a warm, firm clasp. One tepid rookie had a last request of his own, asking that Henry not do what he was determined to do until the men were far enough away.[55] Their resolute NCO granted this request. Soldiers were meant to die in battle. At 02:05, as the ragtag remains of the

once-grand mutinous army marched silently and reverently along
the desolate tracks, they heard a blast from Henry's rifle. *Viva la
muerte.*

7

AFTER THE FLOOD

The white families having fled, we found no more victims to gratify our thirst for blood. . . . [W]e mustered now about forty strong. . . . [T]he gun was fired to ascertain if any of the family were at home; we were immediately fired upon and retreated, leaving several of my men. . . . I never saw them afterwards. Pursuing our course back and coming in sight of Captain Harris' . . . we discovered a party of white men at the house. . . . I scratched a hole under a pile of fence rails in a field, where I concealed myself for six weeks. . . . I began to go about in the night and eavesdrop the houses in the neighborhood . . . and returning every morning to my cave before the dawn of day. I know not how long I might have led this life, if accident had not betrayed me, a dog in the neighborhood . . . was attracted by some meat I had in my cave . . . I immediately left my hiding place, and was pursued almost incessantly until I was taken a fortnight afterwards by Mr. Benjamin Phipps. . . . [H]e cocked his gun and aimed at me. . . . I am here loaded with chains, and willing to suffer the fate that awaits me.—Nat Turner[1]

Though that evening seemed to last a lifetime for the young mutineers, the conflagration lasted for only two hours and ended before 23:00.[2] The final body count was fifteen whites, including four police officers and two national guardsmen. Twelve others were injured, with one policeman later dying and two others losing an arm. Four Buffalo Soldiers were killed, in addition to First Sergeant Henry.[3] Private Watson died by friendly fire. Private Strong was felled in camp before the rioting began when the troops began firing wildly into the sky. Two others, including Private Bivens, later died from their wounds.[4]

Until 1917, only the St. Louis riots were comparable to the Camp Logan mutiny in terms of bloodshed and violence. What made the latter unique was the fact that it was the first uprising in which more whites were killed than blacks and in which no black civilians participated. Moreover, this was the first instance in which white civilians were pitted against black servicemen. Until then, black uprisings were often little more than suicide missions for slaves who had nothing to lose. In many ways, the Houston mutiny was the quintessential uprising: the underclass obtains arms or any other advantage and inflicts revenge upon its oppressors—Texas's storming of the Bastille. America changed after the docile and subservient blacks finally fought back and vowed to continue the fight. Previous generations of blacks ascribed to Booker T. Washington's notions of accommodation and understanding, acceptance into society through education and economic advancement. The Pauline doctrine of submitting meekly to authority and entering into God's kingdom like little children lived on. However, the Buffalo Soldiers now adopted DuBois's concepts of black power and equality.

White supremacists bided their time, and in 1919, they initiated the Red Summer, with the intent of finally scaring blacks back into submission. Their acts of terrorism ignited race riots across three dozen American cities, and the mayhem was covered extensively by the press. Nevertheless, the Ku Klux Klan now butted up against military-trained blacks with firearms.

The federal government feared that the burgeoning black civil rights movement was being usurped by socialist and communist influences in the wake of the 1917 Bolshevik Revolution. It also dreaded the role of foreign anarchists, who regularly bombed the homes and businesses of prominent civic leaders. A century later, the race riots of 2020 reignited the same left-right, Marxist-capitalist antagonism.

Dawn signaled the end of Houston's nightmare. Bagpipes could be heard faintly in the distance. Once again, roosters crowed, and half-starved stray dogs trotted into empty streets. The landscape still was sodden, and the air humid enough to drown out the sound of gunshots. Great white egrets occasionally wandered along the bayous, oblivious of the previous night of violence. By midday, the sun finally baked away the morning's dampness.

Most of the mutineers snuck back into camp unnoticed. Some mingled with those who stayed and formed a defensive battle line against armed mobs—black or white. Other soldiers simply crawled into their bunks and slept off the hangover from a failed insurgency. Whether they reposed with a clear conscience was a different matter. A much smaller offshoot of the main column led by Corporal Brown had not received word of the capitulation or First Sergeant Henry's suicide. The soldiers boldly marched into the San Felipe district but quickly discovered that four hundred national guardsmen secured the area. They were outnumbered and outgunned many times over. Any attempt to raid the quarter would have been suicide. Discipline collapsed after they chose to retreat during the small hours of the morning—soldiers scattered, every man for himself. Most tried desperately to seek refuge from black Houstonians. Either the locals disagreed with the insurgency or they did not want to support the losing side. Few soldiers received assistance, though some were handed civilian clothes. Most mutineers discarded their Springfield rifles, ammunition, and uniforms. When finally captured by the Illinois National Guard, many were wearing nothing but their underpants. They offered no resistance and were most grateful to have avoided capture by the police.[5]

The San Felipe district was eerily silent that late Friday morning, much like a deserted Wild West outpost. Few blacks showed up for work that day. Their reaction to the riots was far more muted than that of the whites. Rather than seek help from government agencies, blacks simply shuttered their homes and buckled down and awaited the storm's passing. A large segment did not want to risk being caught in the crossfire and quit the city. The road south to Galveston was clogged with fleeing refugees with wailing infants, many still in their sleeping clothes. The elderly among them had lived through slavery. The scene suggested the wartime images later seared into America's consciousness, such as Russian peasants fleeing the Nazis or the South Vietnamese clawing their way into American helicopters before the fall of Saigon.

However, the Illinois National Guard had not eased its vigilance. By midmorning, it completely sealed off the San Felipe district. Soon after, with the assistance of the sheriff's posse, it began a meticulous house-to-house search for rioters. The broad dragnet did not discriminate.[6] As with any operation against "enemies of the state" or "unidentified threats," innocents were also snagged as bycatch. Civilians who aided or were suspected of aiding the mutineers were arrested. Anybody caught with so much as a pocket-knife on his person was hauled in. The Houston police continued handing out guns to the sheriff's posse. Though the threat of retribution from whites was a more significant threat to Houston, the Illinois National Guard disarmed all black residents. Even in 1917, there was the age-old debate between civil liberties and security. As long as the rights sacrificed on the altar of security were not those of the whites, there was little backlash. While white and black antagonism played out publicly, the other prominent ethnicity, the brown Latinos, were invisible to both groups.

Uniformed men disregarded the constitutional liberties of citizens as they kicked down doors looking for suspects. The Illinois National Guard was experienced in riot control, but not all troops

were adequately trained. In one instance, a guardsman had cleared
a black woman's home of suspects, but when he checked to ensure
his rifle was not loaded, he shot through the ceiling.[7] In a scene
reminiscent of a Charlie Chaplin reel, a Buffalo Soldier was hiding
in the attic. The shot narrowly missed him, forcing him to jump out
of a window and flee on foot. By nightfall, only two 24th Infantry
suspects were still at large.[8]

The suspects were held in the Bastille, a colorful reference to the
prison used by French kings before the revolution. Officials knew it
as the Harris County Jail. After being booked, every square inch of
their bodies was inspected for traces of blood, cordite, or any other
substance in accord with the uprising.[9] The quarters were cramped
and without air conditioning. The air was thick with human perspi-
ration and flatus—a touch better than the slave ships of centuries
past. Several injured mutineers were sent to St. Joseph's infirmary
close by. In 1895 the Sisters of Charity of the Incarnate Word built
the sick bay in a residential neighborhood on the southern outskirts
of Houston. It included a convent, male and female wards, and,
remarkable for the time, a Negro wing. Decades later, St. Joseph's
Medical Center would pioneer the latest medical procedures in conjunction with the world-class Texas Medical Center.

As the day progressed, bodies of the victims began filling up the
morgues. Of great concern to General Hulen was the crowds that
were milling about the infirmary and county jail. Around the
morgues, there was the expected wailing from loved ones but also
scowls from the menfolk. Hulen feared that these groups could
grow quickly into frenzied mobs determined to seek frontier justice. Sheriff Hammond confirmed that he would not be able to
control the crowds if they grew much larger.[10] As such, Hulen
ordered a hundred and fifty enlistees to guard the county jail and
another several dozen for the infirmary. Mayor Moody then closed
all morgues to the public.[11]

Major Snow now prepared to return to the 24th Infantry camp. Nevertheless, a sticky task awaited him. He met with the commanders of all the companies and discussed how they would go about disarming more than a hundred outpost guards.[12] Luckily for the major and Captain James, a large portion of the sentries had abandoned their posts and sought safety inside the camp, fearing that any invaders would outnumber them. However, they had held on to their weapons in case the white mob did indeed overrun the camp. Luckily, when they were called to surrender their arms, all were cooperative—even relieved—to do so. Under the Illinois National Guard's vigilant eye, the rifles were turned in and stacked with military precision for removal. The men then were marched back to the 24th Infantry camp along the tracks on a route that purposefully avoided Washington Road.[13] For the rest of the day, whites drove by the camp waving weapons and hurling slurs, hoping to provoke the Buffalo Soldiers into violence once again. Many of those harassers worked in government or law enforcement.

Nevertheless, disarming the Buffalo Soldiers' camp itself was a different story. The officers were unanimous in the opinion that resentment still simmered beneath the surface and that any wrong move might rekindle the embers of the previous night. However, there was no good option other than by defusing the bomb carefully and hoping for the best. Just after lunchtime, the 1st Battalion of the 19th Infantry arrived in Houston.[14] It made the rail journey from San Antonio at breakneck speed. Rather than arrange for troop transport, the battalion marched from the train depot directly to the camp. The colonel briefly surveyed the situation. He agreed that the men needed to be disarmed before nightfall. The first rung of his plan was to evacuate residents from the vicinity. He then deployed his men along Washington Street with their rifles aimed directly at the 24th Infantry camp. Two other companies of the Coast Artillery Corps were positioned at right angles along a nearby street. A heavy machine gun was brazenly placed at the point where those two units met. The colonel assured his men that he did not expect any resistance from the Buffalo Soldiers—wishful thinking. He followed up with the more natural order to "annihilate" the Negro troops if they made any sudden moves and reached for their rifles.[15]

Once the 19th Infantry was in place, Major Snow meekly decided to finally enter the camp. He was accompanied by General Hulen and a brigadier general with the Illinois National Guard who was also a veteran of the East St. Louis riots. The 19th Infantry's colonel followed suit and stood atop a crate. His words were measured and firm. He bravely ordered the men to gather peaceably in the streets outside their tents but without their arms. To the officers' relief, the men obeyed. They also expressed a sigh of relief. The colonel confined them to barracks but stressed that all measures were temporary. In what was a half-truth, he added that the 19th Infantry had surrounded the camp to secure it from outside attack or any bad apples who might want to start trouble again. He emphasized his point by stating that the guard was just as quick to shoot "inwards" as they were outward.[16] His homily did not mince words. He assured the throng that he realized that most of them stayed in camp and did not participate in the mutiny. "You whose consciences are clear . . . have no fear."[17] Nevertheless, he did not ignore the damned: "Those of you who took part in the disorders will have to take the consequences, be what they may."[18] The men appreciated a straight-shooting lecture over saccharine platitudes. The disarming of the 24th Infantry continued until the afternoon.[19]

Although disarmament occurred without a hitch, the 24th Infantry was still not out of the woods yet. The generals and colonels from several military branches agreed that they needed to quickly get the Buffalo Soldiers "the hell out of Dodge" and back to their home in Columbus, New Mexico.[20] The War Department did not want any more attention and threw every resource at minimizing the flack. A general phoned Southern Pacific Railroad officials and discussed what they could do to ensure that the soldiers got out of

Houston as safely as possible. There were real fears that saboteurs would blow up the train by mining the tracks. Several flatcars were placed before those carrying troops to mitigate this risk. Designated lookouts scanned the horizon and ensured the train's right of way at every junction and bend.[21]

As the trains rolled out of Houston, past a patch of blood in the soil, and through the lush plains and cattle country, the soldiers dropped personal calling cards written in dull pencil. Some were scribbled notes weighted with used rifle shells. Others were innocent letters to girlfriends living in the county in which the train passed. Still, some took more threatening tones: "To the people of Houston—remember the 23rd of August, 1917. At 8:30, the 24th Infantry gave Houston their first military blowout. The citizens didn't know . . . that a 30 U.S. magazine could shoot so hard."[22] One sad note read: "Take Texas and go to hell. I don't want to go there any more in my life. Let's go East and be treated as people."[23]

Although the War Department thought that making the 24th Infantry vanish into thin air would quell the discontent in Houston, it was mistaken. Whites rankled at the idea of stationing blacks in the South to begin with. The rebellion barely had ended before Congressman Joe Eagle demanded the immediate removal of all black troops from Texas, including guardsmen. Regimental officers were surprisingly sympathetic toward the Buffalo Soldiers. Most felt that Jim Crow laws and the locals' racist treatment were responsible for the troubles. The problem facing army brass was that segregation was not about to be rescinded any time soon. The *Houston Post* wrote, "this measure of separation is absolute and will be maintained."[24] The *Houston Chronicle*, a progressive voice for its time, argued the obvious, that black troops should be allowed anywhere in America, without fear of racial conflict.[25] Other benevolently racist voices considered it Houstonians' patriotic duty to "tolerate the Negro soldiers."[26] Town-hall meetings deteriorated into shouting matches among disgruntled groups, from those who simply wanted federal funds, to racist stalwarts, to the moderates such as the *Chronicle*.[27]

As the weeks passed, Houston went through the stages of grief, from denial that there were preexisting problems that prompted the troubles, anger toward the Buffalo Soldiers, bargaining, depression, and finally, acceptance—but only to a point. The black group in the crosshairs was the local citizens. Although both they and the whites had seen and experienced the same riots, their reactions differed significantly. It was only until the death of George Floyd at the hands of the police that all races finally agreed that the government had committed a grievous wrong and that restorative justice should be sought.

Texans demanded that the guilty be dealt with swiftly and harshly. They refused to pin the blame on any whites or the police. The black citizens did not agree with the soldiers' actions, especially the senseless killings of innocents. However, they felt that the police got what they deserved. The slurs and discrimination that the soldiers withstood for several weeks were what local blacks lived through ad infinitum. Whites who rode the streetcars or sat at the best tables in restaurants could not fathom that the subjugated classes could see the events in a different light. Not all blacks remained tepid. In the spirit of Nat Turner, there were later incidents in which blacks refused to sit in the back of streetcars. In one instance, a white passenger flashed a pistol, which prompted a visiting black soldier to flash a military-issued weapon. The white man fled. Such happenings fueled wild rumors that complicated any reconciliation. Upon mere whisperings of trouble, white mobs gathered en masse downtown. Nevertheless, even the police had tired of their overzealousness by this time.

The black community spoke out in exemplary fashion but with a somewhat defeatist tone. In a melancholy statement, E. L. Blackshear, principal of a predominately black elementary school, pleaded with fair-minded Houstonians not to lump all Negroes with the few bad ones who had rioted.[28] He implored whites to remember all the patriotic black soldiers who defended their country.[29] Leaning on the Baptist faith of many blacks as Martin Luther King later did, leaders called on Negroes to reject violence, if for no other reason than that blacks were victims of mob hostility themselves. They resisted committing evil even to prevent greater ones, knowing that what would be left would still be evil.

During the American racial unrest of 2020, police forces of several major cities were defunded or wholly disbanded.[30] In what could be seen as a historical oddity, in 1917 in Houston, black civilians, fearing for their safety, pleaded with Mayor Moody to offer more policemen and protection. "Some of our people are afraid," lamented the head of a delegation.[31] The sentiment of blacks, or perhaps that of their representatives, changed radically a century later. Moved by the request, the mayor announced in no uncertain terms that all Houstonians would be protected, "regardless of color or creed."[32] The idea that blacks were suddenly seen as dignified humans only after the 1960s' civil rights movement was not accurate. Many Americans held surprisingly enlightened and progressive views on racial equality, even during the Jim Crow era.

As Houston attempted to sweep the insurgency under the rug and carry on with an air of normalcy, few lessons were learned. Blacks and whites continued to live vastly different realities and now had more reasons to mistrust the other. Many blacks simply packed up their belongings and left Houston forever, headed to northern parts unknown and a murky future. Indeed, after the Russian peasants overthrew the unpopular czar, they got Lenin and then Stalin.

All parties mourned the perished innocents, but many blacks were distraught that most of the culpable whites were alive and kicking. Although Officer Daniels, an instigator of brutality, was no more, Officer Sparks was still very much breathing and back to his old ways. Police Chief Brock's inability to fire this bad cop was a testament to the chief's overall ineptitude and abdication of duties during the conflagration. Within two weeks, two blacks were shot and killed by police. Wallace "Snow" Williams was found dead in his backyard, riddled with bullets. It was revealed that the shots came from Sparks's six-shooter. In an eerie repeat of history, an illiterate but eloquent witness, William Johnson, recounted that Wallace was killed after fleeing from police who had broken up a craps game in the now haunted San Felipe district. He had seen Sparks shoot Williams in the back and then kick him in the head before he died. Johnson's love for the country and the American way was evident in his statement. "We are not in Russia. We are in the land of the brave and home of the free where Mr. Wilson, our great president, has on his shoulders the burden of all, black and white. . . . [W]e have not got no law here in the South, or law just for one race, that for Lee Sparks."[33] Ironically, Williams praised President Wilson, benevolently unaware of the executive's racist shortcomings. There was enough evidence for the district attorney to indict Sparks for murder. Not surprisingly, as in many racially charged trials in the South, it took the jury less than a minute to declare Sparks innocent.[34]

Days later, after being called for a domestic violence incident, Houston police shot dead Andrew Hewitt as he fled. The officer claimed that Hewitt had a pitchfork in his hands.[35] It was later revealed that he was grasping a table fork.[36] The same grand jury that indicted Officer Sparks returned no charges against this officer. Weeks later in Goose Creek, outside of Houston, a white woman claimed that Bert Smith, a black cook for an oil company, raped her. A mob of white men beat and then hung him from a tree. Sheriff Hammond filed murder charges against the suspects. A grand jury refused to indict any of them because no witnesses were willing to testify. A white woman's social status was a reflection of the man she attracted. As such, a black man approaching or making eye contact with a white woman was considered an insult for which a polite "no thank you" would not suffice. Though the fairer sex abstained from violence, many women were proficient at committing it by proxy via a chivalrous man. Only on her deathbed in 2008 did Emmett Till's female accuser retract her story, which had resulted in his lynching. In 2020, a video emerged of a white woman, a committed social justice supporter, phoning the police, claiming that her life was in danger. She merely had a minor verbal disagreement in New York City's Central Park with a black man, Christian Cooper. "A white woman lies; a black man dies," was a Southern proverb.

8

INQUISITION

[Rap group] Public Enemy call themselves the prophets of rage, heirs to the mantle of Nat Turner and Malcolm X. They say it proud—they're black and they're loud. Just what makes these muthas so angry?—John Leland, *SPIN*[1]

It was not long after the smoke cleared before Houston officials began looking for their pound of flesh. Twelve hours after the riots had ended, District Attorney John Crooker ran about the West End collecting witness statements. He initiated a tedious period of jurisdictional strife. Although most Houstonians were relieved that the Buffalo Soldiers had left town, Crooker was incensed. If he could not detain individual soldiers from the now vacant camp, he would quench his desire for retribution by indicting all those sitting in the county jail. He aimed to prosecute the lot in the Harris County Courts. Crooker was, however, disappointed to find that the cells where they were to languish like the Count of Monte Cristo were suddenly empty. All suspects were turned over to the army. Crooker and other prominent Houstonians went to great lengths to get the servicemen back to Houston to stand trial. A blanket murder warrant was even issued. Ironically, the soldiers were in no better hands in New Mexico, since the government had its own motives for spiriting the men away. Since the city could not prosecute the men themselves, Crooker would lean on the army to punish them more severely.

Not satisfied with the secretary of war's tepid response, Congressman Eagle told the *Houston Post* that the Buffalo Soldiers had "slaughtered our men, women, and children unprovoked. . . . [T]hese red-handed murders should be shot right here where they killed their victims."[2] One former judge demanded that another congressman not allow the guilty to be let off with a simple dishonorable discharge, as happened in the Brownsville affair.[3]

District Attorney Crooker made a hand calculation and played fast and loose with criminal procedure when he charged forty-one members of the 24th Infantry for the murder of Police Officer Raney. Contrary to the ham-handed performances of past grand juries against white police officers, this mass indictment included nine names that were listed as "unknown."[4] Crooker pressed his congressman to ask President Wilson to return the troops to Houston to face proper adjudication, not a "farce trial in another state."[5] Wilson, a Princeton law professor, considered the request and pondered the tricky question of jurisdiction. He was surely mindful of the landmark 1866 Supreme Court case Ex parte Milligan, which ruled that the application of military tribunals while civil courts are operating is unconstitutional. He wisely opted to allow the army to handle the affair through its courts-martial to maintain military discipline.

Bright and early on Monday, August 27, city council put together the Houston Board of Inquiry composed of seven prominent business and civic leaders for its investigation.[6] Nevertheless, the army was suspicious of this board, as many of the members seemed to have conflicts of interest. Several had contributed indirectly to the riots and were now using the board to shield them from scrutiny. City officials were arguably the most culpable party. They acted for their economic interests and avoided at all costs upsetting their white constituents by, at the very least, not ensuring that the visiting soldiers were treated decently in a segregated city.

The spurned city's efforts bordered on sensational, all in order to elicit mass public support. District Attorney Crooker, representing the state of Texas, was tasked with questioning scared black teenagers, humiliated policemen, and angry racist residents. An accurate and pithy report would be produced from the testimony. For good measure, Brigadier General John Chamberlain, the army's inspector general, also attended the hearings.

Witnesses were compelled to testify under pain of a fine but also were selectively screened. In one instance, Mayor Moody led subsequent witnesses by suggesting that the focus of their testimony should be on four specific questions: Did the Houston police treat the soldiers fairly? Did any black citizens help the rioters? Was alcohol taken into the camp? Were the 24th Infantry officers derelict in their duty? In a gesture of fairness, the Houston Board of Inquiry heard testimony from a select group of black Houstonians, none of whom directly witnessed the rioting. Some were frequent visitors to the camp. One was known to be a splendid fabulist.

However, the main witness called to testify was Major Snow himself. Mayor Moody, with his long arm, went to great lengths to subpoena him. Snow also was eager to set the story straight. Local newspapers painted the major as unfit. The War Department agreed to let him testify in the belief that airing Snow's version of events would rehabilitate the army's image.[7] Nevertheless, just before he was to testify, the Houston Board of Inquiry discovered that he had secretly left town the night before upon orders from above. The War Department realized that the risk of embarrassment was too significant and backtracked on their word.[8]

With the Houston Board of Inquiry even more incensed by the army's belligerence, the citizens' testimony grew even more boisterous and embellished. They described the hundreds of black, teenaged women who loitered inside the camp with Major Snow's full approval, often until 23:00. Both sides agreed that the guests often carried satchels into camp, which probably contained alcohol. The *Houston Chronicle* described the camp as having a "shocking laxity of discipline," going on to compare it to an orgiastic district composed of tents.[9] The critics' metaphors echoed lines from Samuel Taylor Coleridge's ecstatic opium-induced poem of 1813, "In Xanadu did Kubla Khan. A stately pleasure-dome decree." The verse was later incorporated into a song and album by the gay 1980s pop group Frankie Goes to Hollywood. Despite the exaggerations, few guests were known prostitutes, and most were merely looking to secure a husband who might spirit them away from the South.

The amorous and imbibing pursuits of the Buffalo Soldiers were hardly different from those of white units or any other legion since the days of the Roman Empire. However, Houston was carefully constructing a case against the 24th Infantry and Major Snow. The *Houston Chronicle* went so far as to question Snow's honor as an officer by claiming that he indulged his underlings and "failed lamentably to measure up to West Point standards."[10]

Ironically, since many whites never imagined that blacks could exercise free will, they tended to blame the army officers for the lack of discipline and chaos, which they felt motivated the riots. The moderate white view was that black servicemen "should not be treated with brutality, but they must have respect instilled into them."[11] Nevertheless, many Houstonians remained incensed that Major Snow had told his subordinates that the police, not Corporal Baltimore, were responsible for the violence.

Although many residents' complaints about Major Snow were mere bluster, there were substantive accusations that kept him awake at night. He failed to take decisive action before the riots. Furthermore, after the troops left, he neglected to alert the police or senior officers of Camp Logan. Instead, he ran off toward Wash-

ington Street and wandered about in a state of fear and befuddle-
ment.[12]

Even before the Great War, the meritocratic American military
distinguished itself from those of Europe who were still led by
aristocrats and landed gentry. Continental officers were a princely
lot who had scarcely picked up a gardening hoe, much less a mus-
ket. Brigadier General Chamberlain received dozens of letters from
angry citizens. Many were anonymous. Most pinned the blame not
on whites, not on the Buffalo Soldiers, but squarely on Major
Snow. One summed up the sentiment, "[He] was attending too
many Pink Teas and social functions."[13]

Moreover, just when the heat was too much for Major Snow to
handle, the Houston Board of Inquiry came down on Police Chief
Brock. He made for a good scapegoat because the leaders on the
board wanted to fire the chief because he impaired their legal and
illegal dealings. There were clear conflicts of interest that should
have been disclosed or cordoned off. A "Chinese wall" was a legal
term describing the barrier that legal entities erected to isolate individuals from sensitive information that could lead to conflicts of
interest. Brock was a lightning rod for dissent from within his police force, city hall, and Camp Logan across town. A petition circulated calling for his resignation. Mayor Moody, now a lame duck,
kicked the can down the road and did nothing.[14]

What incensed many of Police Chief Brock's enemies was that
he had agreed with the army that Officer Sparks's behavior triggered the violence. His other unpardonable sin was mandating his
officers to address blacks as colored people and not by various
racial slurs. Furthermore, Brock's inability to properly lead on the
night of the riots prompted some to hold him responsible for the
deaths of his policemen.

Police Chief Brock proclaimed that he had ordered his officers
to work closely with the 24th Infantry guards. He went so far as to
reference documents proving as much. To his dismay, all copies of

those memorandums mysteriously went missing from department files. It was impossible to confirm whether his enemies had sabotaged his proof or whether he was lying to avoid blame. The evening *Houston Press* interpreted this peculiarity as an example of a "concerted effort by Brock's adversaries to politically knife him."[15] Other officers backed up Brock, but it was too little, too late for his critics.

Moody left office, and a new mayor took his place. The *Houston Chronicle* and *Press* remained deferential toward Police Chief Brock and his progressive policies. However, the new mayor gave into the rabble and removed him. The *Houston Press* quixotically wrote that the mayor gave in to "people of the underworld and . . . the lawless element, generally."[16] The *Houston Chronicle* came to the same conclusion but by different means, blaming the black soldiers, stating that they were "overbearing and reckless in their disregard of Houston laws and regulations."[17] The new mayor's hands were tied. Brock was quietly and unceremoniously demoted to his previous position as the superintendent of parks. Nevertheless, before he left, he won a small victory for black Houstonians. The mayor amended the civil service rules to allow the police chief to suspend any officer who utilized his gun or club in an act of brutality and permitted the civil service commission to make any suspension permanent.[18] Although police procedure and internal affairs divisions would evolve dramatically in the coming decades, these allowances were strikingly forward-thinking for their time.

Police Chief Brocks's removal placated many—most importantly, the army. Calls to bar the partly black Illinois National Guard from Camp Logan ceased, and the camp carried on as usual— contributing dollops of money into Houston's economy. As part of the overture, Officer Sparks finally was dismissed from the force. Not surprisingly, even as a civilian, he did not mend his ways. Working as a security guard for an oil company, Sparks shot at two blacks sitting idly beside a boxcar, severely wounding one.[19]

In September, the Houston Board of Inquiry finally released its report. Few findings were a surprise to anybody. However, many of the broader assertions were revealing. It posed that the soldiers' altercation with Officers Daniels and Sparks triggered the uprising, citing specifically the brutality used in apprehending Corporal Baltimore. The findings veered somewhat, placing some blame on what they deemed deplorable camp conditions. The soldiers had contact with the "very lowest class of the Houston Negro population."[20] Major Snow's predecessor, Lieutenant Colonel Newman, was answerable for implementing a lax visitation policy for prostitutes and even prepubescent girls, the report concluded. It also held those visitors responsible for smuggling alcohol and other intoxicants into the camp. They partly blamed blacks' "hostile" attitude toward the "laws and customs of the South."[21] It added the bold assertion that the riots would have occurred even in the absence of Sparks's behavior and Police Chief Brock's incompetence. The animosity between the soldiers and police was a convenient excuse for the violence. The report backed up this assertion by pointing out that the soldiers killed whites indiscriminately but harmed not a single black civilian. Though Baltimore was deemed innocent, the report pointed the finger at black Houstonians, claiming they had fed the soldiers a constant stream of racial propaganda to enrage them and prompt them to riot. The *Houston Post* exonerated the city of blame and claimed that the soldiers were not provoked.[22] Although it was easy for whites to stake the killing of innocents as proof of black savagery, the truth was more nuanced. In Nat Turner's rebellion, the killing of white innocents was a means of recruiting more slaves to the cause. Rather than appealing to their sadism, Turner wanted to demonstrate to slaves that blacks could now hold power over their oppressors.

The glaring omission in the report was any word of blame toward the Houston police. It found nothing out of the ordinary with the disproportionate occurrence of black arrests and the incessant

complaints of racism and brutality. Moreover, it condoned those
who felt "that in dealing with the lawless Negroes . . . it is necessary to be severe."[23]

Nearly every interest group conjured into existence its own bo-
geyman. Though previously relegated as harmless prudes and kill-
joys, prohibitionists were back in the public space with a vengeance. They were even more energetic and vindicated, blaming
the evils of alcohol as the direct cause of the conflagration. A
prominent fiery pastor giving the sermon at Officer Raney's funeral
rejected any notion that race was a factor and placed all the blame
on "vice and booze."[24] The temperance movement was still popular
in the South. It stressed that the bloodshed would have been spared
had firewater not been smuggled in by "lewd women."[25] The teeto-
talers had a loose understanding of how different drugs affected
thought and behavior. Alcohol was a social lubricant for soldiers
since the days of Alexander, but sedatives rarely motivated men to
fight. The world's warrior cultures more commonly used an array
of amphetamine stimulants. A familiar maxim was that an addict
and alcoholic would both steal your wallet, but only the alcoholic
would help you try to find it.

The National Association for the Advancement of Colored People (NAACP) was the only black group to investigate the riots. It
sent a white journalist from New York, Martha Gruening, in early
September. As preceded the Freedom Summer murders in Mississippi in 1964, the rush of northerners, eastern seaboard intellectuals, and federal busybodies threatened to fuel the fire and encumber
the pursuit of truth. Gruening was a writer and civil rights activist
born in Philadelphia to a German-speaking Jewish family. After
graduating from Smith College in 1909, she settled in Greenwich
Village, New York, a hothouse incubator of political thought. She
wrote and edited a pacifist magazine and was once arrested for
disorderly conduct after handing out antiwar literature. Gruening
later worked as the assistant secretary in the NAACP at the national

level. She eventually moved to France and continued to advocate for blacks.[26]

When Gruening finished her inquiry, she confirmed that most black witnesses were too scared to speak up. Few participated in the investigation. Several even lied to the Houston Board of Inquiry in order to avoid trouble. They were either neglected by government officials or found it futile to speak against the preconceived narrative. While sympathetic, Gruening's report did nothing to soothe the actual feelings of those who continued to suffer under Jim Crow laws. Blacks felt that the disarming, or emasculating of the black soldiers, was a fundamental cause of the riots and that if Corporal Baltimore were armed, he would not have been assaulted, and there would be peace on the streets. "Southerners do not like to fight Negroes on equal terms," said Sara Travers, the original victim of police brutality, which triggered the rioting.[27] She was the only witness who allowed her name to be used. She had nothing to hide. "I could talk all night . . . but I live here, and my family lives here. . . . I just made up my mind that I didn't know anything."[28] Travers was a mysterious figure herself. In the tradition of Mary Magdalene, she was rumored to be a prostitute and, even decades after her death, was the subject of Houston lore. Nevertheless, for both women, there was scant evidence of that.[29] The Bible confused scholars for millennia due to the prevalence of women named Mary. Gruening proclaimed Travers to be no more than a pious and hardworking mother.

The feisty Jewish journalist did not pull any punches in criticizing the Houston government for its capricious enforcement of the law. White neighborhoods were given special attention. Black citizens were ordered to stay put inside their homes, whereas whites were freely handed guns. After the mutiny, dozens of black residents were rounded up, arbitrarily arrested, and eventually released without charges. Gruening believed wholeheartedly that the riot's cause was not drunkenness or machismo but systematic and institutional injustice.

Newton Baker, the secretary of war, was tasked with addressing Houstonians' disquietude. He was level headed and refused to bend to the emotional demands of others. Baker appeased many critics by making concessions. He removed both 24th Infantry battalions from Texas and promised to "leave no stone unturned" in investigating the riots.

The Brownsville affair occurred a decade earlier and had taken years to adjudicate. Embarrassed by it, the War Department made a great effort to handle this incident speedily. The army promptly appointed two high-ranking officers to investigate, Brigadier General Chamberlain and Colonel G. O. Cress, the Southern Department's inspector general.[30] They both would conduct independent investigations, playing gumshoe in Houston during the following weeks. They were soon on the streets taking depositions from residents and officers who knew of or were parties to the violence.

Yet the army prejudged the situation from the start. In no unclear terms, it wanted Brigadier General Chamberlain to proceed "with a view to fixing responsibility upon individuals concerned in the riot."[31] It was apparent that the army would err toward swift justice, favoring expediency over judicial thoroughness.[32] Chamberlain promptly completed his investigation but was also thorough. Nevertheless, many questioned if his efforts were meant simply to placate the mob. As predicted, his findings placed much of the blame squarely on the soldiers, and he recommended they be prosecuted to the fullest extent of military law. He went on to make prejudicial comments to the press, which critics felt tainted the legal process. A key finding was that officers under Major Snow were generally in agreement with his camp's visitation policy for women. Only once did officers witness females in the men's tents after 23:00. Most, if not all, of the women were known to be respectable companions and not sex workers. The officers agreed with Snow's assertion that allowing females into the camp, a policy started by his predecessor Lieutenant Colonel Newman, diverted the troops from going into town and getting into trouble. The respected camp chaplain, who often organized bible studies, backed up the report and vouched that the females visiting the camp embodied a Christian ethical character. Newman, though no longer camp commander, was nevertheless brought in to defend his policy on discipline standards. He explained that "the Negro is essentially a sociable creature. He likes to be where there are lots of people to talk to and to laugh with."[33] Though his description was condescending, he did rightfully point out that Houstonians' racist attitudes prejudiced them to paint all females entering the camp as prostitutes. "The prevailing opinion [was] . . . that all colored women are immoral," Newman added.[34]

Brigadier General Chamberlain considered Major Snow well-intentioned. However, Chamberlain still came down on him like a hammer and recommended that he be tried under the ninety-sixth article of war "for gross negligence and inefficiency in not taking more effective steps to prevent the mutiny."[35] Chamberlain specified Snow's failure to communicate with Camp Logan and failure to identify or arrest the participants. The army was in a difficult position since the traditions and routines that it imposed and revered, such as tribal loyalty and pride in the uniform, indirectly exacerbated the troubles.

Colonel Cress offered each of the 156 jailed suspects the opportunity to make a voluntary statement, yet he obtained nothing resembling a confession. He concluded that the behavior of the police caused the soldiers to hate whites and fueled a desire for revenge. He stated that "a very considerable number of the men, from the beginning, resolved to assert what they regarded as their rights as . . . United States soldiers" and that "the Police Department . . . resented on the Negro the badge of authority of the United States uniform."[36] In removing segregation signs in the city, Cress added—with an nod to constitutional law—that the soldiers "were not willing to comply with laws repugnant to them."[37] Decades later, during the Nuremberg trials, the notion of obeying commands or laws that were repugnant came to light once again.[38] Brigadier General Chamberlain was less charitable than Cress. He felt that their motivation was not just rage but a sense of pride. Although the enlistees were accustomed to Jim Crow laws, the years of rugged army training empowered them to overcome the emotional trauma of the South's caste system, and they refused to tolerate blatant humiliation. The men were ready to defend the Constitution and the dignity of their comrades. Nat Turner's column rampaged on little more than clubs and knives. Once First Sergeant Henry's file had access to firearms—a rare occurrence for blacks—they fought.

Nevertheless, both officials heavily criticized the 3rd Battalion's leadership for not taking prompt steps to avert disaster after witnessing preparations for the insurrection. Major Snow took no action in the afternoon after seeing soldiers stealing ammunition nor did he account for every man who returned to the camp after the uprising. Likewise, the guards' rifles were not inspected to determine if they had been fired.

The 24th Infantry also started its inquiry. As soon as the trains departed from Houston on Saturday morning, several officers commenced interviewing the prime suspects. When the battalion arrived at Camp Furlong, Columbus, New Mexico, the troops were immediately quartered in the stockade while the 19th Infantry watched them.[39] They eventually would be transferred to Fort Bliss in El Paso, Texas. The extra precautions were in place because Camp Furlong was only several miles from the Mexican border, making desertion a tempting option. In a bold and legally dubious move, the army preemptively allowed the fort's colonel to cross into Mexico in the event of mass desertion. Not coincidentally, a half-century earlier, many deserters from both sides of the American Civil War crossed into Mexico and joined the French

Foreign Legion, aiding Emperor Maximilian I and fighting rebels. Diplomatic relations between the United States and Mexico were still raw after Pershing's failed expedition. In 1970 President Richard Nixon was criticized for allowing U.S. troops to cross into the neutral country of Cambodia to eliminate North Vietnamese forces.

At the more secure Fort Bliss, a regimental board of officers continued interrogating every man individually. From the onset, nothing of value was obtained. However, the inquisitors eventually extracted several valuable leads, which cracked the door open enough to prompt several reluctant soldiers to divulge information. The first piece consisted of lists of men present for several camp tasks between approximately 21:30 to 23:00 on the night of the riots. Furthermore, the Houston police then provided the names of all soldiers arrested within seventy-two hours of the mutiny.[40] By twisting evidentiary standards, those men were, by default, guilty of rioting unless they had rock-solid alibis. Although the lists were useful, they were by no means a smoking gun. Even in the most rudimentary trial setting, more evidence would be needed in order to convict. Oral testimony was the oldest sort of evidence and could exclude or supplement documentary evidence. Under U.S. law, almost anyone could be a witness. Experts, convicted felons, and children could testify.

Nat Turner understood that for a rebellion to succeed, the number of organizers had to be small. The Camp Logan plotters purposefully gave the humble rankers as little information as necessary. The government investigators initially had great difficulty securing useful testimony because of the alleged vows of secrecy the mutiny leaders made both to themselves and others. The blood of First Sergeant Henry sealed their silence. The plotters held fast, regardless of what came. Even the lot's least literate knew that he had no incentive to talk. Worse yet, the rank-and-file soldiers knew less about the insurrection than the white interrogators. Military brass whispered of the Brownsville affair, where the prosecution also ran into a "conspiracy of silence."[41]

Leaders all the way up to President Wilson precariously balanced competing interests. The president abstained from unduly punishing the black troops for fear of turning away black support for the war in France. Nevertheless, he did not want to seem as if he was letting them off too easily, as was felt by many after Brownsville. Whether the army yet realized it, it would do all it could to avoid repeating that outcome.

As expected, white witnesses came forward. In an almost unheard-of occurrence to even seasoned prosecutors, only one black suspect was positively identified, First Sergeant Henry. It was unlikely that a small group of out-of-state blacks had the power to intimidate any white witnesses. There was no suspicion of foul play to explain the mass amnesia among the populace. Witnesses did mention that the humid, drizzly weather that night hampered visibility. Air conditioning and refrigeration technology were still in their infancy. The sight of an overweight white man patting sweat from his brow with a handkerchief became a common Houston trope for a reason. However, a simple sociological phenomenon better explained why no other soldiers were recognized—blacks were invisible to most whites. With little or no contact and Jim Crow laws in effect, blacks lived in a parallel universe. Moreover, to whites, blacks were indistinguishable from one another. "All niggers look alike" was a common cliché.

With little evidence at their disposal, the board of officers did their best to glue the jigsaw puzzle together. Hard interrogation tactics were used. Some soldiers were threatened with hanging if they did not give up any useful information. Some were grilled for hours on end and repeatedly asked the same questions to extract any inconsistencies that would be used against them. The army took various lawful and legally questionable approaches toward extracting information. Coercive interrogations would scandalize the military in the 2000s during the war and occupation of Iraq. [42]

A significant break finally occurred when the army obtained a notepad belonging to Private Ezekiel Bullock, found along Washington Street near where E. M. Jones was killed. Bullock was scheduled for guard duty that night. That prompted the army to deduce that Jones was not killed by First Sergeant Henry's column, but by a few renegade guards who left their Lower A Division posts and wandered onto Washington Street to find trouble. After that, Bullock and most of the sentries reported to the headquarters sergeant at Camp Logan. The noncommissioned officer vividly remembered Bullock because he had ruined his trousers and was a mess. Counter to the narrative that an army of indomitable black supermen overtook Houston, the truth was that those young men defecated themselves out of fear like any other mortal. Confronted with this evidence, Bullock admitted his part in the shooting and finally agreed to testify against the others in exchange for immunity. After the guards on duty with Bullock were interrogated, Private Albert Wright also finally confessed. Nevertheless, this confession wasn't the smoking gun the government investigators were waiting for.

Wright refused to take the stand against his comrades. Playing a careful game of chess, the government investigators used his admission to persuade Bullock to turn on the others. In the 1972 case Kastigar v. United States, [43] the U.S. Supreme Court confronted the appropriateness of granting immunity and confirmed that it is sufficient. Witnesses compelled by subpoena to appear before a grand jury were entitled to accept a deal from the prosecution. [44] However, this grant impaired the witness's right to invoke Fifth Amendment protection against self-incrimination. [45] The army understood that in order to win the war, it sometimes had to give up a few battles. Bullock agreed to come clean. The government investigators did not merely induce Bullock to cooperate; they "flipped" him into an

informer. The information he provided was invaluable during subsequent proceedings, though it was voluminous and often conflict-
ing. Bullock had put his life in danger. Benjamin Franklin quipped,
"Three men can keep a secret if two of them are dead."

Eventually, another young enlistee accepted the board of officers' offer of immunity. Private Henry Peacock was one of the few
soldiers recognized by his colleagues as he returned to camp. As he
was a smoking gun in human form, his decision to flip, and to do so
early, saved him from the gallows. By mid-September, the army
was finally developing a picture of what happened.

Before any court-martial was initiated, Captain James was slated
to be the prosecution's star witness. On the evening of the mutiny,
his actions were exemplary. Although many criticized Major Snow,
James's leadership prevented even greater bloodshed. He kept his
company in place. Of all people, James knew more about the incident and conditions at the camp than anybody else. Nevertheless,
on October 15, he was discovered lying across his crisp and per-
fectly made bed with a bullet in his head. His death was ruled a
suicide, though conspiracy theories circulated questioning what
happened. James's family never accepted the official cause of
death. What drove James to take his life would never be known.
Like so many undisclosed facts about the riots, James took what he
knew to the grave. He also may have been racked with guilt by
having to testify against his boys. Decades later, historians and next
of kin argued that James was about to flip sides and testify for the
defense. The government may have wanted him dead. He was barely twenty-four years old and a respected West Point graduate. Sadly, James was the third brother in his family to die in active service.
One was killed in the Philippines in 1906. The other perished near
the Mexican border. Atop James's flag-draped casket were his officer's cap and sword. Regardless of whether he was to testify for or
against his men, his beloved Buffalo Soldiers sent a magnificent

arrangement of roses with the inscription, "To Our Beloved Captain."

9

THE TRIAL

The judgment does not come suddenly; the proceedings gradually merge into the judgment.—Franz Kafka, *The Trial*[1]

The U.S. Army's judge advocate general (JAG) selected Colonel John Hull, the central department JAG in Chicago, to prosecute the monstrous court-martial. The army realized that for a budding military lawyer, this would be a fiendishly difficult case, but also a potentially rewarding one. To sweeten the deal, they allowed him to select his assistant. He chose reserve officer Major Dudley Sutphin, a corporate lawyer within a prominent firm in Cincinnati who served as a superior court judge.

In short order, the two eager prosecutors were walking the streets of Houston, retracing the route taken by the rioters. In less than two weeks, they then traveled to El Paso to interview the 156 suspects. The following month, trickles of that lot were cleared and sent back to rejoin their battalion in New Mexico. The rest of the battalion, still under guard, was subsequently allowed to bear arms again and return to a sense of normalcy. By early October, Colonel Hull diligently pared down the number of suspects to sixty-four. This development was sufficient for the army to finally issue formal charges.

According to the Constitution, even accused soldiers are allowed
to procure their counsel, select an officer of their choice, or have an
advocate appointed to them. As expected, the defendants had neither the financial resources nor family connections to hire a lawyer.
The Southern Department selected for them Major Harry Grier, an
interesting choice as he was not a lawyer, although he did teach law
at West Point. He was the thirty-seven-year-old inspector general
of the 36th Infantry Division and a career soldier. What he lacked
in courtroom acumen, he made up for in raw experience, as he
served in the 25th Infantry after graduating from West Point in
1903. He was transferred to the 24th in 1915 and accompanied the
unit into Mexico during Pershing's campaign. After six years with
it, he gained an intimate understanding of the black soldiers he was
about to defend. Accolades aside, in true army ham-handedness,
what probably made Grier most qualified was the mere fact that he
was available for the job.[2]

On October 19, Major Grier arrived at Fort Houston, where he
was joined two days later by the sixty-four indicted men. Major
General Ruckman promised to allow Grier as much time as he
needed to cobble together a defense. Yet he also made it clear that
he wanted the court-martial to start as soon as possible, preferably
by the beginning of November. This date only allowed Grier two
weeks to prepare his case and collect evidence. In contrast, the
prosecution had already been working on its case for a generous
two months. Grier selected the talented Captain Shekerjian as his
assistant. As Grier prepared for court-martial, Shekerjian abruptly
resigned due to a glaring conflict of interest. Because of Captain
James's unexpected death, Shekerjian was now the government's
principal witness, as he was the second most knowledgeable officer
about the events in the camp.[3]

Without an assistant, Major Grier was left to manage the full
defense of the sixty-four soldiers on his already overburdened
shoulders. Nevertheless, all was not well with Shekerjian; after the

trauma of the rioting and the death of his respected colleague, he resigned his commission and left the army altogether. For reasons unknown, Grier requested neither a postponement nor the appointment of a replacement. Doubtless, Grier was doing all he could to placate his superior officers. His decisions were informed not only by Major General Ruckman's impatience but also by the unwillingness of the accused to believe that an appointed white army officer was on their side. Grier reported to the same hierarchy as the prosecutors; as such, the soldiers were as uncooperative with him as they were with the inquisitors in El Paso. Unlike the trial judge advocate, Grier lacked the material and financial resources necessary to pursue defense leads outside the base's fences. Under these trying circumstances and despite his lack of formal training, like all gifted advocates, Grier's strategy was to punch holes in the prosecution's case—casting doubt on the witnesses rather than proving his defendants' innocence. In the time-honored constitutional tradition, the prosecution had to prove the defendant's guilt beyond a reasonable doubt. If doubt remained, the accused was acquitted. Even the United Nations adopted this concept under the Universal Declaration of Human Rights, Article 11, in 1948.[4] Similarly, in civil proceedings, the defendant is presumed correct unless the plaintiff presents a preponderance of evidence, which then switches the burden of proof to the defendant. Following this tack, Grier saw no need to ask for a trial postponement.[5] However, this strategy had its risks. The stage was set to convene the largest military court-martial ever held within the United States.

On November 1, the ponderous wheels of justice turned just enough to adjudicate the guilt of the Buffalo Soldiers who rebelled just a few months earlier.[6] Major General Ruckman originally wanted to hold the court-martial in El Paso but agreed to San Antonio for logistical reasons. On that crisp morning, the court commenced United States v. Sergeant William C. Nesbit et al. Since the sergeant was the highest-ranking soldier among the accused, his name headed the list of all defendants. The proceedings convened in the beautiful and recently completed Gift Memorial Chapel at Fort Sam Houston. It was the only building large enough to accommodate a court-martial of that size and with that much national public interest. Many local citizens strongly objected to the venue since the events occurred in Houston and because, in their eyes, a chapel was inappropriate for such a distasteful affair. Houstonians were pleased that the army invited their own firebrand District Attorney Crooker to assist the JAG.

Although the U.S. Constitution guaranteed Americans the right to a jury trial both in its text and in the Bill of Rights, the framers delegated Congress to establish the rules for disciplining the armed forces. Congress exercised the long-standing practice, contrary to a random jury selection, of allowing the military to select the members of a court-martial panel composed of military officers. This practice had always been intensely criticized. The court-martial officers functioned as individuals in hearing testimony and in reaching a verdict. In contrast to a jury in a civil case, the court-martial officers were not restricted to the evidence presented at trial. Any member was free to question a witness. In a civilian criminal setting, a jury verdict had to be unanimous, with every single juror holding the power to veto the entire trial. In a court-martial setting, a simple majority vote was sufficient for a conviction. A two-thirds vote was necessary to invoke the death penalty. With two top-level military lawyers heading the prosecution, the War Department wanted a prestigious panel composed of at least ten officers holding the rank of colonel or above. The army ended up with three brigadier generals, seven colonels, and three lieutenant colonels from a wide swath of the functional specialties and regions of the continental United States. More than half were West Point graduates.

Though the duties of all members were identical, the highest-ranking officer acted as president of the panel and spoke for the court whenever a legal ruling was necessary. The other members sat on either side of him in order of grade. The most important officer in the court-martial was the trial judge advocate, the equivalent of a prosecutor in a civil setting. This role varied somewhat. The army had looser requirements for the defense and specified only that the defense counsel is an army officer who could "perform such duties . . . before civil courts in criminal cases."[7]

One private was mercifully stricken with pneumonia just before the trial, and his name was removed from the list of sixty-four defendants. In the chapel, the soldiers were seated in four rows on a specially built inclined platform. It enabled them to watch the proceedings and also allowed witnesses to better identify them. The accused consisted of privates along with four corporals. Like most revolutionary movements, the foot soldiers, not the cadres, performed the work and bore the brunt of failure. The troops, in pressed uniforms, sat stoically, some scowling, some wearing blank stares. Their grizzled faces were those of hardworking men, prematurely aged from the sun, labor, and rough sleeping. The scene eerily suggested a New Orleans slave hub where the same mass of men would have been oiled, poked, and haggled over.

After the officers of the court-martial were sworn in, the charges were read. The soldiers were accused of violating, in a time of war, four Articles of War. The most serious charge was related to the ninety-second article, "Acting jointly and in pursuance of a common intent . . . with malice aforethought, willfully, deliberately, feloniously, unlawfully and with premeditation . . . shooting [fourteen people] with U.S. rifles loaded with powder and ball."[8] Under the sixty-fourth article, they were accused of willfully disobeying the orders of Major Snow to remain in camp and turn in their arms and ammunition. Under the sixty-sixth article, they were also charged with mutiny in which they "did forcibly subvert and override military authority and break out of camp with the intent of marching upon the city of Houston, Texas to the injury of persons and property."[9] The catchall charge against every soldier under the

ninety-third article was "unlawfully and feloniously" shooting civilians. Somberly, one by one, the sixty-three soldiers entered a
plea of not guilty. [10]

Colonel Hull insisted that the causes of the mutiny were irrele-
vant. Major Grier disagreed and gambled on the chance that an
emotional defense based upon mitigating circumstances would pre-
vail. Oddly enough, he opened the proceedings by reading a crisp
statement jointly prepared by the prosecution and him: "There are
certain underlying, contributing causes which, although neither per-
tinent nor strictly material to the issue about to be tried . . . nevertheless serve to place the court in possession of more accurate
information." [11] The statement was more advantageous to the prosecution, as it specifically ruled out contributing factors as having a
significant bearing over the elements of the crimes. Nevertheless, it
allowed Grier a liberal hand in introducing mitigating evidence.

Colonel Hull now had to prove, beyond a reasonable doubt, each
and every element of the accusations, a meticulous process for all
lawyers. Many a young trial lawyer at least once forgot to prove the
most basic element, the identity of the accused, and lost a case via a
directed verdict. Hull called before the court the white army officers in camp during the insurgency and a dozen black noncommissioned officers (NCOs). The most important of these early witnesses was Major Snow. In a shameful twist of fate, he was to
testify against the boys he swore to lead and protect. On that fateful
night, Snow heard several men roar, "we have got work to do. . . .
[L]et's go and do it." [12] Hull intended to make the major declare that
the entire episode was premeditated.

Major Grier, in turn, worked on eliciting an admission from
Major Snow that the soldiers seized weapons out of fear. However,
Snow did not acquiesce. Grier achieved a small victory in coaxing
him to admit that the night was too dark, "as black as a stack of
black cats," for even those who knew the men to make an identification. Few ajudicators were inclined to consider that the violence

erupted spontaneously after weeks of Jim Crow subjugation. Even after examining all seventeen witnesses, few new facts were revealed. The only other soldier mentioned by name besides Henry was Private Pat McWhorter, who was accused of being the ringleader for M Company.[13]

The army based its case for premeditation upon evidence that the soldiers stole ammunition from the supply tents then stashed it in predetermined locations in the camp and under the homes of several unsuspecting black civilians.[14] Based upon the pandemonium before the mutineers marched out, it was unlikely that any of them had the time or means to take more than a few rounds from the caches. If the men had stored away as much as alleged, the army should have recovered more than just trace amounts when it thoroughly searched the camp the following day.

Major Grier more successfully cast doubt on the accuracy of the head counts made after the soldiers left camp. The authenticity of those lists was crucial, as the prosecution insisted that anyone whose name was not on any of the lists was absent from camp and, by default, a participant in the mutiny. A lieutenant testified that at 21:30, twenty-nine men were missing from K Company. He jotted down the names on a notepad and later transferred that information onto another sheet of paper, which he still possessed. He claimed that the original notepad had fallen apart and that those original sheets were missing. The head counts in the other two companies were completed at 23:00, well after the uprising began. Captain James and another lieutenant rightly feared triggering violence from the soldiers if they made an accounting before that hour. Nevertheless, by then, an accurate tally was near impossible because many men had fallen asleep, and some of the column's deserters had returned to camp. A private testified that he needed only ten minutes to search the bivouac for all men who might be hiding or otherwise unaware of the roll call. In Grier's cross-examination, he attacked this rushed head count and pointed out that the insides of the tents and latrines were not inspected. Scared rookies were tasked with making those checks. The officers were unclear about the exact time the lists were made and the number of soldiers missing. Grier continued to chip away at the prosecution's case. [15]

In furtherance of his guilty-by-default approach, Colonel Hull summoned a handful of policemen and more than a dozen Illinois National Guardsmen. They provided the court with the names of eighteen men whom they arrested and handed over to the Houston police to be booked. Hull then argued that verification of an individual's arrest was prima facie proof of identity and thus enough to establish guilt.

In the following days, Colonel Hull brought forth forty-four Houstonians who were eyewitnesses to one or more of the night's events. However, none of them could identify a single soldier and their statements added little to the prosecution's case. Black resident Courtney Clark, who assisted in the arrest of a fugitive private, pointed to a different soldier when asked to identify the suspect. [16] Most witnesses had widely varied estimates of the number of rioters. However, Hull's intent was not to reveal facts but to elicit anger from the officers of the court-martial. He continued by attempting to precisely retrace the route the soldiers took, but in so doing, the location where several victims were killed cast doubt on that course's accuracy. While the prosecution tried to prove premeditation, Major Grier used Hull's assertions to his advantage, claiming that the existence of a well-organized formation indicated that many soldiers were unwillingly press-ganged into the column.

The prosecution dedicated its remaining efforts to proving the charges. Days later, Colonel Hull finally introduced the first of seven key witnesses, the mutineers who "flipped" in exchange for immunity. [17] Five of them were affirmed participants in the violence. Since the ringleaders refused to confess, the army relied heavily on the witness testimony to convict. The first star witness to take the stand was Private Frank Draper, a five-year veteran.

Even though he had not accompanied the troops into town, he was still valuable because he was present at one of the riot planning sessions. At this meeting, he saw Corporals Baltimore and Brown and Privates Risley Young and McWhorter.[18] The second witness was Private John Denty, who also denied involvement. He identified ten defendants in First Sergeant Henry's column. Nevertheless, Denty was a rookie, and his testimony was considered less compelling than Draper's.[19] Teenager Private Lloyd Shorter fingered Corporals James Wheatley and Jesse Moore, and Private Frank Johnson as key organizers. After some prodding, he disclosed the names of twenty other participants. During Major Grier's hard cross-examination, Shorter freely admitted his involvement and adamantly added that the men who joined Henry did so willingly.[20]

Private Elmer Bandy, a four-year veteran, accused six men in his company of refusing to turn in their rifles when ordered to do so. In describing the march on Houston, he named seventeen others as participants.[21] The most compelling testimony came from Private Cleda Love, with only six months of service. His ability to remember names—he divulged forty—and faces was extraordinary.[22] However, his memory was not perfect, as his list included five soldiers who were arrested elsewhere or could conclusively prove that they stayed behind.[23] The defense accused the prosecution of leading the rookie witness with cleverly crafted questioning.

On November 19, Major Grier began in earnest his defense of his sixty-three defendants.[24] The challenge was daunting since most of the men still mistrusted him. When questioned, Colonel Hull quickly used their words to incriminate them. Many believed that testifying on their own behalf was a waste of time, convinced that the army had the power to convict them regardless of the evidence. Only sixteen defendants took the stand.[25] After explaining their whereabouts on August 23, only two had a verifiable alibi.[26] When the president of the panel asked Private Grover Burns on the stand why so many men claimed that he was in the column, he replied that they "were doing that to save their lives . . . anything the investigation board told them to do."[27] Not only was the veracity of immunity witness statements questioned, but some were allegedly coerced. Men were pressured into testifying for the government, thinking that if they did not, the entire lot would be executed. Grier ultimately found a respected NCO to corroborate Burns's alibi.[28] Private Hawkins, who had penned the poignant good-bye letter to his mother, was one of the accused principals. Nevertheless, a soldier also testified that Hawkins had approached him inside the camp during the rioting and had been hiding in the trees.

On November 25, after all 194 witnesses testified, Colonel Hull's assistant, Major Sutphin, began his noteworthy summary of his case.[29] He took a risk and utilized the legal theory of collective guilt. He maintained that it was not necessary to prove the individual involvement of every defendant for the crimes committed by a mob. "Where a number of persons conspire," he argued, "and death happens in the prosecution of that common design, all and each one of the conspirators is guilty of murder."[30] The concept was expressed in another Coleridge poem, "The Rime of the Ancient Mariner," which recounted the story of a ship's crew who died of thirst after permitting a crew member to kill an albatross. Ethicists argue that collective responsibility violates both the principles of individual responsibility and fairness.[31] Ancient literature is filled with examples of aggrieved men who avenged themselves not only on their tormentor but on the other's entire tribe. Legal theorists go so far as ascribing guilt to nations for crimes carried out by a few, arguing that mens rea (guilty intent) is not limited to the individual. Thirty years after the Camp Logan riots, America dropped an atomic bomb on 360,000 Japanese citizens for the sins of their imperial military. Karl Jaspers's *The Question of German Guilt*, published shortly after World War II, was a seminal work that directly addressed those uncomfortable ethical issues. George Fletcher of the

Columbia University School of Law posited, "No dictator rules in a vacuum. To muster power, he must enjoy the support of the military, the implicit emotional consent of business leaders and professionals, and the tolerance of the public. . . . The failure to protest generates a basis for holding the public at least partially responsible."[32]

In Major Grier's favor was Blackstone's ratio, which espoused that it is better that ten guilty persons escape justice than that one innocent suffer.[33] The principle originated from the Bible, when Abraham pleads with God, "Will you consume the righteous with the wicked? What if there are fifty righteous within the city? Will you consume and not spare the place for the fifty? Or what if ten are found there?"[34]

In Major Grier's closing arguments, he described the violence perpetrated against the black servicemen by the police during their brief stay in Houston.[35] He stressed that the soldiers sought vengeance only against the police and not against Houstonians. Several white bystanders were confronted by the black raiders but were unharmed. "We are no Negroes," a Buffalo Soldier muttered as the column passed, indicating that their vengeance was limited to the police.[36] Grier downplayed the notion of a mass conspiracy, claiming that the soldiers harbored real fears that a white mob was coming to attack them. And as the group left the camp, they shouted like banshees, which undermined the idea that they were led by principled leaders who planned the raid. He asserted that many participants were obeying the orders of their first sergeant, but as soon as they realized the seriousness of the violence, they deserted and returned to camp.[37] Consequently, Grier concluded that fewer than fifty men participated in the raid on San Felipe Street. He also cautioned the court against unquestioning belief in the testimony of those with "unclean hands."[38]

A policeman testified that the initial shots fired near Camp Logan "didn't sound like rifles to me."[39] An examination of those inside the camp who were wounded by gunfire suggested that military rifles did not cause their injuries. An assessment of bullets fired into the surrounding homes also revealed the same conclusion. The evidence corroborated the soldiers' assertion that those who disobeyed orders and left the camp did so only to form a defensive battle line around the camp.

On November 27, the Nesbit court-martial adjourned, and the panel retired to reach a decision. After deliberating an entire day, the officers returned to record their decisions.[40] Fifty-four of the sixty-three defendants were found guilty of all charges.[41] Four were declared guilty of willfully disobeying the order of a superior by leaving camp without permission.[42] Five were acquitted.[43] The president of the panel then read out the sentences. Thirteen enlistees were culpable either of masterminding the riot or leading the column during the raid. As such, they would be "hanged by the neck until dead."[44] Corporal Baltimore, the locus of the entire affair, was both victim and perpetrator. He would lose his life as a result, notwithstanding the painful fact that the Houston Board of Inquiry deemed him innocent. Five of the thirteen men—Nesbit, Baltimore, Brown, Wheatley, and Moore—were NCOs who were held to a higher standard; as such, the court exercised the harshest final judgment.[45] The other eight were Privates James Divins, William Breckenridge, Carlos Snodgrass, Ira Davis, Hawkins, McWhorter, Johnson, and Young.[46] The exculpatory evidence in Hawkins's favor was not enough to save his life.

The other forty-one defendants were found guilty of mutiny and assault with intent to commit murder. They were sentenced to life with hard labor. Although none was accused of being a ringleader or individually responsible for any killing, all were fingered as part of the column.[47] Private First Class John Hudson was convicted on the testimony of an immunity witness.[48] Yet the court was so persuaded by his passionate sworn statement that it entered a plea of clemency. "He impressed us as being an ignorant man, rather stupid and not of high mentality, yet not vicious. . . . We believe . . . that he was puzzled and bewildered."[49] It was better for him, perhaps, to be insulted than executed. Four defendants received lighter sentences of thirty months or less. Taking the stand and defending their whereabouts seemed to have benefited many of those men in this instance. The five who were acquitted simply could not be identified as part of the column beyond a reasonable doubt.

Major General Ruckman ordered that the mass execution take place at Fort Sam Houston on December 11.[50] The army purposely spread a rumor that executions would take place in Leon Springs, twenty miles away. In a maneuver thinly disguised as a security measure but most likely a ploy to placate white civilians, the hangings took place several hours before the general informed the press of his decision.[51] Those sentenced to life in prison would molder away at the U.S. penitentiary in Leavenworth, Kansas.

The immediate public response was to be expected. By now, the story had gained a nationwide following. Nearly every major newspaper in the South felt that justice was served. Even newspapers that would later evolve into beacons of progressive journalism such as the *Atlanta-Journal Constitution* agreed with the prevailing "law and order" sentiment.[52] The *Outlook*, dubbed as a family weekly, boasted of having former President Roosevelt as an associate editor. It called on blacks to condemn the Houston riots in the same way whites condemned the East St. Louis riots.[53] Other northern newspapers were more sympathetic. The *Cleveland Gazette* called the executions "the South's 'Pound of Flesh.'"[54] Chicago's moderate *Broad Ax* regretted that the 24th Infantry had "blown their past splendid record to the winds."[55] A more balanced reaction came from the black press, though some blacks criticized it for not hitting back at the white media and for soft-pedaling arguments of "military justice." In searing fashion, DuBois exposed the contradictions of American justice. In the *Crisis*, he wrote, "They have gone to their death. . . . Thirteen young, strong men; soldiers who have fought for a country which never was wholly theirs; men born to suffer ridicule, injustice, and, at last, death itself. . . . They broke the law. Against them punishment, if it was legal, we cannot protest. . . . [The soldiers] were disciplined men who said—this is enough: we'll stand no more."⁵⁶ The *New York Age* declared, "Strict justice has been done. . . . [But] so sure as there is a God . . . full justice will be done."⁵⁷ Other black intellectuals saw the executions as merely a mass lynching by the federal government. Compared with nonmilitary death penalty cases, the army was exceptionally swift to execute. Most strikingly, there was no possibility of appeal, as America was at war—albeit a distant and perplexing one in which the Ottoman Turks were fighting Russia. In protest, acting JAG Brigadier General Samuel Ansell said, "The men were executed immediately upon the termination of the trial and before their records could be forwarded to Washington or examined by anybody, and without, so far as I can see, any one of them having time or opportunity to seek clemency."⁵⁸ White servicemen who had committed similar crimes received more lenient sentences.

Nevertheless, Houston's sad tale was not over yet. Just as the soldiers sentenced to life were taking their bunks in Fort Leavenworth, Colonel Hull and Major Sutphin were gathering evidence for their next court-martial, United States v. Corporal John Washington et al., which convened on December 17 in the infantry post gymnasium at Fort Sam Houston.⁵⁹ However, even as the court-martial got underway, the public's interest began to wane. On trial this time were fifteen members of the Lower A Division, one of the seven guardhouses. They were charged with quitting their posts and marching along the highway, threatening the lives of civilians, and murdering E. M. Jones on Washington Road. The composition of this court-martial panel was nearly indistinguishable from the United States v. Nesbit case.

Corporal Washington led the fifteen. The unit was well within earshot of the firing orgy at the 24th Infantry camp preceding the insurgency. The prosecution alleged that the men interpreted it as a signal to begin the rampage, after which they proceeded down Washington Road to join the main column. This court-martial was a much simpler affair since most of the facts were undisputed, and there were more witnesses. Several were standing outside Miller's eatery when they saw a group of black soldiers fire into a shared taxi coming down the street. The driver, Jones, and passenger were hit, and the former died. Despite several eyewitnesses, none could identify a single soldier or agree on the group's size. [60] The prosecution overzealously argued that nearly the entire eighteen-man guard detail deserted its post and that all of those on trial fired into the vehicle. Falling back on the theory of collective guilt, Colonel Hull claimed that regardless of whose round killed Jones, by shooting at the car, every man was guilty. [61] Major Grier countered that narrative by first agreeing that more than a dozen men may have left their post, but not all of them proceeded as far as Washington Road. Furthermore, based upon witness accounts, no more than five fired at the automobile. [62] The prosecutor's case rested on its star immunity witness, Private Bullock, himself one of the Lower A Division guards. The government linked Bullock to Jones's murder after he accidentally left his handwritten notepad near the crime scene. Bullock confirmed that he and five other privates were ahead of the other ten defendants when they spotted the taxi on Washington Road. Bullock insisted that he urged the others not to fire but to no avail. It was unclear if only those in his group shot at the vehicle or if all fifteen men did so. Bullock boldly claimed that every man discharged his rifle, adding that he heard bullets pass by his head. Nevertheless, he also contradicted his story at several points during cross-examination. [63]

Major Grier hedged his bets. In what must have been an excruciating ethical decision, he essentially ceded to the prosecution the five guards who were seen firing to save the remaining ten from execution. Colonel Hull tacitly accepted the offer. Finally, the pros-

ecution announced that it anticipated no more indictments and regarded the Washington court-martial closed.

After deliberating only a few hours, the panel found those five
defendants guilty of all charges and sentenced them to hang.[64] Mercifully, the court found the other ten guilty only of leaving their
posts, marching down a public highway in a riotous manner, and
threatening civilians. The prison sentences varied from seven to ten
years.

This time, on January 2, 1918, Major General Ruckman publicly
announced the verdicts and sentences before the troops were
hanged.[65] He also postponed the executions until the secretary of
war had an opportunity to review the case. Fate intervened on behalf of those Buffalo Soldiers, for on January 17, the War Department issued General Order Number 7, proposed by JAG Brigadier
General Ansell himself.[66] It revised the rules concerning the death
penalty and called for all of those cases to be reviewed by the U.S.
president. This last-minute policy change was no mere coincidence,
but the fruit of determined activism by the likes of the National
Association for the Advancement of Colored People (NAACP) and
several progressive newspapers.

Already upset by the lack of transparency before the executions
of the initial thirteen soldiers, black America would not submit to
the second culling of their young men. Middle-class blacks spoke
openly about revenge. "Lord, How Long, O Lord, How Long!"
lamented the *Cleveland Gazette*'s editor, "[Sons sacrificed] on the
altar of Southern prejudice and hate."[67] Petitions for clemency
poured into the White House. Several spokespeople representing
the black community pleaded with President Wilson to commute
the death sentences to life in prison "as a magnificent gift to the
race and nation at this critical time."[68] They made no excuses for
the crimes but reminded the White House of the black community's
historically unwavering patriotism from the battles of Bunker Hill
to Carrizal. With the assistance of Washington State's two senators,

the grand master of Spokane's Colored Lodge appealed to Wilson. On behalf of the "Ancient Craft of Masonry," he felt that "the thirteen men executed some time ago in connection with this awful affair have heroically atoned for this deplorable offense."[69] Senator Knute Nelson of Minnesota forwarded to Wilson a letter from a constituent in a remote, cold, and white community. The author urged the government to halt any proceedings against the black soldiers "until something is done to punish the [white] men that are primarily responsible."[70]

Finally, James Johnson, field secretary of the NAACP, and three prominent black ministers obtained an audience with President Wilson.[71] Johnson and the others were graciously received in the White House; the president rose from his desk and sat in a large comfortable chair while his guests read a prepared statement. Johnson concluded his remarks with a reminder of the injustices suffered by black Americans the previous nine months. He cited the riots at East St. Louis and the grisly lynching of two men in Tennessee. Wilson professed to be moved by Johnson's statement. "After I left the president's office," Johnson wrote, "my hostility toward the president [was] greatly shaken."[72]

However, before President Wilson could decide on the five men's fate, the wheels of justice in Fort Sam Houston turned again. With confidence and zeal, Major Sutphin had pursued every conceivable lead, regardless of probative value. He eventually stumbled upon additional evidence gathered while the first court-martial took place that linked several untried suspects to one of the many crimes committed during the riots. Now a third court-martial would try a group of forty men who rioted in the city in United States v. Corporal Robert Tillman et al. Private William Kane finally "flipped" in exchange for the possibility of an early release from prison.[73] The prosecution also made great use of black informants posing as convicts planted inside Fort Leavenworth. Private Bullock worked undercover until his appearance as a government witness in the first court-martial exposed him. With a wealth of stool pigeons, Sutphin secured indictments. Wilson was advised to hold off on his decision until the verdicts of this court-martial were known.

On February 18, the final court-martial convened again in the Gift Memorial Chapel but with little hope that the trial would bring forth any new or exculpatory findings. Although white America and the press had long ago lost interest, the lives of at least five men still hung in the balance. Colonel Hull left Major Sutphin to prosecute the case on his own. Aside from that, the Tillman court-martial looked very much like the previous two, and many of the same witnesses testified. [74] This time, Sutphin altered the prosecution's strategy and encouraged witnesses to describe in gory detail the atrocities they saw, which included the bayoneting and mutilating of victims. Four local morticians who likely worked on Officer Daniels's battered corpse provided stomach-turning testimony. Describing Carstens's abdominal gash, one stated, "The whole of the intestines were hanging down below the knee, and the man's stool was all over his legs and everywhere."[75]

Of the forty defendants, Major Sutphin had a particular animus toward the four corporals, including Tillman and James Mitchell.[76] The former had a target on his back after testifying for the defense in the first court-martial. Mitchell was on Sutphin's wrong side for a trivial act: complaining to Major Snow that the soldiers in Houston were being treated like dogs. One corporal angered the prosecution by explaining his absence during head count with a preposterous alibi. He claimed that as soon as the shooting began, he lowered himself into the latrine pit with a rope and carefully wedged himself against the walls with his legs and back to keep from falling in. Sutphin doubtless believed him to be full of shit. Private Ernest Phifer described the rampage with a disturbing psychopathic coolness. As he matter-of-factly detailed how the victims died, he lacked any semblance of remorse for participating in their killings.

The prosecution again relied heavily upon the testimony of four immunity witnesses who identified thirty-seven of the forty defendants.

To convict the corporals, Major Sutphin had to first reconcile how they could have participated in the raid when their names were on the checklist. As such, the testimony of Private Shorter proved pivotal. He explained how three of the corporals from I Company were seemingly in two places at the same time. According to Shorter, three corporals left camp with a group during the initial free-for-all of shooting into the sky. Then they fired at an ambulance on Washington Street and immediately returned to camp, expecting to join First Sergeant Henry's column, which had already left. The damning testimony not only fingered the corporals, but it also explained who shot at the ambulance, an incident that did not occur along the route supposedly taken by the Henry column.

The appearance of Private Kane threw the defense into a tailspin. Major Grier immediately objected to him as a witness on the "ground of infamy."[77] He argued that a person found guilty in one court-martial could not testify in another. Major Sutphin countered just as vigorously that a previous conviction does not necessarily disqualify a witness. The court had not often been posed with such procedural questions, and the answer was not immediately apparent. Court clerks, the unsung heroes of law, busied themselves researching every nuance, citation, and case related to this question. In a Supreme Court setting, they would feed their detailed results to a justice, who would reconstitute them into a bible-sized decision. In this instance, the court sided with the prosecution. Kane had the extraordinary ability to connect the defendants with specific events of the night.

The defense had little to discredit him. Private Kane was the most valuable yet most difficult of all the immunity witnesses because he came to the stand as prepared as a first-year law student reciting a familiar case. In the spirit of all jailhouse lawyers throughout history, he was intelligent enough to learn about the law, his rights, and, most importantly, every detail of United States v. Nesbitt. He memorized the transcript, knowing that his testimony had to be consistent to avoid the traps laid by Major Grier.

Private Love was another helpful witness for the prosecution. His description of Private William Boone's actions was damning. On the night of the riot, three men lay in the street, one of whom was on all fours lamenting, "Oh Lord! Oh Lord!"[78] Suddenly, out of nowhere, Boone appeared like the grim reaper and shot the man in cold blood, saying, "Lay down there, you son-of-a-bitch," adding that he should have been dead long ago.[79]

Like Private Love, the other men on trial learned from the Nesbit and Washington court-martials and reckoned that their chances were somewhat better if they took the stand. More than half did so. The alibis given for their absences during head count ranged from fleeing to one of two nearby restaurants to hiding alone in the surrounding woods. Although a few had verifiable alibis, the rest either had nobody to vouch for them or had only close friends who, the prosecution stressed, had an interest in keeping them from the gallows. Major Sutphin was successful in casting significant doubt on the veracity of the defendants' testimony.

Major Grier argued that "it was fear of punishment and not sorrows or regret for their crimes" that motivated the immunity witnesses to cooperate with the government.[80] He went on to discredit Private Phifer's testimony, claiming that since he freely admitted to firing into the Winkler home in "one of the most cold-blooded shootings," then his account should be highly suspect.[81] "Any man who is cowardly enough to fire a high power rifle, with a helpless woman standing in the line of direct aim," Grier claimed, "would not hesitate to commit perjury to save him from the punishment he so richly deserves."[82] Private Love was painted with the same brush. Grier once zealously defended the Sons of Ham, whom he now disparaged. To save the living, perhaps he felt that the dead should be left to bury the dead. Doubtless those same public defender ethical hypotheticals were pondered in law school salons for centuries. Mrs. Winkler eventually would be compensated a paltry $1,000 for her lost son.

Major Grier opened the door to the possibility that none of the immunity witnesses had accurately identified any of the accused. He referred to Private Bullock as a liar since contrary evidence proved that "these irresponsible and untrustworthy witnesses [were] absolutely mistaken . . . [thus presenting] the grave possibility that others among the accused may have likewise been implicated unjustly."[83] The betrayal by men who vowed to fight until the bitter end must have weighed heavily upon the immunity witnesses. Would they ever look their comrades in the eye? Judas tried to undo his wrong by returning the silver to the high priests, but it was too little, too late.

Though the facts of the case did not seem to favor either side, in terms of lawyering talent, the trained Major Sutphin had the advantage. In his closing remarks, Sutphin peppered his commentary with humor, sarcasm, and cynicism, which—to a court bored by two previous trials—was refreshing. Decades later, presidential candidates would be elected based upon their talents at derision, comedic skill, and ability to mesmerize a captive audience. To counter Major Grier's passionate pleas, Sutphin painted the witnesses as Good Samaritans who were somehow misunderstood. In a backhanded compliment, he stated that Private Kane was "a man far above the average intelligence of his race . . . able to communicate his knowledge to others in an intelligent fashion."[84] Sutphin added that the private was not a snitch but wanted "to free his mind from a secret . . . and assist the government."[85]

Major Sutphin praised Private Shorter for his honesty, crediting it primarily to being raised by a doctor father who taught him right from wrong. Shorter was the only man, he argued, who told the truth from the beginning and who stuck to it. Sutphin effectively played on the fact that since the first two courts-martial, the odds and stakes had changed. He added that defense witnesses altered their demeanor and, most likely, some facts. In Shakespearean fashion, he feigned outrage and disgust.

Since Major Sutphin's case rested on the accuracy of the head count lists, he argued that both the men who were counting and those who remained in the camp had every incentive to be completely thorough. He ridiculed the idea that there were men in the trees or above latrine pits. After deliberating most of the day on March 26, the panel found twenty-three of the defendants guilty of all charges and acquitted two.[86] The remaining were convicted of one or both charges of disobeying orders and of mutinous behavior.[87] The sentences were not read out.

The blameworthy went to bed that night terrified of what their punishments would be the following morrow. The court reconvened in a closed session, presumably for a compelling reason. Of the men found guilty of all charges, eleven were to be hanged. The remaining twelve were given life sentences. Since four of them were NCOs—Corporals Quiller Walker, Tillman, Geter, and Mitchell—the court found their behavior more egregious than that of the privates. In the case of Private Boone, his sentence was based solely upon the testimony of Private Love. The exact reasons for condemning the other six defendants were murky. Military law did not require the court to justify its decision to reconvene in a closed session.[88]

The sentences for the remaining men varied from two to fifteen years, proportionate to the number and seriousness of their offenses. For equally nebulous reasons, the Tillman court-martial was much harsher overall than the previous two, despite their similarities in actors and facts. Fortunately for the condemned, President Wilson decided that the execution of these sentences would also await his final approval. The guilty would be in legal limbo for many more weeks. The thirteen executed Buffalo Soldiers from the

Nesbit trial did not die in vain. Subsequent reforms born of that case spared the lives of many others who followed for decades to come—black and white.

Plea bargains are customarily agreements between defendants and prosecutors in which the accused agrees to plead guilty to some or all of the charges in exchange for leniency. Trials always have been prohibitively expensive, and court systems could hear only a small fraction of grievances. Jarndyce v. Jarndyce in Dickens's *Bleak House* was a decades-long suit concerning a large inheritance. Eventually, costs devoured the entire estate, and the case was abandoned. Proving a defendant's guilt beyond a reasonable doubt invariably had been fiendishly difficult, and rightly so, according to the framers of the U.S. Constitution. An often overlooked corollary is that the government only commits to a trial when it has a solid case. Not surprisingly, governments in all jurisdictions have a stellar winning record. Had the Buffalo Soldiers been made aware of the nature of American justice or been somewhat savvier, their fate may have been different. In the government's eyes, the three courts-martial—the largest in American history—were a stunning success. Of the 118 soldiers charged with mutiny, rioting, and murder, 110 were found guilty of at least one charge. Eighty-two men were declared guilty of all charges. [89]

However, not a single army officer was court-martialed, despite Brigadier General Chamberlain's recommendations. In the government's rush to bury this ugly chapter of history, it administered justice unevenly upon blacks and whites, enlisted and non-enlisted. Even the leviathan War Department dodged blame. As expected, the black community took the injustices in stride.

Like Blessed Mary at the feet of her condemned son, blacks never lost interest in the fate of their boys. Each court-martial piqued their passions, but they reached a tipping point when the number of soldiers sentenced to death or long prison terms approached eighty-seven. The NAACP and other black organizations ramped up their efforts. Booker T. Washington died before the fate of the Buffalo Soldiers was decided. Robert Moton replaced him as principal of the Tuskegee Institute and directly pleaded with President Wilson to do something "to change the attitude of these millions of black people."[90] The air of urgency and subtle warning of unrest were noted by Wilson.

Secretary of War Baker carefully reviewed all three courts-martial and, at the very least, concluded that they were conducted without procedural error. His recommendations were passed on to the president. Wilson responded the way most leaders do toward their expert advisers—he accepted their proposals without much afterthought. Wilson even instructed the secretary of war to draft a public statement incorporating the suggestions. Baker advised Wilson, however, to assure Americans that the granting of clemency should not be interpreted as an indication that the president doubted "that full justice was done in the trials." Wilson stressed that "extraordinary precautions [ensured] the fairness of the trials" with the defendants' rights "surrounded at every point [by] a humane administration of the law."[91] Days later, Wilson signed the proclamation commuting the death sentences of the ten soldiers from the Tillman trial. In politically tinged words, he stated that the decision should be viewed "as recognition of the splendid loyalty of the race to which these soldiers belong" and that his clemency should serve as "an inspiration to the people of that race to further zeal and service to the country."[92]

In the bonhomie surrounding President Wilson's act of clemency, the casual observer did not realize that he had approved the execution of the other six remaining men. Private Boone from the Tillman trial, positively identified as having shot an innocent, was to be executed with those from the Washington trial.[93]

On September 16, Father H. F. Kane, pastor of St. Peter's Catholic Church in San Antonio, accompanied five condemned men to the gallows. He ministered to them during their months in lockup.

It was unclear if any of the soldiers were members of the Universal Church of Rome or if they believed in the sacrament they were about to receive. Nevertheless, a priest acting *in persona Christi capitis* was about to see them off into the afterlife. They were clad in parade uniform with their hands cuffed behind them. The indignity of their conviction did not detract from their attention to detail and impeccable appearance.

The scaffolding was made from local mesquite wood, notorious for its warped and challenging grain. "Out of the crooked timber of humanity, no straight thing was ever made,"[94] posited Immanuel Kant. On the platform, the padre performed the ancient rite, the "service for the departure of a condemned soul."[95] No soldier offered any final words. Led by Father Kane, moments before dropping to their deaths, they chanted softly, "Father, into thy hands I commend my spirit, Lord Jesus receive my soul."[96]

As the young soldiers' bodies swung gently in the morning breeze, the hope of ever learning the full truth of that fateful night was extinguished. The government never broke them. Like First Sergeant Henry, they took their own secrets to their graves. The army was left to conclude that the original mutiny plans were derailed by Major Snow's sudden orders to collect the rifles. Those schemes, it was alleged, were more extreme and bloody. Nat Turner's meticulously planned rebellion did not have a tangible goal. Some argued that he wished to establish a rump state in Virginia. The only reason Toussaint Louverture succeeded in Haiti was because slaves outnumbered whites twenty-five to one. The mutiny succeeded in little more than Old Testament revenge on the police. The soldiers overestimated their ability to commit violence without getting caught. Though Henry was painted as the grand traitor, was he actually the fall guy for a much darker conspiracy? Was the real mastermind still among the living? According to Lieutenant Colonel Newman, Henry was one of the few soldiers who enjoyed his stay in Houston, as "he had met more high-class colored people in

Houston than he had ever seen before." Illiterate but courteous, it is unlikely that Sergeant Henry had the will or ability to organize a full-blown uprising against both the army and the city of Houston. Henry's actions were most likely spontaneous, and once he realized the gravity of the events, he took his own life rather than give the government the pleasure of killing him. Alternatively, did the truth follow the second-century Gnostic gospel of Judas? That narrative consisted of a conversation between Christ and Judas, in which they both plotted the betrayal, arrest, and sacrifice of the Son of Man. Without knowing what was in the soldiers' minds, the world never knew what was in their hearts.

As soon as the attending coroner pronounced the men dead, their bodies were lowered into unmarked graves nearby.[97] The scaffolding was quickly dismantled. Due to an administrative oversight, Private Boone was not among those executed.[98] He was yet to be informed of his fate, even after his five comrades were hanged. It must have felt like decades in purgatory. The War Department was determined to rectify the situation. At noon on September 23, Boone was told to prepare for death the following dawn.[99]

In Kafka's *The Trial*, the everyman Josef K is unexpectedly arrested on his birthday by two unidentified agents from an unspecified government bureau for an unnamed crime. He is not imprisoned but is told to appear at court the coming Sunday, without being told the exact time or room. After searching feverishly, Josef finds the court in the attic. He is chastised severely for being late and further infuriates the judge after expressing frustration about the absurdity of the process. Josef later seeks solace in a local cathedral. A priest mysteriously calls him by name and recounts an ancient parable, an early text underpinning secular law. Generations of courts, scholars, and officials had interpreted it differently throughout the centuries. Eventually, two men arrive at Josef's apartment and kill him. Josef's last words were "Like a dog!"[100]

When Father L. J. Welber, pastor of the local Holy Redeemer Catholic Church, arrived, Private Boone was pacing nervously and in a state of panic.[101] As such, the priest counseled him and presumably heard his final confession. Their discussion was private—both spiritually and legally—and privileged, known only to priest and penitent, like the secrets of Fatima. If there was indeed a conspiracy of silence, perhaps the padre knew. Moments later, the soldier "became quiet and met death bravely."[102] As his body tumbled to the earth, he would be in a state of grace. And thus, the mutiny of rage came to its ignominious end. *Omnes præséntis et futúræ vitæ pœnas.*

10

ATONEMENT

> I [Nat Turner] was looking for Margaret. She was hiding around
> the corner of the house. When I finally spied her, she ran light
> and quick as the wind through the rows of corn. I ran, following
> the bright sunlight in her hair. After that flashing face had turned
> to look at me, I ran faster than she and then I caught up with her.
> I must, I must, I must, I must kill you! Because I love you!
> Because you're white! White! White! White!—Gualtiero Jaco-
> petti and Franco Prosperi, *Goodbye Uncle Tom*

Nat Turner was hung, and his body was quartered. Where his
remains were interred remain unknown. It was rumored that he was
castrated, either before or after his death, his loins the symbol of
black masculinity, the object of fear and loathing. His revolt was
quashed, with innocents sacrificed in the wake. His legacy lived on
in history books, with a confusing and clouded legacy of neither
saint nor demon.

George Floyd, a six-foot-two black man, was a well-liked
bouncer at a Minneapolis, Minnesota, Mexican-Latino club. He
regularly drove patrons home if they had too much to drink. On
Memorial Day, May 25, 2020, he walked into a small corner store.
The Middle Eastern clerk was initially wary but said nothing. After
Floyd left, the police were alerted about a counterfeit $20 bill that
he used to buy cigarettes. David Chauvin, a white police officer,

and three others were dispatched. Floyd, who was sitting in his car when they arrived, was suspected to be under the influence of drugs or alcohol. He was also believed to have a weakened heart. After a brief struggle, he was handcuffed. Floyd fell to the pavement, and Chauvin then pinned him down with a knee to his neck. "Please, please, please, I can't breathe. . . . [E]verything hurts!" muttered Floyd repeatedly.[1] American volunteer Alan Seeger, who died in the Battle of the Somme on July 4, 1916, called out for his mother as he lay in a crater, waving his comrades on. As life agonizingly left the body, a soldier sought the safety of the womb that gave him life, *O clement, O loving.* Floyd, too, called out for his mother before he died. His mother was long deceased.

Though Floyd committed grave wrongs earlier in his life, he came to Minneapolis to mend his ways.[2] The day after his death, that city was in flames, and several people lay dead after riots erupted.[3] Violent protests spread to nearly every major American city, even many European capitals. The inferno created oxygen-deprived vortexes that howled like demons. Burning cars shot fire high into the sky, fixtures from hell. Floyd was a son of Houston, Texas.[4] He was buried not far from the San Felipe district and the carcass of Camp Logan.

David Dorn, seventy-seven, was black and a proud thirty-seven-year veteran of the St. Louis Police Department. Known for dedicating much of his time mentoring local at-risk youth, the second-hand lion refused to live the idle life of a retiree. Only days after Floyd's death, he valiantly responded to the alarm of a friend's pawn shop. He attempted to protect the business from looters but was murdered by a young assailant just a few years older than Princip was in 1914. Dorn was felled on the sidewalk in front of the ransacked shop. His death was streamed on Facebook live. "They just killed this old man . . . over some TVs . . . c'mon, man, that's somebody's granddaddy," a voice is heard saying.[5] Nobody both-

ered to hold his hand or offer aid before he died. Eventually, a
bystander suggested calling the police.

In the last letter to his mother, Private Hawkins wrote, "I will meet
you by the river."[6] Appropriately enough, he and the other Sons of
Ham were laid to rest along the banks of Salado Creek, "and if the
tree fall toward the south, or toward the north, in the place where
the tree falleth, there it shall lie."[7] They remained undisturbed until
1937 when Fort Sam Houston needed the land for training purposes. In an interesting twist of fate, it was discovered that the
executed men had not been dishonorably discharged before their
deaths, as was expected. As such, the men were authorized to be
buried in the national cemetery close by. In doing so, they were the
first and paved the way to desegregate all of the hallowed of
grounds for servicemen. A familiar aphorism states that blacks and
white are equal only twice in a lifetime: at birth and in death.
According to military custom, the surrounding headstones note
each serviceman's name, rank, birth, death, and honors. Those for
this lot included only the name and date of death.

Nevertheless, nearly two decades later, federal bureaucracy,
blundering, and misplacement of records made it impossible for
families of the deceased to find their loved ones. Private Hawkins's
father never recovered from the emotional trauma. Private Moore's
brother even went to Washington, D.C., to seek answers. All his
family received was a box with a dog-eared Bible, coat, and a
dollar. The private's brother died before Moore's body was found,
which was only discovered in 1987 after the Freedom of Information Act enabled his descendants to sift through Kafkaesque piles
of documents.

Like the French Foreign Legion, the 24th Infantry henceforth
was relegated to isolated and obscure postings in the American
West, far from major population centers. The government now
avoided posting black units of any kind in the South. In a sad twist,

the army's attempt at racial justice had the opposite effect. To increase the number of Negro officers, they stripped noncommissioned officers (NCOs) from the 24th Infantry and sent them for training in Iowa. This decision resulted in a dearth of effective leadership in Houston and the eventual mutiny. The NCOs who skipped Houston made it known that they would have traded their commissions for the chance to avert the riots and maintain the regiment's good name. The *Outlook* threatened to protest their commissions until blacks apologized en masse for the rioting. After keeping the thorny 3rd Battalion within the 24th Infantry on life support for several years, the army finally disbanded it in 1921. Other Negro regiments remained underutilized until World War II, when manpower concerns prompted a pragmatic change in policy. Executive Order 9981 finally integrated the military and called for equal opportunity for all races. It also made racist remarks a punishable offense. The 24th Infantry as a whole carried on and fought in the Korean conflict, yet scandal plagued it again. After several battles in which many units performed poorly, several enlisted men faced court-martial once again. A handful of white officers were relieved of command, and the entire regiment was disbanded in 1951. It was partly reinstated in 1995, but as of 2021, only one battalion with little semblance of the proud original regiment remains.

The rampage made public the injustices and simmering rage that blacks suffered in private. Nevertheless, not all black voices were sympathetic. Lieutenant Henry Flipper, the first black West Point graduate, opined, "the men of the 24th Infantry are gamblers, thugs, bums, and the scum of our people." Flipper, of all those wronged by the judicial and military establishment, should have been more sympathetic. In 1881, he was put in charge of a large sum of his superior's funds. Either from an accounting error or oversight, he soon realized that a considerable amount had gone missing. Fearful that hostile commanders would use the incident to expel him from the army, Flipper attempted to hide the discrepancy and was arrested for embezzling government funds. Many felt that he was framed. Friends within the army and Good Samaritans in the surrounding community replaced the missing money within days. However, Flipper was still court-martialed. Letters exchanged with a white woman were used against him. He was eventually drummed out of the army with the equivalent of a dishonorable discharge. In two prior situations involving white officers who were found guilty of the same offense, neither was dismissed nor dishonored.

One of the few green shoots to sprout after the violence was the establishment of the Houston branch of the National Association for the Advancement of Colored People (NAACP) in 1918.[8] In the coming decades, its influence would rival that of the New York City chapter.[9] While the NAACP was still smarting from its failure to save the lives of the last six soldiers, its strong Houston presence reinvigorated its efforts to seek early release for the remaining imprisoned men. The riots enabled the NAACP to grow into the most respected and organized black civil rights association. Through 1924, it conducted an extensive campaign to raise awareness of the condemned soldiers and lobbied the president to pardon them.[10]

Nevertheless, eventually, NAACP officers had progressed as far as possible with President Wilson and opted to wait until Warren Harding's election to take their efforts to the next level. By that time, none of the twenty-three men sent to Fort Leavenworth for less than ten years was still confined. Fifteen had even been restored to military duty. However, all but five of the original sixty-eight soldiers who were sentenced to life remained incarcerated. The controversial Private Kane was pardoned for his testimony in the Tillman court-martial.[11] Another soldier was released due to a terminal illness, and three died—one by his own hand.[12]

In the spring of 1920, the military went so far as to have all sixty-three prisoners evaluated by a psychiatrist to tease out any additional evidence for clemency. [13] This special investigation looked into "the whole life both civil and military, and including their behavior while in confinement." [14] After "carefully questioning" each of them, the government uncovered nothing of value while neglecting mitigating circumstances and the fact that the accused had not been identified as participants in the rioting. Nevertheless, it did affirm that the soldiers continued with their "conspiracy" to withhold evidence. Not surprisingly, clemency was not recommended.

On September 28, 1921, James Johnson again met with the commander in chief. He and a delegation of thirty prominent black leaders armed with fifty thousand signatures met with President Harding. [15] As he had done in the earlier meeting with President Wilson, Johnson served as the delegation's spokesman. He did not base his convictions on emotion or outrage but on three very sound jurisprudential principles. Johnson claimed that the Buffalo Soldiers' "previous record for discipline, service, and soldierly conduct" merited special consideration. [16] He added that offenses should be mitigated due to the conditions under which they had served. Finally, Johnson argued that the troops had already suffered enough, asserting that the executions bordered on vengeance rather than justice.

Although reserved, President Harding was exceptionally polite and promised the delegation that "he would do what he could." [17] Johnson did not buy into the niceties and decorum and suspected that Harding had no plans to take any action. Not surprisingly, none of the sixty-three men was released that year. The only men set free during the next two years were five who were initially given fifteen-year sentences.

With little help from President Harding, the NAACP turned to Congress. Representative Daniel Anthony of Kansas introduced a resolution directing the secretary of war to furnish the House of Representatives with information about whether the evidence against the executed men and those given life sentences proved their "direct participation" or if some were convicted solely because they were absent from the head count.[18] He also wanted the severity of their sentences reviewed.

In response, on December 6, Secretary of War John Weeks wrote to the chairman of the House Committee on Military Affairs. Weeks was not an elected politician, and he did not fret over reelection. He reiterated that all of the men still in the penitentiary were found guilty of serious offenses and that "the evidence of guilt . . . was overwhelming and stands without explanation or contradiction. [The defendants] had a fair and impartial trial. . . . [No soldier was guilty] merely because he was absent from roll call."[19] In addition to reviewing all three courts-martial, the JAG's office had set aside three months to examine the record of each prisoner with a view toward clemency. He summarized coolly that the clear and convincing evidence did not justify the mitigation of their sentences. An old Italian adage about obeying traffic law suggests that if everybody is guilty, then nobody is guilty. Weeks's Calvinist interpretation of culpability differed from the Latin one.

The temporary appointment of Colonel Hull as the army's acting JAG in 1921 was an additional setback for the activists. Since he was the prosecutor in all three courts-martial, the army should have immediately recognized his assignment as a conflict of interest. However, time can often impart wisdom on even the hardest of men. In 1922, Hull undertook a year-long review of the individual cases of the fifty-seven men serving life terms.[20] As a sample of all prisoners grouped by race or socioeconomic class, the Buffalo Soldiers received clemency less frequently than all others. Hull realized, years after the courts-martial, that some men were followers rather than leaders. He teased out the probability that after leaving with First Sergeant Henry's column, Corporals Tillman, Mitchell, and possibly Geter returned to camp.[21] Hull was convinced that Private Hezekiah Turner was not a raging killer after all, but little more than the column's medic.[22] Furthermore, he discovered that on the whole, the Buffalo Soldiers were disproportionately model prisoners and had "rendered marked service in the upholding and supporting the authorities in the maintenance of prison discipline and order."[23] As such, Hull recommended that the sentences of six men be reduced to twenty years. In an ode to Augustinian and Thomistic thought, Hull stated that redemption should not be denied for a "prisoner who is willing to work for his own salvation."[24]

Just when some members of the NAACP considered giving up, Colonel Hull's act of clemency empowered the organization to continue the fight for the next few years. The sudden death of President Harding in 1923 provided additional hope that President Calvin Coolidge might be more amenable. Nevertheless, they were mistaken. Though Johnson again earned an audience with the highest officer in the land, Coolidge refused to meddle in a matter that remained politically incendiary. The NAACP finally overplayed its hand. Its annual meeting, not coincidentally, was held in Kansas City, merely forty miles from Fort Leavenworth. NAACP officers referred to the soldiers as "martyrs of the Houston Riot," and planned to send a delegation to visit them.

Black activism prompted a countermovement by white Houstonians who petitioned the president not to grant clemency. Acting somewhat independently, the War Department nonetheless approved the parole of nineteen prisoners and reduced the sentences of eight others nearly to time served.[25] This King Solomon–like gesture not only angered white Houstonians but left black Americans frustrated. However, the trickle of parole granting continued. By 1927 twenty-seven more men were released.[26] The early release of Private Tyler embodied the uneven application of the law and hypocrisy toward black athletes. The naturally sportive Tyler played in the penitentiary's segregated baseball league. With an astonishing 0.607 batting average and a close friendship with boxer

Jack Johnson—also locked up at that time—Tyler was paroled to play professionally for the Chicago American Giants.

By the decade's end, only a handful of soldiers remained incarcerated. Most of those still inside either had broken the law in- or outside of prison and were promptly returned. One such incorrigible, Private Stewart Philips, had broken out of the penitentiary. Though eventually caught, he nevertheless was the final prisoner to be paroled, quietly, in 1938. By then, he was a middle-aged man, and the world was then on the brink of a second world war. Houston's darkest day, whenever spoken of, was discussed in hushed tones of guilt and embarrassment. Blacks and whites made a pact to keep this secret to themselves. Sadly, several men who had been released requested to be reincarcerated.[27] The penitentiary obliged them. They had been locked up for so long that their mind and soul remained imprisoned.

Nevertheless, the possibility of a posthumous presidential pardon lived on through the decades. In act 2, scene 3 of *Hamlet*, Shakespeare's protagonist urges the villain Polonius to treat well the performers who came to entertain the king. As such, clemency power historically had been used to entrench a kingdom by endearing the sovereign to his subjects. On February 19, 1999, President Bill Clinton granted the first posthumous presidential pardon in U.S. history. The recipient was none other than Lieutenant Flipper.[28] The gesture was without historical precedent, and legal hurdles needed to be overcome. Law clerks got busy. It had long been the policy of the pardon attorney of the U.S. Department of Justice not to accept or process posthumous pardon applications, stating that such power could not and should not be granted the president.

The government's position was rooted in cases decided during the republic's early days. The pardoning power of England was applied in individual American colonies and subsequently incorporated into the U.S. Constitution. Pardon powers were originally more commonly exercised by state governors. Indeed, the power in state constitutions is at least as expansive as the broad authority given to the president in article 2, section 2, clause 1.[29] The British crown traditionally delegated this pardon power to its direct representatives in the New World. This English model influenced the colonies during the prerevolutionary period. Since many of these colonies-turned-states had issued posthumous pardons, they supported the idea that this power should also reside with the president.

In 2016, one hundred years after the riots, the descendants of Corporal Nesbit and Privates Moore and Hawkins petitioned the U.S. government for posthumous pardons, arguing they "suffered grave injustices at the hands of the United States when they were executed by hanging after a defective trial."[30] The petitions were filed with the Justice Department, near the end of President Barack Obama's second term. To the descendants' dismay, officials reportedly responded that the Justice Department did not handle posthumous pardons. Not discouraged, the petitions were subsequently sent to the Trump White House. The descendants gathered that in light of the list of requests, preference was given to living petitioners. Retired Lieutenant Colonel Geoffrey Corn, professor of law at South Texas College of Law, reviewed the petition. He recognized that it was improperly filed, as pardon petitions for soldiers had to be submitted through the secretary of the army. It had not even reached the desk of President Donald Trump. The White House was amenable to organizing a meeting with Trump and the descendants, but the idea was ultimately rejected by one of the participants.

Yet President Trump did not hesitate in posthumously pardoning Jack Johnson. Boxer Mike Tyson and Senators Harry Reid and John McCain—a Naval Academy pugilist—had lobbied the Obama administration to pardon Johnson of his racially dubious 1913 felony conviction but to little effect. After speaking with committee members of the World Boxing Council and *Rocky* actor Sylvester Stallone, Trump pardoned Johnson 105 years after his conviction.

Retired Colonel Frederic Borch, a historian for the JAG Corps and the first prosecutor of terrorists at Guantanamo Bay in 2004, also pressed for a presidential pardon for the Buffalo Soldiers. Citing well-established civil and military law, he argued that "No black soldier was going to get a break in the Jim Crow Army of 1917." He was equally critical of the collective guilt theory: "Some were [guilty]. Were some also innocent? Highly likely." Borch bridled at the idea that one officer who was not a lawyer, with only two weeks to prepare, could adequately represent sixty-three soldiers. "While everything about the court-martial was legal," Borch said, making a relativist reference to the evolving understanding of the Constitution and the protections it offered, "it was not fair. Not a fair trial then. Certainly, not a fair trial now."[31]

The soldiers' descendants began to wonder if a presidential pardon would genuinely heal the wounds. As in Catholic theology, repentance, which results in forgiveness, wipes away sin, yet the consequences of said sin may remain and require atonement through penance or purifying fire after death. As such, a presidential pardon removed, either conditionally or unconditionally, the punitive legal effects of an offense. Nevertheless, it could not erase the conviction as a historical fact or prove that the pardoned individual did not commit a crime. In the 1833 case United States v. Wilson, Justice John Marshall said of the presidential pardon, "it is considered as a public law; having the same effect on the case as if the general law punishing the offense had been repealed or annulled."[32] This diktat ultimately led to a coordinated effort between the Houston NAACP Veterans Affairs Committee, the Buffalo Soldiers Museum, and South Texas College of Law Houston. Together they began a new initiative to seek restoration of honor for the men of the 24th Infantry.

As of 2020, South Texas College of Law Houston, in conjunction with its Actual Innocence Clinic, worked to submit pardon petitions for all convicted soldiers through the proper channels. The law school housed the most comprehensive collection of the riot's associated court documents, historical records, personal annals, and recently declassified government papers. The clinic also initiated a project to secure action by the army to upgrade all of the convicted rioters' dishonorable discharges to honorable. Cadets studying law at West Point also collaborated in these efforts. The initiative already bore fruit. The secretary of the army requested the secretary of veteran's affairs to place proper military headstones on the graves of the executed men.

Moral support for a presidential pardon even came from the most unexpected sides of the uprising. English poet John Donne wrote: "Any man's death diminishes me because I am involved in Mankind; And therefore never send to know for whom the bell tolls; it tolls for thee."[33] In that same spirit, Sandra Hajtman, great-granddaughter of slain Police Officer Raney, proclaimed, "The men did not have a fair trial. I have no doubt the men executed had nothing to do with the deaths."[34] She also recounted how Raney was a good man who regularly took into his home abandoned black children. His wife nursed the youngest of them. "You have to . . . learn from it—both sides bear responsibility."[35] Even in 1917, most Houston police were fair-minded and decent. Even a voice from a descendant of the 24th Infantry officers was heard. "The soldiers were a hundred percent wrong for rioting, but I don't blame them," said Jules James, the great-nephew of Captain James, beloved by his boys.[36] "The unit had sixty years of excellent service, was full of experienced veterans, but couldn't endure seven weeks of Houston."[37]

One perspective that neither side considered was the notion that acquiescing to racist sentiments and not sending black troops into southern cities was itself racist. Recruits joined the army with the knowledge that they would be sent where they were needed. They were not poker chips for the War Department to weigh against the preferences and dislikes of segregationists. The presence of the

Arkansas National Guard escorting black students in Little Rock schools in 1957 was a testament to the more rational racists-be-damned position.

Absent a pardon, in 2017, the descendants successfully procured gravestones in Houston's historic College Park Cemetery for three of the soldiers killed in the mutiny, including First Sergeant Henry. They also organized a rededication of a Texas Historical Commission marker where Camp Logan once stood—now Memorial Park—to mark the event's one hundredth anniversary. It was attended by Houston Mayor Sylvester Turner and other dignitaries. That same year, the marker was vandalized with red paint.

On one nondescript day, Hajtman met with two friends, Amanda Holder, the great-niece of Corporal Moore, and Charles Anderson, the great-nephew of Sergeant Nesbit. They strolled through Houston, retracing the route taken by the rioting troops. Enveloped in a great white light, the souls of the departed Buffalo Soldiers, Houston police, and civilians followed in tow, in perfect formation—all were friends. Trumpets sounded. In their afterlife, the lions and lambs lived in harmony.

None of the Buffalo Soldiers were ever cleared. Most newly freed men quietly returned or relocated to the many northern ghettos, integrated with the local blacks, and tried to live anonymous lives. Some married and started families and lived upstanding lives. Some became vagrants. Some turned to God and others to drink. These men without a country had been stationed in the Wild West, ran into troubles in the South, and wanted only to be forgotten in the frigid north.

> When we heard at first [John Brown] was dead, one of my townsmen observed that "he died as the fool dieth"; which, pardon me, for an instant suggested a likeness in him dying to my neighbor living.—Henry David Thoreau, "A Plea for Captain John Brown"

NOTES

I. GALLOWS AND UNMARKED GRAVES

1. Robert V. Haynes, *A Night of Violence: The Houston Riot of 1917* (Baton Rouge: Louisiana State University Press, 1976), 1. C. E. Butzer of Houston Heights, who was a member of the quartermaster corps at Fort Sam Houston, was the only eyewitness of the execution to write a description. His letter was published in the *Houston Chronicle*, December 13, 1917.

2. Nat Turner, *The Confessions of Nat Turner, the Leader of the Late Insurrection in Southampton, VA* (Baltimore: Thomas R. Gray, 1831), 20–21.

3. *Houston Chronicle*, December 13, 1917; *Cleveland Gazette*, December 15, 1917; *Topeka Plaindealer*, December 14, 1917; *Chicago Broad Ax*, December 15, 1917.

4. United States v. Sergeant William C. Nesbit et al., RG 153, FRC, 2129-60; *Houston Post*, December 4, 1917; *A Manual for Courts-Martial: Corrected to April 15, 1917* (Washington, DC, 1917), 182–85; M. M. Hoffman, "Court-Martial Conversion," *Catholic World*, October 1950, 45–51; Ephesians 2:8–9 (Authorized King James Version).

5. *Houston Chronicle*, December 13, 1917; *Cleveland Gazette*, December 15, 1917; *Topeka Plaindealer*, December 14, 1917; *Chicago Broad Ax*, December 15, 1917.

6. Haynes, *A Night of Violence*, 4, who states, "This description of the execution is based largely on C. E. Butzer's account in the *Houston*

Chronicle, December 13, 1917." See also *Cleveland Gazette*, December 15, 1917. *A Manual for Courts-Martial* stated that "death by hanging is considered more ignominious than death by shooting" (160).

7. Haynes, *A Night of Violence*, 3–4.

8. *Chicago Broad Ax*, December 15, 1917.

9. Description by C. E. Butzer, *Houston Chronicle*, December 13, 1917; *Cleveland Gazette*, December 15, 1917; *Chicago Broad Ax*, December 15, 1917.

10. *Catholic World*, "Court-Martial Conversion," October 1950, 45–51.

11. *Chicago Defender*, March 2, 1918; *Topeka Plaindealer*, December 14, 1917; *New York Age*, December 29, 1917.

12. Letter by Private Hawkins, December 11, 1917; James Jeffrey, "A 100-Year-Old US Riot Only Now Being Talked About," BBC News, November 25, 2017, www.bbc.com/news/world-us-canada-42116688.

13. *Houston Chronicle*, December 13, 1917.

14. Haynes, *A Night of Violence*, 5.

15. Haynes, *A Night of Violence*, 5.

16. Haynes, *A Night of Violence*, 2, 5.

17. Haynes, *A Night of Violence*, 5.

18. Haynes, *A Night of Violence*, 5.

19. Haynes, *A Night of Violence*, 5.

20. Ambrose Bierce, "An Occurrence at Owl Creek Bridge," *San Francisco Examiner*, 1890.

21. Haynes, *A Night of Violence*, 6.

22. Haynes, *A Night of Violence*, 5–6; Celebration Road Show and John Newton, *Amazing Grace Hymn* (Celebration Records, 1970).

23. *Houston Chronicle*, December 13, 1917; *Chicago Broad Ax*, December 15, 1917.

24. *Chicago Broad Ax*, December 15, 1917.

25. *Houston Chronicle*, December 12, 1917; *Houston Post*, December 12, 1917.

26. *Houston Chronicle*, December 12, 1917; *Houston Post*, December 12, 1917.

27. *Houston Chronicle*, December 12, 1917; *Houston Post*, December 12, 1917.

28. *Houston Chronicle*, December 12, 1917; *Houston Post*, December 12, 1917. The *Houston Chronicle* noted that "The remains were interred near the place of execution."

29. Isaaiz N. Nutter to Senator Joseph Frelinghuysen (NJ), December 18, 1917, General Court Martial Case 109018, Records of Judge Advocate General, RG 153, FRC.

30. *Houston Chronicle*, December 13, 1917; *Atlanta Constitution*, December 13, 1917; *El Paso Morning Times*, December 14, 1917.

31. Gregg Andrews, *Thyra J. Edwards: Black Activist in the Global Freedom Struggle* (Columbia: University of Missouri Press , 2011).

32. Robert H. Ferrell, *America's Deadliest Battle: Meuse-Argonne, 1918* (Lawrence: University Press of Kansas, 2007).

33. Carol R. Byerly, *Fever of War: The Influenza Epidemic in the U.S. Army during World War I* (New York: New York University Press, 2005).

34. "Memorial Park," www.houstontx.gov/parks/parksites/memorial-park.html, accessed March 24, 2020.

35. Ed Mayberry, "Historical Marker, Head Stones Commemorate 1917 Riots," Houston Public Media, August 23, 1917, www.houstonpublicmedia.org/articles/news/2017/08/23/232510/historical-marker-head-stones-commemorate-1917-riots.

36. Texas Historic Sites Atlas, Details for Camp Logan (Atlas Number 5201010624), https://atlas.thc.state.tx.us/Details/5201010624, accessed October 14, 2020.

2. BUFFALO SOLDIERS

1. Frank N. Schubert, "Ten Troopers: Buffalo Solider Medal of Honor Men Who Served at Fort Robinson," *Nebraska History* 78 (1997), 151–57.

2. Indian War Period Medal of Honor Recipients, Medal of Honor Citations, United States Army Center of Military History, September 22, 1890.

3. Medal of Honor Recipients: Arlington National Cemetery, Arlington National Cemetery.

4. William T. Bowers, William M. Hammond, and George L. Mac-Garrigle, *Black Soldier White Army* (Washington, DC: Government Printing Office, 1996), 12.

5. *Philadelphia Ledger*, November 1901; Howard Zinn, *A People's History of the United States*. (New York: Harper Perennial, 2016), 308.

6. Ray L. Burdeos, *Filipinos in the U.S. Navy & Coast Guard during the Vietnam War* (Bloomington, IN: AuthorHouse, 2008), 14.

7. David Ryan and Michael Patrick Cullinane, eds., *U.S. Foreign Policy and the Other* (New York: Berghahn, 2014), 114–15.

8. Joseph Ryan, " The Saga of David Fagen: Black Rebel in the Philippine Insurrection," Socialist Action News and Views, https://web.archive.org/web/20091027112545, http://www.geocities.com/mnsocialist/fagen.html, accessed May 1, 2020.

9. Ryan, " The Saga of David Fagen."

10. Lawrence P. Scott and William M. Womack, *Double V: The Civil Rights Struggle of the Tuskegee Airmen* (East Lansing: Michigan State University Press, 1998).

11. *United States Statutes at Large*, 39th Cong. (1866), 332.

12. Larry Shaughnessy, "Oldest Buffalo Soldier to Be Buried at Arlington," CNN, September 19, 2005.

13. Herman Lehmann, *Nine Years among the Indians 1870–1879* (Austin, TX: Von Boeckmann-Jones, 1927), 121.

14. *House Executive Documents*, 41st Cong., 2nd Sess., Pt. 1 (1969–1970), 96–99.

15. Marvin E. Fletcher, *The Black Soldier and Officer in the United States Army*, 1891–1917 (Columbia: University of Missouri Press, 1974).

16. Henry Ossain Flipper, *Black Frontiersman: The Memoirs of Henry O. Flipper, First Black Graduate of West Point* (Fort Worth: Texas Christian University Press, 1997).

17. Hilary Coston, *The Spanish American War Volunteer* (Freeport, N Y : Books for Libraries Press, 1971), 7.

18. *Tampa Morning Tribune*, June 8, 1898.

19. Gail Buckley, *American Patriots: The Story of Blacks in the Military from the Revolution to Desert Storm* (New York: Random House, 2001), 152.

20. Buckley, *American Patriots*, 146.

21. War with Spain Medal of Honor Recipients, Medal of Honor Citations, United States Army Center of Military History, September 1, 2004.

22. Buckley, *American Patriots*, 146.

23. Frank N. Schubert, *Black Valor: Buffalo Soldiers and the Medal of Honor* (Wilmington, DE: Scholarly Resources, 1977), 164–65.

24. Willard B. Gatewood Jr., *"Smoked Yankees" and the Struggle for Empire: Letters from Negro Soldiers, 1898–1902* (Fayetteville: University of Arkansas Press, 1987), xi.

25. Gatewood, *"Smoked Yankees" and the Struggle for Empire*, xi.

26. Gatewood, *"Smoked Yankees" and the Struggle for Empire*, 239–40.

27. *Salt Lake City Tribune*, October 22, 1896. See also *St. Paul Broad Axe*, October 31, 1896.

28. *Salt Lake City Tribune*, October 22, 1896. See also *St. Paul Broad Axe*, October 31, 1896.

29. Leon Wolff, *Little Brown Brother: How the United States Purchased and Pacified the Philippine Islands at Century's Turn* (Garden City, New York: Doubleday, 1961).

30. Douglas Henry Daniels, *Afro-Americans, the San Francisco Bay Area 1950–1960, A Report for the Golden Gate National Recreation Area*, March 13, 1980, 18.

31. Flipper, *Black Frontiersman*.

32. Erik Carlson, "Ellington Field: A Short History, 1917–1963," February 1999, https://historycollection.jsc.nasa.gov/JSCHistoryPortal/history/ellington/Ellington.pdf.

33. William G. Muller, *The Twenty-fourth Infantry: Past and Present* (Fort Collins, Colorado: Old Army Press, 1972), 82.

34. Robert V. Haynes, *A Night of Violence: The Houston Riot of 1917* (Baton Rouge: Louisiana State University Press, 1976), 90–91.

35. *Houston Post*, July 26, 29, 30, 1917; Thomas Richard Adams, "The Houston Riot of 1917" (M.A. Thesis, Texas A & M University, 1972), 21–22.

36. Testimony of Major Snow, United States v. Sergeant William C. Nesbit et al., 31–33.

37. Testimony of Captain Shekerjian, United States v. Corporal John Washington et al., 27–29, General Courts Martial Case 109018, Records of Judge Advocate General, RG 153, FRC.

38. Quoted in David M. Kennedy, *Over Here: The First World War and American Society* (New York: Oxford University Press, 1980), 159.

39. Kennedy, *Over Here*, 159.

40. Newton D. Baker, Secretary of War, to President Woodrow Wilson, August 17, 1917, in *The Papers of Woodrow Wilson*, vol. 43 (Washington, DC: Library of Congress, 1955), 506.

41. Haynes, *A Night of Violence*, 53.

42. Statement of Colonel Newman, September 20, 1917, Records of Inspector General, File 333.9, RG 159, FRC; Houston Post, July 26, 1917; *Houston Chronicle*, August 8, 1917.

43. *Houston Press*, May 25, 1917; *Houston Chronicle*, May 20, 1917.

44. *Houston Chronicle*, July 29, 1917.

45. Haynes, *A Night of Violence*, 38.

46. Haynes, *A Night of Violence*, 37–38.

47. Haynes, *A Night of Violence*, 39–40.

48. *Houston Chronicle*, July 29, 1917.

3. THE WHITE MAGNOLIA

1. Marilyn McAdams Sibley, *Port of Houston: A History* (Austin: University of Texas Press, 1968), 151–53, 159–61.

2. *Houston Press*, February 7, 12, 1917.

3. *Houston City Directory*, 1918, 7–8; Sibley, *Port of Houston*, 146–48; *Texas Almanac*, 1972–1973, 162–65.

4. Robert V. Haynes, *A Night of Violence: The Houston Riot of 1917* (Baton Rouge: Louisiana State University Press, 1976), 24n34.

5. Bruce A. Glasrud and Michael N. Searles, eds., *Buffalo Soldiers in the West* (College Station, Texas: A&M University Press, 2007), 200.

6. *Houston Press*, March 13, April 12, 23, 1917; *Houston Chronicle*, April 26, May 1, 1917.

7. David G. McComb, *Houston: The Bayou City* (Austin: University of Texas Press, 1969), 154–55.

8. Thomas Richard Adams, "The Houston Riot of 1917" (Master's thesis, Texas A & M University, 1972), 23.

9. See, for example, Nicole Maurantino, "Remembering Rodney King: Myth, Racial Reconciliation & Civil Rights History," *Journalism & Mass Communication Quarterly* 91, no. 4 (2014): 740–55: "Rodney King's place within history was secured on March 3, 1991, when King, a black motorist, was brutally beaten by several white Los Angeles police officers following a car chase. The videotaped beating, recorded by white

bystander George Holliday, was played and replayed by news media, making the footage 'one of the most watched pieces of amateur video in history.'" Also see Victor A. Matheson and Robert A. Baade, "Race and Riots: A Note on the Economic Impact of the Rodney King Riots," *Urban Studies* 41, no. 13 (December 2004): 2691–96: "Following the announcement of the verdict, riots erupted throughout the city of Los Angeles for several days resulting in 53 deaths, 10,000 arrests, 2,300 injuries, more than 1,000 buildings lost to fire, thousands of jobs lost and an estimated cost to the city of $1 billion in damages. The LA Riots gained a place in history as the worst riots the U.S. has seen in modern years."

10. See, for example, Radkey Balko, *Rise of the Warrior Cop: The Militarization of America's Police Forces* (New York: PublicAffairs, 2013): "No one made a decision to militarize the police in America. The change has come slowly, the result of a generation of politicians and public officials fanning and exploiting public fears by declaring war on abstractions like crime, drug use, and terrorism."

11. Dionnem Searcy and David Zucchino, "Protests Swell across America as George Floyd Is Mourned Near His Birthplace," *New York Times*, June 6, 2020, www.nytimes.com/2020/06/06/us/george-floyd-memorial-protests.html.

12. McComb, *Houston*, 154–55.

13. *Houston Press*, February 3, 17, 19, July 13, 24, 1917.

14. *Houston Post*, August 20, 1917.

15. Adele B. Looscan, " Harris County, 1822–1845," *Southwestern Historical Quarterly* 19 (1914): 37–64.

16. Chandler Davidson, *Biracial Politics: Conflict and Coalition in the Metropolitan South* (Baton Rouge: Louisiana State University Press, 1973), 11–18.

17. Davidson, *Biracial Politics*, 14–15.

18. Dewey W. Granthan Jr., "The Progressive Movement and the Negro," *South Atlantic Quarterly* 54 (October 1955): 461–77.

19. *Houston Chronicle*, July 26, 1917.

20. *Houston City Directory*, 1917. For a description of the city's six wards, which were officially abolished in 1915, see page 1005.

21. *Houston City Directory*, 1917, 43– 44.

22. Haynes, *A Night of Violence*, 28.

23. John Strausbaugh, *Black Like You: Blackface, Whiteface, Insult and Imitation in American Popular Culture* (New York: Jeremy P. Tarcher/Penguin, 2006).

24. C. Vann Woodward, *The Strange Career of Jim Crow* (Oxford: Oxford University Press, 2001), 7.

25. Charles W. Rhodes, *The Texas Constitution in State and Nation: Comparative State Constitutional Law in the Federal System* (Lake Mary, FL: Vandeplas Publishing, 2014).

26. Plessy v. Ferguson, 163 U.S. 537, 540 (1896).

27. Arnoldo De León and Robert A. Calvert, "Segregation," in *Handbook of Texas*, Texas State Historical Association, www.tshaonline.org/handbook/entries/segregation, accessed October 14, 2020.

28. 104th Cong., 1st Sess., H.R. 2730.

29. Plessy v. Ferguson .

30. Plessy v. Ferguson.

31. Plessy v. Ferguson.

32. Plessy v. Ferguson, 163 U.S. 542.

33. Plessy v. Ferguson, 163 U.S. 544.

34. Plessy v. Ferguson.

35. Hans Vought, "Division and Reunion: Woodrow Wilson, Immigration and the Myth of American Unity," *Journal of American Ethnic History* 94, no. 13 (1994): 3, 24.

36. Vought, "Division and Reunion," 3, 24.

37. A. Scott Berg, *Wilson* (New York: Berkley, 2014).

38. Berg, *Wilson*.

39. Chandler Davidson, *Biracial Politics: Conflict and Coalition in the Metropolitan South* (Baton Rouge: Louisiana State University Press, 1973), 11–18.

40. "Dixon's Play Is Not Indorsed by Wilson," *Washington Times* , April 30, 1915, 6.

41. Mark E. Benbow, "Birth of a Quotation: Woodrow Wilson and 'Like Writing History with Lightning,'" *Journal of the Gilded Age and Progressive Era* 9, no. 4 (2010): 509–33.

42. Saul Friedländer, *Nazi Germany and the Jews, 1933–1945* (New York: Harper Perennial, 2009).

43. *Houston Press*, June 11, 12, 1917.

44. *Houston Press*, June 11, 12, 1917.

45. *Houston Press*, June 11, 12, 1917; *Houston Chronicle*, June 11, 12, 1917.

46. *Houston Press*, May 25, 1917; *Houston Chronicle*, May 20, 1917.

47. *Houston Chronicle*, July 15, 25, 1917; *Houston Press*, July 18, 19, 24, August 22, 1917; *Houston Post*, July 25, August 12, 1917.

48. *Houston Chronicle*, July 15, 25, 1917.

49. *Houston Chronicle*, July 18, 1917.

50. Haynes, *A Night of Violence*, 53.

51. McLemore to Secretary of War Baker, August 8, 1917, in Jeff McLemore Collection; *Houston Post*, August 1, 1917.

52. Martin Luther King Jr., "Why Jesus Called a Man a Fool," sermon delivered at Mount Pisgah Missionary Baptist Church, August 27, 1967, https://kinginstitute.stanford.edu/king-papers/documents/why-jesus-called-man-fool-sermon-delivered-mount-pisgah-missionary-baptist.

53. Nat Turner, *The Confessions of Nat Turner: The Leader of the Late Insurrection in Southampton, VA* (Baltimore: Thomas R. Gray, 1831), 9.

54. *Chicago Defender*, October 6, 1917.

55. Turner, *The Confessions of Nat Turner*, 9.

4. EAST TEXAS STORM CLOUDS

1. James SoRelle, "The 'Waco Horror': The Lynching of Jesse Washington," in *The African American Experience in Texas: An Anthology*, ed. Bruce A. Glasrud and James Smallwood, 188–89 (Lubbock: Texas Tech University Press , 2007).

2. Patricia Bernstein, *The First Waco Horror: The Lynching of Jesse Washington and the Rise of the NAACP* (College Station: Texas A&M University Press, 2006).

3. Bernstein, *The First Waco Horror*.

4. Bernstein, *The First Waco Horror*.

5. Bernstein, *The First Waco Horror*.

6. Bernstein, *The First Waco Horror*, 189–91.

7. Bernstein, *The First Waco Horror*, 189–91.

8. Joseph Conrad, *Heart of Darkness and the Secret Sharer*, ed. Albert J. Guerard (New York: New American Library of World Literature, 1964), 152–53.

9. Chin Kim and Theodore R. LeBlang, "The Death Penalty in Traditional China," *Georgia Journal of International and Comparative Law* 77 (1975): 77.

10. Andy McNab, *Bravo Two Zero* (London: Bantam Press), 1993.

11. "The Negro Silent Protest Parade organized by the NAACP, Fifth Ave., New York City, July 28, 1917," *The Making of African American Identity*, vol. 2: 1865–1917 (2014), https://nationalhumanitiescenter.org/pds/maai2/forward/text4/silentprotest.pdf.

12. See, for example, Thomas C. Schelling, "Dynamic Models of Segregation," *Journal of Mathematical Sociology* 1 (2) (1971): 143–86, 181: "'Tipping' is said to occur when a recognizable new minority enters a neighborhood in sufficient numbers to cause the earlier residents to begin evacuating . . . for the vast majority of white Americans a tipping point exists, and cites 20% Negroes as a commonly estimated upper limit in some Eastern cities . . . as an empirical generalization that, once an urban area begins to swing from mainly white to mainly Negro, the change is rarely reversed."

13. Thomas Sowell, *Intellectuals and Race* (Philadelphia: Basic Books, 2013), 32.

14. Winston James, *Holding Aloft the Banner of Ethiopia* (New York: Verso, 1998), 95.

15. Elliot M. Rudwick, *Race Riot at East St. Louis, July 2, 1917* (Carbondale: Southern Illinois University Press, 1964).

16. Rudwick, *Race Riot at East St. Louis*.

17. Robert V. Haynes, *A Night of Violence: The Houston Riot of 1917* (Baton Rouge: Louisiana State University Press, 1976), 200.

18. *Houston Post*, August 26, 28, 1917; *Houston Chronicle*, August 29, 31, September 19, 1917.

19. John D. Weaver, *The Brownsville Raid* (New York: W. W. Norton, 1970).

20. Arthur Ruhl, "The Gallery at San Antonio," *Collier's Weekly*, April 29, 1916, 13; *Chicago Defender*, April 15, 1916, July 8, 22, 27, August 5, 12, 19, 1916; *San Antonio Express*, July 25, 26, 1916.

21. Ann J. Lane, *Brownsville Affair: National Crisis and Black Reaction* (Port Washington, NY: Kennikat Press, 1971).

22. Lane, *Brownsville Affair*.

23. C. Calvin Smith, "The Houston Riot of 1917, Revisted," *Houston Review* 13, no. 2 (1991): 85–102. http://studythepast.com/civilrightsundergraduate/materials/houstonriot1917_houstonreview.pdf.

24. *Houston Post*, August 20, 1917.

25. William G. Muller, *The Twenty-fourth Infantry: Past and Present* (Fort Collins, CO: Old Army Press, 1972).

26. Mary Berry and John W. Blassingame, *Long Memory: The Black Experience in America* (New York: Oxford University Press, 1982), 308.

27. *Houston Post*, May 29, June 28, 1917.

28. *Houston Post*, August 20, 1917.

29. Haynes, *A Night of Violence*, 68.

30. Al-Tony Gilmore, "Jack Johnson and White Women: The National Impact," *Journal of Negro History* 58, no. 1 (1973): 18–38.

31. Statement of Colonel Newman, September 20, 1917, Records of Inspector General, File 333.9, RG, 159, FRC.

32. Testimony of Oliver J. Charboneau, conductor, Cress Report, Appendix B, 21–23; statement of L. E. Gentry, police officer, Cress Report, Appendix B, 27–28.

33. Statement of L. E. Gentry, 27–28.

34. Statement of Colonel Newman, September 20, 1917.

35. *Houston Chronicle*, July 30, 1917.

36. Arica L. Coleman, "When the NRA Supported Gun Control," *Time*, July 29, 2016, https://time.com/4431356/nra-gun-control-history/.

37. Salim Boss, *They Are Either Extremely Smart or Extremely Ignorant* (N.p.: n.p.: 2010), available at www.scribd.com/doc/139909281/They-Are-Either-Extremely-Smart-or-Extremely-Ignorant5.

38. *Houston Press*, August 1, 1917.

39. Thomas Richard Adams, "The Houston Riot of 1917" (M.A. Thesis, Texas A & M University, 1972), 26; statement of Captain Haig Shekerjian, August 30, 1917, Cress Report, Appendix A, 62.

40. Testimony of Captain Ralph C. Woodward, August 26, 1917, Cress Report, Appendix A, 155.

41. Testimony of Sergeant William Nesbit, August 31, 1917, Cress Report, 11.

42. Statement of Captain Rothrock, August 29, 1917, Chamberlain Report, 5–6.

43. T. H. Dixon to editor, *Houston Chronicle*, August 28, 1917.

44. *Houston Chronicle*, July 23, 1917.

45. Testimony of Colonel John S. Hoover, August 26, 1917, Cress Report, Appendix A, 4.

46. Haynes, *A Night of Violence*, 76.

47. Rudwick, *Race Riot at East St. Louis*, 74–86.

48. *Houston Press*, June 18, 1917; *Houston Chronicle*, June 14, 1917.

5. GOMORRAH

1. Vladimir Dedijer, *The Road to Sarajevo* (New York: Simon and Schuster, 1966).

2. Tony Fabijančić, *Bosnia: In the Footsteps of Gavrilo Princip* (Edmonton: University of Alberta, 2010).

3. Margaret MacMillan, *The War That Ended Peace: How Europe Abandoned Peace for the First World War* (Profile Books, 2013).

4. Joachim Remak, *Sarajevo: The Story of a Political Murder* (New York: Criterion Books, 1959).

5. Remak, *Sarajevo*, 137–42.

6. Luigi Albertini, *Origins of the War of 1914* (Oxford: Oxford University Press, 1953), 120–121.

7. *Houston Post*, July 29, 1917.

8. *Houston Post*, July 29, 1917.

9. Statement of Colonel Newman, September 20, 1917, Records of Inspector General, File 333.9, RG 159, FRC.

10. Thomas Richard Adams, "The Houston Riot of 1917" (master's thesis, Texas A & M University, 1972), 30.

11. Martha Gruening, "Houston: An N.A.A.C.P. Investigation," *Crisis* 15 (November 1917): 14; Phocion Samuel Park Jr., "Twenty-fourth Infantry and Houston Riot of 1917" (Master's thesis, University of Wisconsin, 1971), 96–97.

12. Interview with William Orange, July 23, 1972.

13. Robert V. Haynes, *A Night of Violence: The Houston Riot of 1917* (Baton Rouge: Louisiana State University Press, 1976), 94.

14. Testimony of Lee Sparks, August 26, 1917, Cress Report, Appendix A, 21.

15. Testimony of Major Kneeland S. Snow, United States v. Sergeant William C. Nesbit et al., 33–34; testimony of Captain Shekerjian, United States v. Nesbit, 122–23.

16. Testimony of Private John T. Long, United States v. Corporal John Washington et al., 169–70.

17. Testimony of Miss Edna Tucker, United States v. Nesbit, 950–52.

18. Testimony of Captain Shekerjian, United States v. Corporal Robert Tillman et al., 240–42.

19. Statement of Captain Shekerjian, September 5, 1917, Chamberlain Report, 70.

20. Haynes, *A Night of Violence*, 101.

21. Testimony of Captain Shekerjian, United States v. Tillman, 240–42.

22. Testimony of Captain Shekerjian, August 30, 1917, Cress Report, Appendix A, 63–64.

23. Testimony of Captain Shekerjian, United States v. Tillman, 240–42.

24. Testimony of Lee Sparks, Cress Report, Appendix B, 274–86; testimony of Clarence Brock, Cress Report, Appendix B, 217–20; statement of detective Edward F. Dougherty, August 31, 1917, Chamberlain Report, 144.

25. Richard Peace, *Dostoyevsky: An Examination of the Major Novels* (Cambridge, UK: Cambridge University Press, 1971), 59–63.

26. Haynes, *A Night of Violence*, 108.

27. Testimony of Mrs. C. B. Moy, United States v. Tillman, 1064–68; testimony of R. M. Owens, September 19, 1917, Cress Report, Appendix A, 177.

28. Testimony of Mrs. C. B. Moy, United States v. Tillman, 1064–68; testimony of R. M. Owens, September 19, 1917, Cress Report, Appendix A, 177.

29. Testimony of Ed F. Pickering, Cress Report, Appendix B, 43–47; testimony of Frank A. Shaffer, Cress Report, Appendix B, 29–33; testimony of Ed F. Pickering, United States v. Tillman, 1094–98; *Houston Post*, August 29, 1917.

30. Testimony of Ed F. Pickering, Cress Report, Appendix B, 43–47; testimony of Frank A. Shaffer, Cress Report, Appendix B, 29–33; testimony of Ed F. Pickering, United States v. Tillman, 1094–98; *Houston Post*, August 29, 1917.

31. Testimony of Ed F. Pickering, Cress Report, Appendix B, 43–47; testimony of Frank A. Shaffer, Cress Report, Appendix B, 29–33; testi-

mony of Ed F. Pickering, United States v. Tillman, 1094–98; *Houston Post*, August 29, 1917.

32. Statement of Major Snow, September 5, 1917, Chamberlain Report, 84.

33. Testimony of Lee Sparks, Cress Report, Appendix B, 274–86; testimony of Clarence Brock, Cress Report, Appendix B, 217–20; statement of detective Edward F. Dougherty, August 31, 1917, Chamberlain Report, 144.

34. Testimony of Major Snow, August 25, 1917, Cress Report, Appendix A, 34–35; testimony of Captain Silvester, August 31, 1917, Cress Report, Appendix A; testimony of Captain Shekerjian, August 30, 1917, Cress Report, Appendix A, 64; testimony of Major Snow, United States v. Nesbit, 36–37.

35. Testimony of Private Frank Draper, United States v. Nesbit, 1029–31, 1041–42.

36. Testimony of Private Ernest E. Fields, August 31, 1917, Cress Report, Appendix A, 82; statement of Captain James, September 5, 1917, Chamberlain Report, 57; testimony of Captain Shekerjian, United States v. Tillman, 242.

37. Testimony of Major Snow, United States v. Nesbit, statement of B. A. Calhoun, August 29, 1917, Chamberlain Report, 166–67; testimony of Captain Haig Shekerjian, United States v. Tillman, 242.

38. Testimony of Major Snow, United States v. Nesbit, statement of B. A. Calhoun, August 29, 1917, Chamberlain Report, 166–67; testimony of Captain Haig Shekerjian, United States v. Tillman, 242.

39. Adams, "The Houston Riot of 1917," 37. Some of this information is from Henry's military service record, which is in the Military Records Center, St. Louis, Missouri.

40. Adams, "The Houston Riot of 1917," 37.

41. Testimony of Private E. E. Fields, August 31, 1917, Cress Report, Appendix A, 83; Colonel Newman to Colonel Cress, October 1, 1917, Records of Inspector General, RG 159, FRC.

42. Testimony of Major Snow, United States v. Nesbit, 39; testimony of Captain Shekerjian, United States v. Nesbit, 127; testimony of Private Joseph Alexander, United States v. Nesbit, 1125; testimony of Private Lloyd Shorter, United States v. Tillman, 1469–70; testimony of Private Cleda Love, United States v. Tillman, 1554–55.

43. Testimony of Major Snow, United States v. Nesbit, 39; testimony of Captain Shekerjian, United States v. Nesbit, 127; testimony of Private Joseph Alexander, United States v. Nesbit, 1125; testimony of Private Lloyd Shorter, United States v. Tillman, 1469–70; testimony of Private Cleda Love, United States v. Tillman, 1554–55.

44. Testimony of Major Snow, United States v. Nesbit, 39; testimony of Captain Shekerjian, United States v. Nesbit, 127; testimony of Private Joseph Alexander, United States v. Nesbit, 1125; testimony of Private Lloyd Shorter, United States v. Tillman, 1469–70; testimony of Private Cleda Love, United States v. Tillman, 1554–55.

45. Testimony of Captain Bartlett James, August 31, 1917, Cress Report, Appendix A, 58; testimony of Sergeant Samuel Venters, United States v. Nesbit, 229–31.

46. Testimony of Major Snow, United States v. Tillman, 75; testimony of Major Snow, United States v. Nesbit, 37–38.

47. Testimony of Captain Shekerjian, United States v. Nesbit, 244–45; testimony of Major Snow, United States v. Tillman, 87–88. Corporal James H. Mitchell's recollection of this exchange is somewhat different. See his testimony in United States v. Tillman, 2535–36.

48. Testimony of Captain Shekerjian, United States v. Nesbit, 244–45; testimony of Major Snow, United States v. Tillman, 87–88.

49. Testimony of Private Frank Draper, United States v. Nesbit, 1029–31, 1041–42.

50. Testimony of Private Frank Draper, United States v. Nesbit, 1029–31, 1041–42.

51. Testimony of Private Frank Draper, United States v. Nesbit, 1038–41; testimony of Mrs. Eugenia Draper, United States v. Tillman, 1179–80.

52. Testimony of Private Denty, United States v. Tillman, 1238–40, 1250.

53. Testimony of Major Snow, United States v. Tillman, 89–90; testimony of Sergeant Willie Scott, United States v. Tillman, 381–82; testimony of Major Snow, August 25, 1917, Cress Report, Appendix A, 29–30.

54. Testimony of Major Snow, United States v. Tillman, 89–90; testimony of Sergeant Willie Scott, United States v. Tillman, 381–82; testimony of Major Snow, August 25, 1917, Cress Report, Appendix A, 29–30.

55. Testimony of Major Snow, United States v. Tillman, 89–90; testimony of Sergeant Willie Scott, United States v. Tillman, 381–82; testimony of Major Snow, August 25, 1917, Cress Report, Appendix A, 29–30.

56. *Houston Chronicle*, August 27, 1917; testimony of Frank B. Dwyer, September 20, 1917, Cress Report, Appendix A, 165; statement of Captain Rothrock, August 29, 1917, Chamberlain Report, 4.

57. *Houston Chronicle*, August 27, 1917; testimony of Frank B. Dwyer, September 20, 1917, Cress Report, Appendix A, 165; statement of Captain Rothrock, August 29, 1917, Chamberlain Report, 4.

58. Testimony of Private Ernest Phifer, United States v. Tillman, 1292–93, 1345; testimony of Private Lloyd Shorter, United States v. Tillman, 1475–76; memorandum, Major Snow to General John A. Hulen, August 24, 1917, Cress Report, Appendix A, 145; Report of Colonel Cress to Commanding Officer, Southern Department, September 1917, 9–10.

59. Testimony of Private Charlie Banks, United States v. Tillman, 1835.

60. Testimony of Private Wiley L. Strong, August 28, 1917, Cress Report, Appendix A, 127; testimony of Lieutenant William Chaflin, September 5, 1917, Chamberlain Report, 32.

61. Testimony of Captain Haig Shekerjian, United States v. Tillman, 250–53; *San Antonio Express*, November 3, 1917.

62. Testimony of Private Grant H. Mems, United States v. Nesbit, 1635–37; testimony of Corporal Quiller Walker, United States v. Tillman, 2402–4.

63. Testimony of Sergeant Rhoden Bond, United States v. Tillman, 2204–10; testimony of Private Frank Draper, United States v. Tillman, 1200–1203; testimony of Captain Shekerjian, August 30, 1917, Cress Report, Appendix A, 66.

64. Testimony of Sergeant Rhoden Bond, United States v. Tillman, 2204–10; testimony of Private Frank Draper, United States v. Tillman, 1200–203; testimony of Captain Shekerjian, August 30, 1917, Cress Report, Appendix A, 66.

65. Testimony of Sergeant William U. Fox, United States v. Nesbit, 198–202; testimony of Private Joseph Alexander, United States v. Nesbit, 1126–27, 1146–47; testimony of Private Ernest Phifer, United States v. Tillman, 1295–98, 1346–48; testimony of Private Cleda Love, United

States v. Tillman, 1609–10; testimony of Private Kane, United States v. Tillman, 1396–97; testimony of Private James Divins [August 24, 1917], Cress Report, Appendix B, 323.

66. Testimony of Sergeant William U. Fox, United States v. Nesbit, 198–202; testimony of Private Joseph Alexander, United States v. Nesbit, 1126–27, 1146–47; testimony of Private Ernest Phifer, United States v. Tillman, 1295–98, 1346–48; testimony of Private Cleda Love, United States v. Tillman, 1609–10; testimony of Private Kane, United States v. Tillman, 1396–97; testimony of Private James Divins [August 24, 1917], Cress Report, Appendix B, 323.

67. Testimony of Sergeant Rhoden Bond, United States v. Tillman, 2208–10; testimony of Sergeant William U. Fox, United States v. Tillman, 2237–38.

68. Testimony of Mrs. Eugenia Draper, United States v. Tillman, 1182–83; testimony of Private Phifer, United States v. Tillman, 1347–48; testimony of Private First Class Henry H. Peacock, United States v. Nesbit, 1236, 1258.

69. Testimony of Mrs. Eugenia Draper, United States v. Tillman, 1182–83; testimony of Private Phifer, United States v. Tillman, 1347–48; testimony of Private First Class Henry H. Peacock, United States v. Nesbit, 1236, 1258.

70. Testimony of Mrs. Eugenia Draper, United States v. Tillman, 1182–83; testimony of Private Phifer, United States v. Tillman, 1347–48; testimony of Private First Class Henry H. Peacock, United States v. Nesbit, 1236, 1258.

71. Testimony of Mrs. Eugenia Draper, United States v. Tillman, 1182–83; testimony of Private Phifer, United States v. Tillman, 1347–48; testimony of Private First Class Henry H. Peacock, United States v. Nesbit, 1236, 1258.

72. Testimony of Mrs. Eugenia Draper, United States v. Tillman, 1182–83; testimony of Private Phifer, United States v. Tillman, 1347–48; testimony of Private First Class Henry H. Peacock, United States v. Nesbit, 1236, 1258.

73. Testimony of Captain Shekerjian, United States v. Nesbit, 134–35; testimony of Private Cleda Love, United States v. Nesbit, 1308; *Houston Chronicle*, August 24, 1917.

74. Testimony of Captain Shekerjian, United States v. Nesbit, 134–35; testimony of Private Cleda Love, United States v. Nesbit, 1308; *Houston Chronicle*, August 24, 1917.

75. Testimony of Private First Class Clyde F. Gojode, United States v. Tillman, 488–95; statement of Lieutenant John H. Jack, September 5, 1917, Chamberlain Report, 45–46; testimony of Captain Shekerjian, August 30, 1917, Cress Report, Appendix A, 57–68.

76. Testimony of Private First Class Clyde F. Gojode, United States v. Tillman, 488–95; statement of Lieutenant John H. Jack, September 5, 1917, Chamberlain Report, 45–46; testimony of Captain Shekerjian, August 30, 1917, Cress Report, Appendix A, 57–68.

77. Testimony of Private Ezekiel Bullock, United States v. Washington, 309.

78. Testimony of Private Willie Blunt, United States v. Washington, 283–85; testimony of Private Ezekiel Bullock, United States v. Washington, 310–13.

6. VIVA LA MUERTE

1. Testimony of H. F. Juenger, August 29, 1917, Records of the Inspector General, General Correspondence File 333.9, RG 159; testimony of E. J. Hargraves, United States v. Corporal Washington et al., 112–14; testimony of Private Bullock, United States v. Washington, 314–15.

2. Testimony of H. F. Juenger, August 29, 1917, Records of the Inspector General, General Correspondence File 333.9, RG 159; testimony of E. J. Hargraves, United States v. Washington, 112–14; testimony of Private Bullock, United States v. Washington, 314–15.

3. Robert V. Haynes, *A Night of Violence: The Houston Riot of 1917* (Baton Rouge: Louisiana State University Press, 1976), 168.

4. Haynes, *A Night of Violence*, 168.

5. Testimony of Private First Class Frank Beebe, United States v. Washington, 38–44; testimony of First Lieutenant William B. Barton, United States v. Washington, 78–79, 83–84; testimony of Charles Clayton, United States v. Washington, 147–54.

6. Testimony of Private First Class Frank Beebe, United States v. Washington, 38–44; testimony of First Lieutenant William B. Barton,

United States v. Washington, 78–79, 83–84; testimony of Charles Clayton, United States v. Washington, 147–54.

7. Testimony of Keith Dudley Wright, United States v. Corporal Robert Tillman et al., 754–57.

8. Testimony of E. H. Neumeyer, United States v. Tillman et al., 663–76; testimony of G. W. Butcher, United States v. Tillman, 678–83.

9. *Houston Chronicle*, August 26, 1917.

10. *Houston Chronicle*, August 26, 1917.

11. *Chicago Defender*, January 26, 1918; testimony of Private First Class Henry H. Peacock, United States v. Sergeant William C. Nesbit et al., 1238; Robert V. Haynes, "The Houston Mutiny and Riot of 1917," *Southwestern Historical Quarterly* 76 (1973): 429.

12. Haynes, *A Night of Violence*, 140.

13. Testimony of Private Bullock, United States v. Washington, 130. See also Phocion Samuel Park Jr., "The Twenty-fourth Infantry and Houston Riot of 1917" (master's thesis, University of Houston, 1971), 127–28.

14. Thomas Richard Adams, "The Houston Riot of 1917" (master's thesis, Texas A & M University, 1972), 45; Park, "The Twenty-fourth Infantry and Houston Riot of 1917," 129.

15. Testimony of Miss Winkler, United States v. Tillman, 706–11; testimony of William J. Drucks, United States v. Tillman, 711–16; testimony of Mrs. J. W. Kennedys, United States v. Tillman, 700–703; *Houston Post*, August 24, 1917.

16. Testimony of Miss Winkler, United States v. Tillman, 706–11; testimony of William J. Drucks, United States v. Tillman, 711–16; testimony of Mrs. J. W. Kennedys, United States v. Tillman, 700–703; *Houston Post*, August 24, 1917.

17. Testimony of Miss Winkler, United States v. Tillman, 706–11; testimony of William J. Drucks, United States v. Tillman, 711–16; testimony of Mrs. J. W. Kennedys, United States v. Tillman, 700–703; *Houston Post*, August 24, 1917.

18. Testimony of Willard A. Wise, United States v. Nesbit, 437–43; testimony of T. A. Binford, United States v. Nesbit, 444–51; Haynes, *A Night of Violence*, 143; personal interview with T. A. Binford, March 30, 1970.

19. Testimony of C. W. Butcher, United States v. Tillman, 680–83; testimony of Willard A. Wise, United States v. Tillman, 760–62; testimo-

ny of Charles E. Carter, August 29, 1917, Records of Inspector General, General Correspondence File 333.9, RG 159, FRC.

20. Testimony of C. W. Butcher, United States v. Tillman, 680–83; testimony of Willard A. Wise, United States v. Tillman, 760–62; testimony of Charles E. Carter, August 29, 1917, Records of Inspector General, General Correspondence File 333.9, RG 159, FRC.

21. Testimony of J. D. Dixon, United States v. Nesbit, 491–95.

22. Testimony of Fred Scofield, United States v. Tillman, 785–92; testimony of C. W. McPhail, United States v. Tillman, 802–3; testimony of Private Phifer, United States v. Tillman, 1304–5; statement of T. C. McLaurin, August 28, 1917, Cress Report, Appendix B, 316; testimony of Fred Scofield, United States v. Nesbit, 451–53; testimony of F. W. Bartlinger, August 28, 1917, Records of Inspector General, File 333.9, RG 159, FRC.

23. Testimony of Private Kane, United States v. Tillman, 1402–5; testimony of Private Shorter, United States v. Nesbit, 1088–89.

24. Testimony of Private Kane, United States v. Tillman, 1402–5; testimony of Private Shorter, United States v. Nesbit, 1088–89.

25. Testimony of Jacob F. Walters, August 24, 1917, Cress Report, Appendix A, 1–2; testimony of Clarence Brock, August 24, 1917, Cress Report, Appendix B, 161; *Houston Post*, August 24, 1917.

26. Testimony of Jacob F. Walters, August 24, 1917, Cress Report, Appendix A, 1–2; testimony of Clarence Brock, August 24, 1917, Cress Report, Appendix B, 161; *Houston Post*, August 24, 1917.

27. *Houston Post*, August 25, 1917.

28. *Houston Chronicle*, August 24, 1917.

29. *Houston Chronicle*, August 24, 25, 1917.

30. Testimony of Colonel Hoover, August 26, 1917, Cress Report, Appendix A, 3; statement of Colonel Hoover, August 30, 1917, Chamberlain Report, 161.

31. Testimony of Major Snow, August 25, 1917, Cress Report, Appendix A, 32; *Houston Post*, August 24, 1917; *Houston Press*, August 24, 1917.

32. Statement of Captain Rossiter, September 20, 1917, Army Commands, Southern Department, Headquarters, RG 393, NA; *Houston Post*, August 26, 1917; testimony of Private Alphens D. Jones, United States v. Tillman, 891–94.

33. Statement of Captain Rossiter, September 20, 1917, Army Commands, Southern Department, Headquarters, RG 393, NA; *Houston Post*, August 26, 1917; testimony of Private Alphens D. Jones, United States v. Tillman, 891–94.

34. Testimony of C. W. Hahl, United States v. Nesbit, 550–55; testimony of Private Phifer, United States v. Tillman, 1372–75.

35. Testimony of W. C. Wilson, United States v. Tillman, 841–47; testimony of C. E. Carter, United States v. Nesbit, 560–68.

36. Testimony of Abe Blumberg, United States v. Nesbit, 586–88; testimony of Private Cleda Love, United States v. Tillman, 1546; *Houston Press*, August 25, 27, 1917.

37. Testimony of Abe Blumberg, United States v. Nesbit, 586–88; testimony of Private Cleda Love, United States v. Tillman, 1546; *Houston Press*, August 25, 27, 1917.

38. Haynes, *A Night of Violence*, 150.

39. Testimony of Private Kane, United States v. Tillman, 1405, 1411; testimony of Private Shorter, United States v. Tillman, 1510–14.

40. Testimony of Mrs. Isaac Siegel, August 26, 1917, Cress Report, Appendix A, 24; testimony of Private First Class Peacock, United States v. Nesbit, 1219–20; Arthur Chappel to Phocion Park, March 14, 1970; Park, "The Twenty-fourth Infantry and Houston Riot of 1917," 146–47.

41. Dying statement of Private George Bivens, August 25, 1917, Army Commands, Southern Department, Headquarters, RG 393, NA; memorandum Lieutenant Louis C. Sauter to Captain John L. Thompson, August 25, 1917, Army Commands, Southern Department, Headquarters, RG 393, NA.

42. Haynes, *A Night of Violence*, 158.

43. Testimony of James Lyon, United States v. Tillman, 850–60; *Houston Post*, August 24, 1917; *Houston Chronicle*, August 26, 1917.

44. Testimony of Asa Bland, United States v. Nesbit, 599–606; testimony of Private First Class Peacock, United States v. Nesbit, 1241–42, 1256–61; testimony of John E. Richardson, United States v. Tillman, 881–85, 888.

45. Testimony of Asa Bland, United States v. Nesbit, 599–606; testimony of Private First Class Peacock, United States v. Nesbit, 1241–42, 1256–61; testimony of John E. Richardson, United States v. Tillman, 881–85, 888.

208   NOTES

46. Testimony of Asa Bland, United States v. Nesbit, 599–606; testimony of Private First Class Peacock, United States v. Nesbit, 1241–42, 1256–61; testimony of John E. Richardson, United States v. Tillman, 881–85, 888.

47. Testimony of Private Alphens D. Jones, United States v. Tillman, 894–95; *Houston Post*, August 26, 1917; Report of Special Board of Investigation in the Death of Captain Joseph Mattes to Commanding General, Camp Logan, August 27, 1917, Records of Inspector General, File 333.9, RG 159, FRC; testimony of Corporal Zemmie Foreman, United States v. Nesbit, 644–48.

48. Testimony of Private Alphens D. Jones, United States v. Tillman, 894–95; *Houston Post*, August 26, 1917; Report of Special Board of Investigation in the Death of Captain Joseph Mattes to Commanding General, Camp Logan, August 27, 1917, Records of Inspector General, File 333.9, RG 159, FRC; testimony of Corporal Zemmie Foreman, United States v. Nesbit, 644–48.

49. Testimony of Private Alphens D. Jones, United States v. Tillman, 894–95; *Houston Post*, August 26, 1917; Report of Special Board of Investigation in the Death of Captain Joseph Mattes to Commanding General, Camp Logan, August 27, 1917, Records of Inspector General, File 333.9, RG 159, FRC; testimony of Corporal Zemmie Foreman, United States v. Nesbit, 644–48.

50. Testimony of Corporal Zemmie Foreman, United States v. Tillman, 908–10; testimony of Private Jones, United States v. Tillman, 894–95; *Houston Post*, August 26, 1917.

51. Testimony of Private Jones, United States v. Tillman, 896–98; testimony of Corporal Foreman, United States v. Tillman, 913; testimony of Mrs. Sarah Everton, United States v. Nesbit, 704–805.

52. Testimony of Private Elmer Bandy, United States v. Nesbit, 1189–91.

53. Testimony of Private Elmer Bandy, United States v. Nesbit, 1189–91.

54. Testimony of Private Phifer, United States v. Tillman, 1322–23; testimony of Private Love, United States v. Tillman, 1550; statements of Sergeant William D. Carrier and Private Arthur Reynolds, September 25, 1917, Army Commands, Southern Department, Headquarters, RG 393, NA; testimony of Major Snow, United States v. Nesbit, 68.

55. Testimony of Private Phifer, United States v. Tillman, 1322–23; testimony of Private Love, United States v. Tillman, 1550; statements of Sergeant William D. Carrier and Private Arthur Reynolds, September 25, 1917, Army Commands, Southern Department, Headquarters, RG 393, NA; testimony of Major Snow, United States v. Nesbit, 68.

7. AFTER THE FLOOD

1. Nat Turner, *The Confessions of Nat Turner, the Leader of the Late Insurrection in Southampton, VA* (Baltimore: Thomas R. Gray, 1831), 18.

2. Robert V. Haynes, *A Night of Violence: The Houston Riot of 1917* (Baton Rouge: Louisiana State University Press, 1976), 167.

3. Haynes, *A Night of Violence*, 169.

4. Robert V. Haynes, "The Houston Mutiny and Riot of 1917," *Southwestern Historical Quarterly* 76 (1973): 430–31n53.

5. Haynes, *A Night of Violence*, 148.

6. *Houston Post*, August 25, 1917; *Houston Press*, August 25, 1917.

7. Haynes, *A Night of Violence*, 187.

8. Haynes, *A Night of Violence*, 187.

9. *Houston Press*, August 24, 25, 1917.

10. *Houston Chronicle*, August 24, 1917; statement of Major Marcellus G. Spinks, n.d., Army Commands, Southern Department, Headquarters, RG 393, NA.

11. *Houston Chronicle*, August 24, 1917; statement of Major Marcellus G. Spinks, n.d., Army Commands, Southern Department, Headquarters, RG 393, NA.

12. Haynes, *A Night of Violence*, 188.

13. Statement of Captain James, September 5, 1917, Chamberlain Report, 54–55.

14. Haynes, *A Night of Violence*, 189.

15. *Houston Chronicle*, August 25, 1917; statement of Colonel Millard F. Waltz, September 7, 1917, Chamberlain Report, 106; testimony of Major Snow, August 25, 1917, Cress Report, Appendix A, 33.

16. Statement of Colonel Millard F. Waltz, September 7, 1917, Chamberlain Report, 107–9; testimony of Major Snow, August 25, 1917, Cress Report, Appendix A.

17. Statement of Colonel Millard F. Waltz, September 7, 1917, Chamberlain Report, 107–9; testimony of Major Snow, August 25, 1917, Cress Report, Appendix A.

18. Statement of Colonel Millard F. Waltz, September 7, 1917, Chamberlain Report, 107–9; testimony of Major Snow, August 25, 1917, Cress Report, Appendix A.

19. *Houston Post*, August 25, 1917; *Houston Chronicle*, August 25, 1917; telegram, General Hulen to General Parker, August 24, 1917, Army Commands, Southern Department, Headquarters, RG 393, NA.

20. Haynes, *A Night of Violence*, 191.

21. Telegram, General Parker to General Hulen, August 24, 1917, telegram, General Hulen to General Parker, August 24, 1917, in Army Commands, Southern Department, Headquarters, RG 393, NA.

22. *Houston Chronicle*, August 25, 26, 1917; statement of Major Snow, September 5, 1917, Chamberlain Report, 102.

23. Jacob Wolters to [Commanding General] Southern Department, August 27, 1917, with enclosures, Henry Sengelmann to Wolters, August 26, 1917, and pass of Private Hankins, signed by Captain James Reisinger, August 21, 1917, Army Commands, Southern Department, Headquarters, RG 393, NA.

24. *Houston Post*, August 25, 26, 1917; *Houston Chronicle*, August 25, 1917.

25. *Houston Chronicle*, August 29, 31, September 19, 1917.

26. *Houston Post*, August 26, 28, 1917.

27. Haynes, *A Night of Violence*, 200; *Houston Post*, August 30, 1917; *Houston Press*, August 30, 1917.

28. *Houston Press*, August 24, 1917; *Houston Chronicle*, August 26, 1917.

29. *Houston Press*, August 24, 1917; *Houston Chronicle*, August 26, 1917.

30. See, for example, Jay Willis, "Minneapolis City Council Members Announce Intent to Disband the Police Department, Invest in Proven Community-Led Public Safety," *The Appeal*, June 7, 2020, https://theappeal.org/minneapolis-city-council-members-announce-intent-to-disband-the-police-department-invest-in-proven-community-led-public-safety/.

31. *Houston Post*, August 28, 1917.

32. *Houston Post*, August 28, 1917.

33. *Houston Post*, August 27, 28, 1917; *Houston Chronicle*, August 27, 1917; *Houston Press*, October 16, 1917; William Johnson to General John L. Chamberlain, August 30, 1917, Records of Inspector General, File 333.9, RG 159, FRC.

34. *Houston Post*, August 27, 28, 1917; *Houston Chronicle*, August 27, 1917; *Houston Press*, October 16, 1917; William Johnson to General John L. Chamberlain, August 30, 1917, Records of Inspector General, File 333.9, RG 159, FRC.

35. *Houston Press*, September 1, 3, 1917; *Houston Chronicle*, September 2, 7, 1917.

36. *Houston Press*, September 1, 3, 1917; *Houston Chronicle*, September 2, 7, 1917.

8. INQUISITION

1. John Leland, "Public Enemy: Our 1988 Interview with Chuck D," *SPIN*, September 1988.

2. Telegram, Congressman Joe H. Eagle to the Secrtetary of War, August 24, 1917, Records of Inspector General, File 333.9, RG 159, FRC; *Houston Post*, August 26, 1917; *Houston Chronicle*, August 25, 1917.

3. Telegram, S. H. Brashear to Jeff McLemore, August 24, 1917, W. S. Sinclair to Jeff McLemore, August 27, 1917, in Jeff McLemore Collection, Archives, University of Texas Library, Austin.

4. Telegram, Congressman Joe H. Eagle to the Secretary of War, August 24, 1917, Records of Inspector General, File 333.9, RG 159, FRC; *Houston Post*, August 26, 1917; *Houston Chronicle*, August 25, 1917.

5. Telegram, Congressman Joe H. Eagle to the Secretary of War, August 24, 1917, Records of Inspector General, File 333.9, RG 159, FRC; *Houston Post*, August 26, 1917; *Houston Chronicle*, August 25, 1917.

6. *Houston Post*, August 26, 1917; *Houston Chronicle*, August 27, 1917.

7. *Houston Post*, August 29, 1917; testimony of Major Snow, Cress Report, Appendix B, 1–3.

8. *Houston Post*, August 30, 1917; *Houston Press*, August 30, 1917; Cress Report, Appendix B, 309.

9. *Houston Chronicle*, August 31, 1917; *Houston Post*, August 30, 1917; *Houston Press*, September 1, 1917.

10. *Houston Chronicle*, August 31, 1917; *Houston Post*, August 30, 1917; *Houston Press*, September 1, 1917.

11. W. B. Sinclair to Jeff McLemore, August 27, 1917, in Jeff M. McLemore Collection, University of Texas Library, Austin.

12. *Houston Press*, August 27, 1917; testimony of R. McDaniel, Cress Report, Appendix B, 128–31.

13. These clippings with notations are in Records of the Inspector General, File 333.9, RG 159, FRC.

14. *Houston Chronicle*, September 2, 1917.

15. *Houston Press*, September 1, 5, 1917; *Houston Chronicle*, September 2, 1917.

16. *Houston Chronicle*, September 2, 1917.

17. *Houston Chronicle*, September 2, 1917.

18. *Houston Press*, September 7, 18, 1917.

19. Telegram, General Chamberlain to Adjutant General of the Army, September 4, 1917; General Chamberlain to W. J. Johnson, September 21, 1917, in Records of the Inspector General, File 333.9, RG 159, FRC; *Houston Press*, March 8, 1918.

20. Robert V. Haynes, *A Night of Violence: The Houston Riot of 1917* (Baton Rouge: Louisiana State University Press, 1976), 229.

21. Haynes, *A Night of Violence*, 229.

22. *Houston Post*, August 26, 1917.

23. *Houston Chronicle*, September 13, 1917.

24. *Houston Chronicle*, September 13, 1917.

25. Haynes, *A Night of Violence*, 229–30.

26. Martha Gruening, "Houston: An N.A.A.C.P. Investigation," *Crisis* 25 (November 1917): 14–19.

27. Haynes, *A Night of Violence*, 233.

28. Haynes, *A Night of Violence*, 232–33.

29. Haynes, *A Night of Violence*, 234; interview with Will Price, July 17, 1973.

30. *Official Army Register*, January 1, 1922, 392.

31. *Houston Chronicle*, August 27, 1917; Gruening, "Houston: An N.A.A.C.P. Investigation."

32. *Houston Post*, August 30, 31, 1917; *Houston Press*, August 30, 31, 1917; *Houston Chronicle*, September 4, 1917.

33. Statement of Colonel William Newman, September 20, 1917, Records of Inspector General, File 333.9, RG 159, FRC.

34. Statement of Colonel William Newman, September 20, 1917, Records of Inspector General, File 333.9, RG 159, FRC.

35. Haynes, *A Night of Violence*, 242.

36. Haynes, *A Night of Violence*, 241.

37. Haynes, *A Night of Violence*, 241.

38. International Committee of the Red Cross (ICRC), *Principles of International Law Recognized in the Charter of the Nüremberg Tribunal and in the Judgment of the Tribunal*, 1950. Principle 4: "The fact that a person acted pursuant to order of his Government or of a superior does not relieve him from responsibility under international law, provided a moral choice was in fact possible to him."

39. Telegram, Colonel Stockle to Commanding General, Southern Department, August 27, 1917, telegram, Colonel Barnum to Adjutant General of the Army, August 28, 1917, in Army Commands, Southern Department, Headquarters, RG 393, NA.

40. Testimony of Lieutenant Charles Snider, September 5, 1917, Chamberlain Report, 40; testimony of Captain Preston, United States v. Sergeant William C. Nesbit et al., 2034–38; copies of the checklists are in United States v. Nesbit, Prosecution's Exhibits Nos. 10-1§4; copy of memorandum of prisoners at county jail, Harris County, Texas, August 24, 1917, Cress Report, Appendix A, 179–80.

41. Ann J. Lane, *Brownsville Affair: National Crisis and Black Reaction* (Port Washington, NY: Kennikat Press, 1971).

42. See, for example, Philip Zimbardo, *The Lucifer Effect: Understanding How Good People Turn Evil* (New York: Random House, 2007); Richard B. Jackson, "Interrogation and Treatment of Detainees in the Global War on Terror," in *The War on Terror and the Laws of War: A Military Perspective*, ed Geoffrey S. Corn (Oxford: Oxford University Press, 2015).

43. 406 U.S. 441 (1971).

44. Kastigar v. United States, 271 U.S. 441, 453–52.

45. Kastigar v. United States, 271 U.S. 441, 453–52.

9. THE TRIAL

1. Franz Kafka, *The Trial*, trans. Breon Mitchell (New York: Schocken Books, 1998), 149.

2. Telegram, Colonel Ralph Harrison to Commanding Officer, Fort Bliss, October 12, 1917, telegram, General John Ruckman, to Adjutant General of the Army, October 14, 1917, Army Commands, Southern Department, Headquarters, RG 393, NA.

3. General John Ruckman to Adjutant General of the Army, October 14, 1917, Army Commands, Southern Department, Headquarters, RG 393, NA.

4. UN General Assembly, Universal Declaration of Human Rights, 10 December 1948, 217 A (III).

5. General John Ruckman to Adjutant General of the Army, October 14, 1917, Army Commands, Southern Department, Headquarters, RG 393, NA.

6. *San Antonio Express*, November 1, 1917.

7. *A Manual for Courts-Martial, Corrected to April 15, 1917* (Washington, DC: Government Printing Office, 1917), 44–51, 145, 160; *Houston Post*, November 18, 1917.

8. Review of record of trial, United States v. Sergeant William C. Nesbit et al., January 29, 1918, prepared by Colonel James J. Mayes, Court-Martial Case 109045, Records of Judge Advocate General, RG 153, FRC.

9. Review of record of trial, United States v. Nesbit, January 29, 1918, prepared by Colonel James J. Mayes, Court-Martial Case 109045, Records of Judge Advocate General, RG 153, FRC.

10. Review of record of trial, United States v. Nesbit, January 29, 1918, prepared by Colonel James J. Mayes, Court-Martial Case 109045, Records of Judge Advocate General, RG 153, FRC.

11. United States v. Nesbit, 8–13.

12. *Houston Chronicle*, November 2, 3, 4, 6, 1917; testimony of Major Snow, United States v. Nesbit, 44, 47–48, 60–68.

13. *Houston Chronicle*, November 2, 3, 4, 6, 1917; testimony of Major Snow, United States v. Nesbit, 44, 47–48, 60–68.

14. See testimony of Leonard B. Booth, United States v. Nesbit, 322; testimony of O. H. Reichert, United States v. Nesbit, 382–83; testimony

of Hattie M. Bennett, United States v. Nesbit, 402–3; interview with Mrs. J. W. Kennedy, July 18, 1973; *Houston Chronicle*, November 5, 1917.

15. Testimony of Louis Thiel, United States v. Nesbit, 325; testimony of Mrs. J. W. Kennedy, United States v. Nesbit, 329–30; testimony of William J. Drucks, United States v. Nesbit, 342–43; testimony of Jeanette Thiel, United States v. Nesbit, 394; testimony of Mrs. F. D. Scott, United States v. Nesbit, 403.

16. Robert V. Haynes, *A Night of Violence: The Houston Riot of 1917* (Baton Rouge: Louisiana State University Press, 1976), 263.

17. Haynes, *A Night of Violence*, 264.

18. Testimony of Private Draper, United States v. Nesbit, 1025–41; *Houston Post*, November 15, 1917.

19. *Houston Chronicle*, November 16, 1917; testimony of Private John Denty, United States v. Nesbit, 1099–112.

20. Testimony of Private Shorter, United States v. Nesbit, 1046–92; *Houston Chronicle*, November 15, 16, 1917.

21. *Houston Post*, November 16, 1917; testimony of Private Bandy, United States v. Nesbit, 1159–88.

22. Testimony of Private Love, United States v. Nesbit, 1266–88; *Houston Chronicle*, November 18, 1917.

23. Testimony of Private Love, United States v. Nesbit, 1268–88; Thomas Richard Adams, "The Houston Riot of 1917" (master's thesis, Texas A & University, 1972), 94. These five were Privates Oliver Fletcher, Grover Burns, Robert Brownfield, Henry Green, and Allie C. Butler.

24. Haynes, *A Night of Violence*, 267.

25. Haynes, *A Night of Violence*, 267.

26. Haynes, *A Night of Violence*, 267–68.

27. *Houston Post*, November 23, 1917; testimony of Private Burns, United States v. Nesbit, 1834–42, 1861–68.

28. Haynes, *A Night of Violence*, 269.

29. Haynes, *A Night of Violence*, 270.

30. Address by assistant judge advocate, United States v. Nesbit, 2056–74.

31. Marion Smiley and Edward N. Zalta, eds., *The Stanford Encyclopedia of Philosophy* (Stanford, CA: Metaphysics Research Lab, Stanford University, 1995).

32. George P. Fletcher, *Romantics at War* (Princeton, NJ: Princeton University Press, 2002).

33. William Blackstone, *Commentaries on the Laws of England* (Philadelphia: J. B. Lippincott, 1893).

34. Genesis 18:24 (Authorized King James Version).

35. Haynes, *A Night of Violence*, 270.

36. Testimony of R. E. Lewis before the Houston Civilian Board of Inquiry, 97, August 24, 1917, RC 393.

37. "There was not 'one iota of evidence' of the existence of a conspiracy." Testimony of R. E. Lewis before the Houston Civilian Board of Inquiry, 97, August 24, 1917, RC 393.

38. Address by judge advocate, United States v. Nesbit, 2119–26.

39. Testimony of Patrolman L. E. Gentry before the Houston Civilian Board of Inquiry, transcript, 25; Major K. S. Snow to Brigadier General John A. Hulen, "Report on Circumstances Attending the Mutiny," August 24, 1917, Record Group 39, United States Army, Southern Department, Box 364, National Archives.

40. Haynes, *A Night of Violence*, 271.

41. *Houston Post*, December 1, 1917; United States v. Nesbit, 2129–69.

42. *Houston Post*, December 1, 1917; United States v. Nesbit, 2129–69.

43. *Houston Post*, December 1, 1917; United States v. Nesbit, 2129–69.

44. Haynes, *A Night of Violence*, 271.

45. Haynes, *A Night of Violence*, 271.

46. Haynes, *A Night of Violence*, 271.

47. Review of record of United States v. Nesbit, January 29, 1918, Court Martial Case 109045, Records of Judge Advocate General, RG 153, FRC; Summary of Evidence against Each Defendant, United States v. Nesbit, exhibit §36.

48. Review of record of United States v. Nesbit, January 29, 1918, Court Martial Case 109045, Records of Judge Advocate General, RG 153, FRC; Summary of Evidence against Each Defendant, United States v. Nesbit, exhibit §36.

49. Recommendation for clemency for Private First Class John Hudson, n.d., Court Martial Case 109045, Records of Judge Advocate General, RG 153, FRC.

50. *Houston Post*, December 4, 1917; approval of proceedings and findings by General Ruckman, December 10, 1917, United States v. Nesbit, 2170–72.

51. *Houston Post*, December 12, 1917.

52. *Atlanta Constitution*, December 13, 1917.

53. *Outlook* 67 (December 19, 1917): 632.

54. *Cleveland Gazette*, December 15, 1917.

55. *Chicago Broad Ax*, December 15, 1917.

56. *Crisis* 15 (January 1918): 114.

57. *New York Age*, December 15, 1917.

58. United States Army Judge Advocate General's Corps, *The Army Lawyer: A History of the Judge Advocate General's Corps 1775–1975* (Washington, DC: U.S. Government Printing Office, 1975), 127.

59. Haynes, *A Night of Violence*, 275.

60. This testimony is in United States v. Corporal John Washington et al., 38–154. See also *San Antonio Express*, December 18, 19, 1917.

61. Address by assistant judge advocate, United States v. Washington, 477–91; *San Antonio Express*, December 23, 1917.

62. Address by Counsel, United States v. Washington, 492–503; *Houston Post*, December 22, 1917.

63. *San Antonio Express*, December 21, 1917; Testimony of Private Bullock, United States v. Washington, 316–71.

64. Haynes, *A Night of Violence*, 278.

65. *Houston Post*, January 3, 1918.

66. *New York Age*, February 9, 1918; *Crisis* 15 (April 1918): 283.

67. *Cleveland Gazette*, January 5, 1918.

68. W. F. Cozart et al. to President Woodrow Wilson, January 10, 1918, Court Martial Case 109045, Records of Judge Advocate General, RG 153, FRC.

69. E. H. Holmes to Senator W. L. Jones, January 16, 1918, Court Martial Case 114575, Records of Judge Advocate General, RG 153, FRC; Senator Miles Poindexter to President Wilson, January 22, 1918, Records of Judge Advocate General, RG 153, FRC.

70. Charles W. Scrutchin to Senator Knute Nelson, February 25, 1918, Records of Judge Advocate General, RG 153, FRC; Senator Knute Nelson to President Wilson, March 1, 1918, Records of Judge Advocate General, RG 153, FRC.

71. Haynes, *A Night of Violence*, 282–83; *Crisis* 15 (April 1918): 283; *New York Times*, February 20, 1918.

72. James Weldon Johnson, *Along This Way: The Autobiography of James Weldon Johnson* (New York: Viking, 1933), 323–25.

73. Haynes, *A Night of Violence*, 285–86, 288.

74. Haynes, *A Night of Violence*, 287.

75. These were Leo H. Weadock, Frank H. Snell, Edward P. Corbett, and Private Harry Goldstein; testimony of Private Goldstein, United States v. Corporal Robert Tillman et al., 984–88.

76. Haynes, *A Night of Violence*, 287.

77. Testimony of Private Shorter, United States v. Tillman, 1381–87.

78. Testimony of Private Love, United States v. Tillman, 1555–59, 1560–67.

79. Testimony of Private Love, United States v. Tillman, 1555–59, 1560–67.

80. Address by counsel, United States v. Tillman, 3011–18.

81. Address by counsel, United States v. Tillman, 3011–18; *San Antonio Express*, March 28, 1918.

82. Address by counsel, United States v. Tillman, 3011–18; *San Antonio Express*, March 28, 1918.

83. Address by counsel, United States v. Tillman, 3011–18; *San Antonio Express*, March 28, 1918.

84. Haynes, *A Night of Violence*, 292.

85. Haynes, *A Night of Violence*, 292.

86. Findings of the court, United States v. Tillman, 3132–45; *Houston Chronicle*, March 28, 1918.

87. Sentences or acquittals by court, United States v. Tillman, 3147–60.

88. Memorandum by Major General John A. Ruckman, May 2, 1918, Court Martial Case 114575, Records of Judge Advocate General, RG 153, FRC.

89. Haynes, *A Night of Violence*, 296.

90. Haynes, *A Night of Violence*, 300.

91. *New York Times*, September 15, 1918.

92. Wilson to Baker, August 24, 1918, Wilson Papers. A typescript of Wilson's proclamation, dated August 31, 1918, is in Court Martial Case 109018, Records of Judge Advocate General, RG 153, FRC.

93. Telegram, Colonel Ansell to Judge Advocate, Southern Department, September 18, 1918, Court Martial Case 114575, Records of Judge Advocate General, RG 153, FRC; telegram, Judge Advocate, Southern Department to Ansell, September 18, 1918, Court Martial Case 114575, Records of Judge Advocate General, RG 153, FRC.

94. Immanuel Kant, *Idea for a General History with a Cosmopolitan Purpose* (1784), Proposition 6.

95. Telegram, Colonel Ansell to Judge Advocate, Southern Department, September 18, 1918, Court Martial Case 114575, Records of Judge Advocate General, RG 153, FRC; telegram, Judge Advocate, Southern Department to Ansell, September 18, 1918.

96. Haynes, *A Night of Violence*, 303.

97. Memorandum, Colonel S. T. Ansell to Adjutant General, September 23, 1918, Court Martial Case 114575, Records of Judge Advocate General, RG 153, FRC; *Houston Post*, September 18, 1918; *New York Age*, September 21, 1918.

98. Memorandum, Colonel S. T. Ansell to Adjutant General, September 23, 1918, Court Martial Case 114575, Records of Judge Advocate General, RG 153, FRC; *Houston Post*, September 18, 1918; *New York Age*, September 21, 1918.

99. *Houston Post*, September 25, 1918.

100. Kafka, *The Trial*, 162.

101. *Houston Post*, September 25, 1918.

102. *Houston Post*, September 25, 1918.

10. ATONEMENT

1. Shubham Kalia and Kanishka Singh, "Police Ignored George Floyd's 'I Can't Breathe' Plea: Transcript," Reuters, July 9, 2020, https://reut.rs/3feaQxU.

2. Manny Fernandez and Patricia Mazzei, "Houston Bids Goodbye to George Floyd, Whose Killing Galvanized a Movement," *New York Times*, June 9, 2020, https://nyti.ms/3cOvvqe.

3. Daniel Nichanian, "How Unequal Perceptions of Protest and Violence Shape Black Lives Matter," *The Appeal*, June 4, 2020, https://theappeal.org/politicalreport/black-lives-matter-protests-images-juliet-hooker/.

4. Fernandez and Mazzei, "Houston Bids Goodbye to George Floyd."

5. Marc A. Thiessen, "The Deaths That Don't Fit the 'Defund the Police' Narrative," editorial, *Washington Post*, June 9, 2020, www.washingtonpost.com/opinions/2020/06/09/deaths-that-dont-fit-de-fund-police-narrative/.

6. Letter by Private Hawkins, December 11, 1917; James Jeffrey, "A 100-Year-Old US Riot Only Now Being Talked About," BBC News, November 25, 2017, www.bbc.com/news/world-us-canada-42116688.

7. Ecclesiastes 11:3 (Authorized King James Version).

8. M. B. Patten to Walter F. White, June 26, 1918, C. F. Richardson to NAACP, June 26, 1918, E. O. Smith to White, June 10, 1918, Records of National Association for the Advancement of Colored People, Branch Files, Houston 1915-1918, Box G-203, Manuscript Division, Library of Congress.

9. Robert V. Haynes, *A Night of Violence: The Houston Riot of 1917* (Baton Rouge: Louisiana State University Press, 1976), 307–8.

10. Report of Executive Secretary to Board of Directors, NAACP, May 1921, 4–5, Arthur Barnett Spingarn Papers, Box 41, Manuscript Division, Library of Congress; *Crisis* 23 (November 1921), 21.

11. Report of Executive Secretary to Board of Directors, NAACP, May 1921, 4–5, Arthur Barnett Spingarn Papers, Box 41, Manuscript Division, Library of Congress; *Crisis* 23 (November 1921): 21.

12. Report of Executive Secretary to Board of Directors, NAACP, May 1921, 4–5, Arthur Barnett Spingarn Papers, Box 41, Manuscript Division, Library of Congress; *Crisis* 23 (November 1921), 21.

13. Haynes, *A Night of Violence*, 310.

14. Executive Secretary's Report to Board of Directors, NAACP, October 1921, Spingarn Papers, Box 41.

15. *Crisis* 23 (November 1921): 21; Executive Secretary's Report to Board of Directors, NAACP, October 1921, Spingarn Papers, Box 41.

16. Delilah L. Beasley to editor, *Crisis* 15 (March 1918): 240; *Chicago Defender*, October 6, 1917.

17. Delilah L. Beasley to editor, *Crisis* 15 (March 1918): 240; *Chicago Defender*, October 6, 1917.

18. Congressional Record, 67th Cong., lst Sess., 7833.

19. Haynes, *A Night of Violence*, 310.

20. Colonel John A. Hull to Colonel William O. Gilbert, Fort Sam Houston, December 16, 21, 1921, Court Martial Case 104095, Colonel Hull to Adjutant General of the Army, April 19, 1922, Court Martial Case 114575.

21. Memorandum, Colonel Hull to Secretary of War, August 8, 1922, Records of Adjutant General, Project Files, 1917–1925, Box 343, 94, NA.

22. Memorandum, Colonel Hull to Secretary of War, August 8, 1922, Records of Adjutant General, Project Files, 1917–1925, Box 343, 94, NA.

23. Memorandum, Colonel Hull to Secretary of War, August 8, 1922, Records of Adjutant General, Project Files, 1917–1925, Box 343, 94, NA.

24. Memorandum, Colonel Hull to Secretary of War, August 8, 1922, Records of Adjutant General, Project Files, 1917–1925, Box 343, 94, NA.

25. Haynes, *A Night of Violence*, 314.

26. Haynes, *A Night of Violence*, 314.

27. *Crisis* 45 (May 1938): 150; V. J. Perisich to Judge Advocate General, September 2, 1955, Court Martial Case 114575, Records of Judge Advocate General, Box 56497, RG 153, FRC.

28. The White House Office of the Press Secretary, "President William J. Clinton's Comments Honoring L. T. Henry O. Flipper," February 19, 1999, https://history.army.mil/html/topics/afam/clinton_flipper.html.

29. "[H]e [the President] shall have Power to grant Reprieves and Pardons for Offences against the United States, except in Cases of Impeachment."

30. DeNeen Brown, "Vandals Damage Historical Marker Commemorating 1917 Uprising by Black Soldiers," *Washington Post*, September 8, 2017, www.washingtonpost.com/news/retropolis/wp/2017/08/24/i-am-not-guilty-the-mass-hanging-of-13-black-soldiers-after-the-bloody-1917-houston-riots/.

31. DeNeen L. Brown, "Vandals Damage Historical Marker Commemorating 1917 Uprising by Black Soldiers," *Washington Post*, September 8, 2017, www.washingtonpost.com/news/retropolis/wp/2017/08/24/i-am-not-guilty-the-mass-hanging-of-13-black-soldiers-after-the-bloody-1917-houston-riots.

32. United States v. Wilson, 32 U.S. 150, 151 (1833).

33. John Donne, *Donne's Devotions* (Cambridge: Cambridge University Press, 1923).

34. James Jeffrey, "Remembering the Black Soldiers Executed after Houston's 1917 Race Riot," Public Radio International, February 1, 2018, www.pri.org/stories/2018-02-01/remembering-black-soldiers-executed-after-houstons-1917-race-riot.

35. Jeffrey, "Remembering the Black Soldiers Executed after Houston's 1917 Race Riot."

36. Jeffrey, "Remembering the Black Soldiers Executed after Houston's 1917 Race Riot."

37. Jeffrey, "Remembering the Black Soldiers Executed after Houston's 1917 Race Riot."

INDEX

Winkler, Freddie, 98, 164–165
World War I, 3, 6–7, 17–18; beginning of,
   69–70; black volunteers for, 51–54
World War II, 176
Wright, Albert, 141
Wright, Charles, 95

X, Malcolm, 62–63, 127
Xenophon, 96

Yaqui, 13
Young, Risley, 153, 156

Zimmermann Telegram, 17